MARCUS AU~~RELIUS:~~
A GUIDE FOR THE PERPLEXED

Continuum *Guides for the Perplexed*

Continuum's Guides for the Perplexed are clear, concise and accessible introductions to thinkers, writers and subjects that students and readers can find especially challenging. Concentrating specifically on what it is that makes the subject difficult to grasp, these books explain and explore key themes and ideas, guiding the reader towards a thorough understanding of demanding material.

Guides for the Perplexed available from Continuum:

Aristotle: A Guide for the Perplexed, John Vella
Plato: A Guide for the Perplexed, Gerald A. Press
Socrates: A Guide for the Perplexed, Sara Ahbel-Rappe
Stoics: A Guide for the Perplexed, M. Andrew Holowchak
Suetonius: A Guide for the Perplexed, Tristan Power

MARCUS AURELIUS:
A GUIDE FOR THE PERPLEXED

WILLIAM O. STEPHENS

continuum

Continuum International Publishing Group

The Tower Building	80 Maiden Lane
11 York Road	Suite 704
London	New York
SE1 7NX	NY 10038

www.continuumbooks.com

© William O. Stephens 2012

British Library Cataloguing-in-Publication Data
A catalogue record for this book is available from the British Library.

ISBN: HB: 978-1-4411-2561-3
PB: 978-1-4411-0810-4

Library of Congress Cataloging-in-Publication Data
Stephens, William O., 1962-
Marcus Aurelius: a guide for the perplexed/William O. Stephens.
p. cm.
Includes index.
ISBN 978-1-4411-0810-4 (pbk.) – ISBN 978-1-4411-2561-3 (hardback)
1. Marcus Aurelius, Emperor of Rome, 121–180. 2. Marcus Aurelius, Emperor of Rome, 121-180. Meditations. 3. Stoics. I. Title.
B583.S74 2011
188–dc23

2011017882

Typeset by Newgen Imaging Systems Pvt Ltd, Chennai, India
Printed and bound in India

For my father

CONTENTS

CONTENTS

LIST OF ILLUSTRATIONS

ACKNOWLEDGMENTS

Many are to thank for helping me complete this book. I am grateful to the Graduate School of Creighton University for the 2010 Summer Faculty Research Scholarship that supported this project. I thank the Kripke Center for the Study of Religion and Society of Creighton University for the grant that funded a course release for time to work on the book Fall semester 2010. Jeff Hause's comments on Chapter 2, Scott Rubarth's comments on Chapter 3, Anne Ozar's comments on the Appendix, and Ryan Wallenstein's comments on all the chapters and the Appendix all considerably improved the book. Tony Long kindly directed me to the introduction to Hutcheson's translation of the *Meditations*. I greatly appreciate the stalwart production of the Subject Index by Jack Dudley. Cartographer extraordinaire Dave Helm has my deep gratitude for the patient, good humored artistry, and long hours he lavished on the maps. Thanks also go to the editors at Continuum who invited me to propose this book for their Guides for the Perplexed series and patiently awaited its delivery. I am especially grateful to Greg Bucher for his wise advice on Chapter 1 and for gently prodding me to provide the glossary, the genealogical diagram, the maps, and the photograph. Selecting and obtaining the right to reproduce the photograph from the Deutsches Archäologisches Institut, Universität zu Köln, and composing the description of it would have been impossible without his assistance. All of these friends were generous with their time, talents, and encouragement, and all have my gratitude. Naturally, I am responsible for the shortcomings of the book that remain.

W. O. S.
Omaha, July 2011

Bust of Marcus Aurelius in the first portrait type, circa 140 CE.
Rome Museo Capitolino, Stanza degli Imperatori 29. Inv. 450.
Negative: FittCap81-66-01 16055.

Marcus is portrayed as a handsome, intelligent crown prince of about nineteen years of age, with oval-shaped eyes, a strong nose, highly arched brows, and a well-formed mouth. Typically for his time, the sculptor contrasts the smooth, polished skin with the rough, textured hair. The locks of hair are sculpted with fine, careful detail. The grooves of the sculptor's drill are very thin. The individual hairs of the crinkle of curls are suggested with a meticulous technique of the chisel. The sculptor has enlivened the face by different sizes of the upper eyelids and has sought a certain degree of naturalism through fluid contouring. On the center of the forehead a few ends of the locks of hair are split, amplifying the naturalistic effect. The artist's tremendous talent is conspicuous in this splendid and almost completely preserved bust, which stands 0.775 m. The bust is possibly from a villa in Lanuvio.*

*See Paul Zanker, Katalog der römischen Porträts in den Capitolinischen Museen und den anderen kommunalen Sammlungen der Stadt Room, Band I: Text Kaiser- und Prinzenbildnisse, Aufnahmen von Gisela Fittschen-Badura. Von Zabern: Mainz am Rhein, 1985, p. 68.

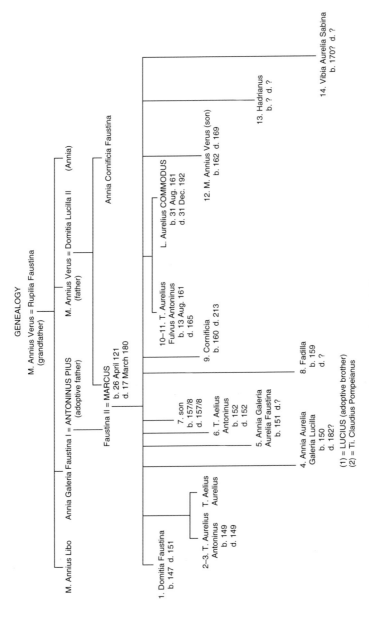

GENEALOGY

Genealogical diagram

Marcus' Roman Empire

CHAPTER 1

THE MAN, THE EMPEROR, THE THINKER

THE MAN

Marcus Aurelius was one of the most interesting figures in the ancient world. For the historian, this is largely because he was the last of what were regarded as the five good emperors of the Roman Empire and the man who presided over the first stirrings of the flood of troubles which would nearly destroy the empire in the next century. These emperors, Nerva, Trajan, Hadrian, Antoninus Pius, and Marcus Aurelius, ruled from CE 96 to 180, a period believed to be a happy, prosperous, golden age of antiquity. Marcus lived during nearly three-quarters of this period, from CE 121 to 180, and reigned from 161 to 180. For the historian of philosophy, on the other hand, Marcus is of particular interest as the only full-blown philosopher ever to have been a king. He was the last of the great Stoic philosophers of antiquity to have bequeathed to posterity—in his case, unintentionally, it seems—a substantial body of philosophical writing. These thinkers, Lucius Annaeus Seneca (c. 4 BCE–CE 65), Gaius Musonius Rufus (CE c. 25–c. 95), Epictetus (CE c. 55–c. 135), and Marcus Aurelius, not only wrote *about* Stoicism, as the great Roman statesman and orator Cicero had. They themselves *were* Stoics and sought to live their lives in accordance with Stoic philosophy. For the last nineteen years of Marcus' life, living by Stoic ideals also meant ruling as a Stoic should. The Roman empire of Marcus' time was vast. It was populated by millions of people of many ethnicities and stretched from North Africa to the rivers Rhine and Danube, from northern England (Britannia) and Germany (Germania) to Egypt (Aegyptus), and from Morocco (Mauretania) to eastern Turkey (Cappadocia) and

Syria. Accordingly, we cannot help but suppose that the responsibility of ruling such an enormous empire would have been felt to be tremendously heavy by a principled, philosophically serious man of solemn duty. This *Guide for the Perplexed* will offer evidence that Marcus Aurelius was such a man.

JUDGING A BOOK BY ITS TITLE

We do not know what title, if any, Marcus himself gave to the collection of philosophical notes attributed to him. Many centuries after he wrote these notes, "To Himself" (*Eis heauton*) appeared as the title of the subsequently lost Greek manuscript used for the first printed edition. Titles English translators have used include *His Meditations Concerning Himself, His Conversation with Himself, To Himself, Thoughts, The Communings with Himself,* and the most popular, *Meditations.* But though the custom of referring to the work by this last title is now firmly entrenched, caution about this custom is warranted for two reasons. First, there is no evidence that Marcus himself used this title or anything like it. Second, the customary title may lead an unsuspecting reader to expect either a unified treatise of introspective reflections akin to René Descartes' *Meditations on First Philosophy*, or a program of contemplative exercises containing Zen Buddhist kōans, or mantras from the Vedic tradition of India aimed at transcendental spiritual transformation. None of these expectations, nor hybrids of them, resembles what Marcus produced. C. R. Haines describes it as a "small but priceless book of private devotional memoranda."[1] Gregory Hays agrees that "Memoranda" is a better, more descriptively accurate title because it "suggests both the miscellaneous character of the work and something about its intended function."[2] Repeatedly throughout the twelve books the entries begin with injunctions to *remember* and to *keep in mind.* They explicitly function as reminders of what to do, what not to do, and of lessons learned that must not be forgotten. For these reasons I have seen fit to depart from custom and to refer to Marcus' work as the *Memoranda* throughout this guide.

The remainder of this chapter gives an overview of Marcus' biography. I sketch his family lineage and adoptions, upbringing and education, his accession to the throne, legal work, military campaigns, political reign, and philosophical legacy. Chapter 2 explores the influence of the philosophies of Heraclitus and Epictetus on Marcus' thought. Each subsequent chapter examines a persistent philosophical theme in his *Memoranda*. The book concludes with an appendix on Stoicism in Ridley Scott's film *Gladiator* (2000). The goal is to make Marcus Aurelius more intelligible and more engaging to the perplexed reader in need of a guide.

THE FAMILY AND BOYHOOD OF "TRUEST"

Annia is the name of the family (*gens* in Latin) into which Marcus was born.[3] In the mid-first century CE Marcus' family was settled in the southern Spanish province of Baetica, in the town of Ucubi, near Córdoba.[4] Annius Verus (I), Marcus' paternal grandfather, was a young neo-patrician who married into a family of high standing. Annius Verus' wife was Rupilia Faustina, daughter of Libo Rupilius Frugi.[5] Annius Verus (I) and Rupilia Faustina had two sons, Annius Verus (II) and Libo, and a daughter, Annia Galeria Faustina. The elder son, Annius Verus (II), married Domitia Lucilla (II), daughter of another patrician, Calvisius Tullus Ruso and the elder Domitia Lucilla (I). Domitia Lucilla (II) the younger, Marcus' mother, acquired much of her mother's fortune, including large and thriving brickworks on the outskirts of Rome.

Lucilla (II) the younger and her husband Annius Verus (II) had two children, Marcus, born on April 26, 121 CE, and his younger sister, Annia Cornificia Faustina, born probably within the next two years. After giving birth to her son, Lucilla probably had little to do with his earliest upbringing. Assuming the traditional ceremony of purification was performed for Marcus, nine days after his birth his father would have acknowledged the child Marcus as his own by lifting him up from the hearth and naming him. He was given the *praenomen* Marcus, which was to be the only one of his names he would carry throughout his life. At this ceremony a Roman boy would receive the gifts of a rattle made of a string with tinkling objects attached to it (*crepundia*) and a golden amulet charm against the evil eye (*bulla*) which the boy would wear round his neck until he donned the *toga virilis*, marking his passage into manhood at the age of fourteen.

Since Marcus' father died young, during his praetorship, probably in 124, Marcus could scarcely have known him. Yet later, in his *Memoranda*, Marcus wrote that from his father's reputation and from his own memories of him he learned modesty and manliness (i. 2). Lucilla did not remarry after her husband's death. Had he lived, Marcus' father Verus (II) surely would have had a distinguished career in Roman public life. A wet-nurse cared for baby Marcus, fed him, and taught him Greek. When his father died, Marcus was adopted by his grandfather Annius Verus (I). In 126 Marcus' grandfather was greatly honored when the emperor Hadrian made him consul for the third time. The historian Cassius Dio reports that Marcus, "while still a boy, so pleased all his many powerful and wealthy relations that they all loved him" (Dio 69. 21. 2).

Marcus was raised in his parents' house on the Caelian, one of Rome's seven hills. Its prominent families and many splendid aristocratic mansions made the Caelian Rome's fashionable district. The most imposing mansion of all was the Lateran Palace, which was next to the estate of Marcus' grandfather, where the boy spent much of his childhood. Situated on the southern edge of Rome, if one looked from the Caelian to the north one could see the Circus Maximus, the Palatine hill with its imperial palaces, the Forum, the Colosseum, and the Baths of Trajan.

One man who played an important role in Marcus' early upbringing was Catilius Severus. Severus married into Marcus' family by marrying the widow of Domitius Tullus, thus becoming the stepfather of the elder Lucilla (I) and Marcus' maternal step-great-grandfather. Marcus thanks his grandfather Verus (I) for his good character and avoidance of bad temper (*Mem.* i. 1). Some time after his wife Rupilia Faustina died, grandfather Verus (I) took a mistress to live with him in his house. In his later years Marcus expressed gratitude that the course of events spared him from being brought up in the same household as this woman any longer than he was. Remarks like these reveal Marcus' sensibilities and are consistent with the report of the biographer in the *Historia Augusta* that Marcus was "a solemn child from his earliest infancy" (*HA Marc.* 2.1). Marcus' mother Lucilla (II) played a considerable role in his life, impressing him with "her reverence for the divine, her generosity, her inability not only to do wrong but even to think of doing it, to live a simple life, far removed from the lifestyle of the rich" (*Mem.* i. 3). This last remark is notable, since Lucilla (II) had inherited considerable wealth. In middle age Marcus was grateful that although his mother was fated to die young, she spent her last years with him. His correspondence with Fronto contains many

4

affectionate references to her. Lucilla (II) was a talented, educated woman, well-versed in Greek.

In 127 at age six, Marcus was enrolled in the order of the *equites* by the nomination of the emperor Hadrian. This equestrian rank entitled him to wear a gold ring and a tunic with a narrow border. Marcus was unusually young to receive this honor. Although he had probably already been taught to read by then, at age seven in 128 Marcus began his elementary education. Catilius Severus, Marcus' maternal step-great-grandfather, convinced the rest of the family that the boy should be taught at home by tutors, not sent off to school. Later, in his *Memoranda*, Marcus thanked his great-grandfather for allowing him to enjoy good teachers at home, and for having learned that it is a duty to spend liberally on such things. Marcus' elementary lessons were in reading and writing Latin and in arithmetic. His first teachers were family slaves or freedmen of the Annii Veri named Euphorio and Geminus. Euphorio probably taught Marcus the Greek language and Greek literature. Geminus, an actor, perhaps supervised Marcus' Latin pronunciation and elocution in general. A third teacher, Marcus' *educator*, supervised the boy's moral welfare and general development. Marcus speaks of him with gratitude: "From my tutor: to support neither the Greens nor the Blues at the chariot races, and neither the Thracian nor the Samnite gladiators; to endure pain and be content with little; to work with my own hands, to mind my own business, to have no time for slander" (*Mem.* i. 5). These comments suggest that Marcus' *educator* inculcated an identifiably Stoic bent in his young pupil. To favor one competitor over another is inappropriate, the Stoics believed, since any such contest is a matter of indifference (of the most trivial kind, at that). Enduring pain without complaint, striving for self-sufficiency, and focusing on one's own self-improvement rather than criticism of others are all Stoic goals.

At age seven Marcus was enrolled by Hadrian into the priestly college of the Salii. This indicates that the Emperor showed the young boy special favor. The Salii priests in Rome were associated with the worship of Mars, the god of war. They wore the archaic Italian war-uniform, the *tunica picta*, with a short military cloak over a breastplate, and a conical-shaped felt hat. They wore a sword, carried a figure-eight-shaped shield (*ancilium*) on their left arm, and carried a spear or staff in their right hand. The Salii priests played a prominent role in religious ceremonies marking the opening of the campaigning season at the Quinquatrus, and perhaps also its close at the Armilustrium. On some other days in March and October they processed through Rome, periodically stopping to perform their ritual dances, beating their shields with their spears and singing their hymn, the Carmen Saliare, an obscure religious chant in archaic, and by then nearly unintelligible, Latin.

Marcus was very serious about his duties as a Salian priest. His offices included being the leader of the dance, the *vates* (prophet), and the master of the order. As master he initiated new members and formally discharged those leaving the order. Marcus learned the archaic formulas by heart, so that he never needed to be prompted to deliver them correctly. On one occasion, when the Salii were following the custom of tossing their crowns on the banqueting couch of the god Mars, Marcus' crown fell directly atop the head of Mars, as if he had deliberately placed it there, whereas the crowns of his fellow priests fell haphazardly. This unlikely event was later interpreted as an omen signifying that Marcus would one day rule Rome.

By age eleven Marcus would have been ready for secondary education under *grammatici*. Marcus was instructed in mathematics and music, perhaps mainly singing. At about this time the painting-master Diognetus also began to teach Marcus. Diognetus seems to have been the first to show Marcus the attractions of philosophy as a way of life. Marcus writes:

> From Diognetus: not to waste time on trivial matters; to distrust the stories of miracle-mongers and magicians about incantations and exorcism of demons and such things; not to attend quail-fights or to get excited about such things; to tolerate outspokenness; and to make philosophy my own; to hear first the lectures of Baccheius, then of Tandasis and Marcianus; to write dialogues as a boy; to opt for the camp-cot and the rough cloak and the other rigors of the Greek regimen. (*Mem.* i. 6)

Marcus adopted the habits of "the Greek regimen" early on, because he was only twelve (in April 132) when he first eagerly embraced the austere way of life of the philosopher. The biographer reports that "He adopted the dress, and a little later the habits of endurance, of the philosopher. He followed his studies clad in a rough Greek cloak. He slept on the ground, and it was only at his mother's insistence that he reluctantly consented to sleep on a little bed covered with skins" (*HA Marc.* 2.6).

Marcus' firm dedication to his studies impressed Hadrian, who closely monitored his upbringing. "Verissimus," meaning "truest," is the nickname Hadrian gave this boy named Marcus Annius Verus. The nickname stuck with him and has been found on coins and on an inscription. Hadrian could not have spent much time with Verissimus during his boyhood, however, because of the Emperor's travels from one end of the empire to the other between 121 and 136.

In about 132 or 133, Marcus was assigned new tutors, one Greek, Alexander of Cotiaeum, and two Latin, Trosius Aper, from Pola (in northeast Italy) and Tuticius Proculus, from Sicca Veneria (in Africa). These *grammatici* had Marcus read aloud and learn by heart passages from classical authors, and they would comment on matters of style and impart philosophical lessons drawn from this literature. Tuticius Proculus was later rewarded by Marcus with senatorial rank and a proconsulship. Alexander of Cotiaeum was a prominent literary figure and the foremost scholar of Homer of the time. Marcus remembers him fondly:

> From Alexander the *grammaticus*: not to find fault and not to criticize in a pestering way those who make an error of usage, or a grammatical mistake, or mispronounce something, but to use the right phrase tactfully oneself, by way of answer or confirmation, or to offer a graceful reminder, or debate the subject itself, not their wording of it. (*Mem.* i. 10)

His *grammaticus'* emphasis on content rather than fancy style, deliberate choice of words, and occasional quotations of Homer are evident in Marcus' *Memoranda*.

When Marcus was fourteen in 135 he donned the *toga virilis*. As a full citizen he could now take an active part in public life. Hadrian wanted the betrothal of Marcus and the daughter of his friend Lucius Ceionius Commodus. Ceionius Commodus was the husband of the daughter of Avidius Nigrinus, whom Hadrian had executed in 118 for "plotting against the emperor's life." So in about 136, after turning fifteen, Marcus became engaged to Ceionia Fabia. Soon after the betrothal Marcus was appointed prefect of Rome, probably by Ceionius Commodus. Although it was an archaic position without administrative importance, it remained a prestigious office for young aristocrats and members of the imperial family. The biographer reports that Marcus "conducted himself very brilliantly when acting on behalf of the magistrates and at the banquets of the emperor Hadrian" (*HA Marc.* 4.6).

An older teacher of Ceionius Commodus was Apollonius of Chalcedon. Stoicism was the leading school of philosophy of the day and Apollonius was one of its prominent proponents. The introduction of this Stoic to Marcus by Ceionius Commodus would prove to be very important in the young man's life. Marcus later studied regularly with Apollonius (*Mem.* i. 8). Apollonius is one of only three people whom Marcus specifically thanks the gods for having met (*Mem.* i. 17).

At about this time Marcus' younger sister, Annia Cornificia, married her first cousin, Ummidius Quadratus. Domitia Lucilla (II) asked her son if he would share his father's inheritance with his sister. Marcus insisted that Annia get it all. He was content with his grandfather's fortune. He also generously suggested that his mother could leave all of her own estate to his sister, so that she would not have less wealth than her husband.

Late in 135 a hemorrhage nearly killed Hadrian, occasioning serious deliberation about the Emperor's successor. Eventually he chose Ceionius Commodus and adopted him in 136, a decision made "against everyone's wishes." Hadrian's reasons for the adoption are uncertain and disputed. Commodus took the name Aelius Caesar. Hadrian sent him to Carnuntum, on the Danube frontier, to quell unrest among the German tribes in Slovakia. Aelius Caesar returned to Rome in the winter of 137. He was to address the senate on January 1, 138, but the night before he fell ill. Medical treatment failed and the next day he died.

Saddened by this loss, suffering from dropsy, and weary of life, Hadrian again had to select an heir. On January 24, 138—his sixty-second birthday—Hadrian announced that Aurelius Antoninus, Marcus' maternal uncle, would succeed him as emperor. Antoninus was amiable, benevolent, calm-tempered, cultured, well-spoken, thrifty, and quite wealthy. His public service included a quaestorship, praetorship, and consulship in Rome, and he had been a consular administering justice in Italy and proconsul of Asia for a year. He was a man of peace without military ambitions. On February 25 Hadrian adopted Antoninus, on the condition that Antoninus in turn adopt the surviving seven-year-old son of the previous heir,

Lucius Aelius Caesar, and his own nephew, Marcus. Marcus became M. Aelius Aurelius Verus and Lucius became L. Aelius Aurelius Commodus. Hadrian arranged for the surviving daughter of Antoninus, Faustina, to be betrothed to Lucius.

The night he was adopted Marcus dreamt that he had shoulders of ivory, and when asked if his shoulders could bear a burden, he discovered that they were much stronger than before. Yet when he learned that he had been adopted into the imperial family, Marcus was appalled. He reluctantly moved from his mother's house on the Caelian to Hadrian's private house. The biographer reports that Marcus was sorry to be adopted into the imperial family because of "the evils that the imperial power contained in itself." The biographer describes Marcus at this age as follows:

He was so complaisant that he allowed himself to be taken, at times, to hunt or the theater or the spectacles. He loved boxing, wrestling, running, and fowling. He played the ball-game well and hunted well too. But the zeal for philosophy led him away from all these pursuits and made him serious and reserved. Still, this did not spoil the friendliness in him which he showed to his household and his friends, and even to those less well known to him. He was austere but not unreasonable, modest but not inactive, reserved but not gloomy. (*HA Marc.* 4. 8–10)

He adds that Marcus

had such a high regard for his reputation, moreover, that even as a boy he always used to warn his procurators—those in charge of his estates and financial affairs—not to do anything in a high-handed fashion. He also often refused legacies that were left to him, returning them to the next of kin. (*HA Marc.* 7.1)

Marcus was intent on preserving his modesty and dignity. The prospect of accumulating more wealth did not entice him, as he was quite wealthy throughout his life.

In the spring of 138 Hadrian appointed Antoninus consul for the second time. The senate consented to the Emperor's request to exempt Marcus from the law barring him from serving as quaestor before the age of twenty-four. In April, at age seventeen, Marcus took office as the quaestor of his adoptive father Antoninus.

Henceforth Marcus' career path separated him from his contemporaries. Yet according to the biographer "he still showed the same respect to his relations as he had when he was an ordinary citizen, and he was as thrifty and careful of his possessions as he had been when he lived in a private household; and he was willing to act, speak, and think according to the principles of his father [Antoninus]" (*HA Marc.* 5. 6–8).

Worn down by years of illness, Hadrian tried to kill himself, but was thwarted by Antoninus. Hadrian retired to the seaside resort of Baiae on the Campanian coast to try to convalesce, leaving Antoninus to rule the empire. Failing to improve, Hadrian sent for Antoninus. Hadrian abandoned the diet prescribed by his physicians and indulged in unsuitable food and drink. With his adopted son Antoninus at his side, Hadrian died on July 10, 138. He was buried in a private ceremony at Puteoli above the Bay of Naples, at a villa once owned by Cicero.

THE PHILOSOPHER-PRINCE

Immediately after Hadrian's death, the new emperor Antoninus asked Marcus if he would agree to annul his betrothal to Ceionia Fabia and to be betrothed to Antoninus' daughter, Marcus' first cousin, the eight or nine-year-old Annia Galeria Faustina (II). This arrangement would require the dissolution of the betrothal of Faustina (II) and Ceionia's brother Lucius Commodus. The seventeen-year-old Marcus would also have to wait seven years before he could have a bride, but he agreed to the new engagement.

In 138, "against universal opposition" of the senate, Antoninus decreed that Hadrian be deified. Yet Antoninus also released the political prisoners, recalled the exiles, and commuted the death sentences imposed by Hadrian during the final tortured months of his life, having already prevented executions from being carried out before Hadrian died. For his dignified, dutiful conduct, the Emperor was asked to accept the name "Pius," meaning "dutiful." Antoninus Pius did not replace any of Hadrian's nominees, and his accession was peaceful and stable.

In 139 Pius appointed his nephew and elder adopted son Marcus consul for 140 with Pius as his fellow consul. Moreover, as heir to the throne, Marcus was *princeps iuventutis*, head of the equestrian order. His name now became Marcus Aelius Aurelius Verus Caesar.

But he refused to allow this newest, powerful name to inflate his ego, as he wrote years later: "See that you don't turn into a Caesar, don't be dyed purple. For it can happen" (*Mem.* vi. 30). The senate made Marcus a member of the priestly colleges. Pius insisted that Marcus now live in the House of Tiberius, the imperial palace on the Palatine hill. Despite Marcus' protests, Pius also required him to assume the visible signs of his new station, the *aulicum fastigium* (pomp of the court). The challenge of preserving his Stoic ideals while living in an imperial court is reflected in the following syllogism in the *Memoranda*: "Where life is possible, it is possible to live well. Life is possible in a palace, so it is possible to live well in a palace" (v. 16). Marcus thanks the gods that he had Pius

> as a ruler and as a father, who could rid me of all arrogance and made me realize that one can live in a palace without needing bodyguards, sumptuous clothes, candelabra, statues, and things like that, all such pomp; but that one may live very nearly as an ordinary citizen, without thereby losing any dignity or being careless in the duties necessary for a ruler on behalf of the state. (i. 17)

As consul in 140 Marcus presided over meetings of the senate, conducted official and religious ceremonies, and performed important administrative functions in the senate. He attended meetings of the imperial council to see how the business of the empire was conducted. Marcus played an increasingly important role in Pius' administration as he was being prepared to rule the state.

The emperor Pius exerted a huge influence on Marcus, as is plain in the first book of the *Memoranda*. There Marcus thanks his adoptive father for his compassion, unwavering resoluteness in judgments reached after thorough investigation, diligence, perseverance, his readiness to listen to any who could contribute to the public good, and his determination to treat everyone impartially as he deserved. Marcus admired Pius' tact in social relations, his carefulness, constancy, equanimity, cheerfulness, and foresight in planning. Pius was above all flattery, self-controlled, sober, deliberate, orderly, circumspect, affable, good humored, and never rude, mean, harsh, or violent. Marcus praises Pius' respect for people sincere about philosophy, his lack of superstition, and his respect for tradition. Marcus praises Pius' conscientious management of the empire, effective stewardship of its resources, and his readiness to be guided without ill will by experts in those fields in which he lacked experience, for example military and legal matters. Marcus also admires Pius' healthy eating habits, rarely needing medical attention, and, like Socrates, that he knew how to enjoy and abstain from things that most people have trouble abstaining from and enjoy too easily (i. 16).

Marcus' studies in philology, literature, history, and philosophy continued. His tutors in Greek were Aninius Macer, Caninius Celer, and Herodes Atticus, a fabulously wealthy Athenian and the most celebrated Greek orator of the age. The prince's tutor in Latin oratory was its preeminent living practitioner, Marcus Cornelius Fronto. Oratory was a key part of Marcus' education, since making public speeches was the only means of communicating to a mass audience prior to the invention of printing. To be trained as "a good man skilled in speaking," as Cato the Elder defined the word *orator*, included the formation of moral character, and thus encompassed training for the whole of public life. Lucius Volusius Maecianus tutored Marcus in law.

Having earlier attended classes given by the Stoic Apollonius, Pius sent for Apollonius to return to Rome from his native Chalcedon. Though Pius is said to have considered Apollonius greedy over his salary, Marcus greatly respected him. From Apollonius Marcus writes that he learned

> Freedom and unvarying reliability. To look to nothing else, even briefly, except the *logos*. To be always the same, in intense pain, in the loss of a child, in chronic illness. To see clearly from his living example that a man can be at the same time strong and gentle. His patience in instructing others. To see a man who obviously regarded his experience and his ability to teach philosophical principles as the least of his gifts. And to learn how to accept the seeming favors of friends without either losing self-respect or receiving them ungratefully. (i. 8)

Herodes Atticus, on the other hand, goes unmentioned in the *Memoranda*. At times tactless and hot-headed, Herodes harshly criticized the Stoics for their ideal of *apatheia* (passionlessness):

> these disciplines of the cult of the unemotional, who want to be considered calm, brave, and steadfast because they show neither

desire nor grief, neither anger nor pleasure, cut out the more active emotions of the spirit and grow old in a torpor, a sluggish, enervated life. (Aulus Gellius, *Attic Nights* 19.12)

Marcus had frequent contact with Herodes for the rest of their lives. Yet given Marcus' allegiance to Stoicism, it is little surprise that Marcus nowhere mentions Herodes by name in the *Memoranda*. One wonders whether Marcus had Herodes in mind when he reminds himself not to be bothered by obstreperous, outspoken critics (cf. v. 3, ix. 27, ix. 34). As a young man when Marcus was mourning the death of one of his educators, he was restrained by some members of the palace staff. According to the biographer, Pius stepped in and said: "Let him be human for once—for neither philosophy nor the empire takes away natural feelings" (*HA Pius* 10.5). Pius evidently did not share the same enthusiasm for Stoic self-mastery that was growing in the maturing Marcus.

Fronto was such a highly esteemed orator that he was regarded a close second only to Cicero. Fronto was extremely learned, precise about Latin usage, brilliant in argument, and a demon for details. He had been a courtier since the court of Hadrian. Fronto disliked his flashy rival Herodes, but in time Marcus succeeded in getting his two eminent teachers to be politely civil to one another. Fronto was little enthused by Marcus' study of philosophy. But many letters of correspondence between Marcus and Fronto have been preserved. Their correspondence reveals an extremely close and intensely affectionate relationship. In a letter celebrating Fronto's birthday, the pupil writes to the master, "I love you as I love myself," and "if ever I know anything of literature this knowledge may enter my heart above all from the lips of Fronto," and prays that "in every journey of mine you may accompany me and that I may not be worn out by so fierce a longing for you" (*Ad MC* 3. 10–11). In his letters Marcus often prays for Fronto's health, as his master was often ill. Once in a legal case Fronto was defense counsel opposing Herodes Atticus, the chief prosecutor. Marcus' diplomatic balm averted antipathies. Fronto later commends Marcus for his conciliation:

If anyone ever had power by his character to unite all his friends in mutual love for one another, you will surely accomplish this much more easily, since you were born to practice all the virtues before you had any training in them. For before you were old enough to begin education you were already perfect and complete in all noble accomplishments. . . . But of all your virtues this is the most admirable: that you unite all your friends in harmony. I cannot conceal my opinion that this is much more difficult than to tame wild beasts and lions with the lyre. (*Ad MC* 4.1)

On January 1, 145, Marcus became consul for the second time—an extraordinary honor for a man of twenty-two. He suffered from a spell of chest pain at this time. The extreme diligence he devoted to his studies even damaged his health, which, along with physical strength, was never robust. But he wrote that his Stoic teacher Apollonius had taught him to endure illness with equanimity. Finally, after a seven-year engagement, Faustina was old enough to marry Marcus in April 145. Since she was Marcus' adoptive sister, Pius had to formally release one of them from his paternal authority (*patria potestas*) for the wedding to occur. As *pontifex maximus*, Emperor Pius officiated at the ceremony. Marcus thanks the gods that he had the wife that he did, describing her as "obedient, affectionate, humble" (i. 17).

By age twenty-five, Marcus grew tired of his study of jurisprudence. He sank into a general malaise. He was tired of homework exercises of arguing both sides in imaginary debates. Though his formal education drew to a close, Marcus had never failed to honor all of his many teachers. Fronto's disdain for philosophy in no way diminished Marcus' commitment to it. The person who exerted the greatest direct influence on Marcus' philosophical formation seems to have been Quintus Junius Rusticus. Rusticus was a descendant of one of the martyrs killed by the tyrant Domitian. It was Rusticus and Stoic philosophy, not Fronto and Latin oratory, which won Marcus' heart and mind. Marcus writes:

From Rusticus: to realize that my character needed reform and treatment; not to be led astray into zeal for rhetoric, or to write treatises on speculative topics, or preach little moralizing sermons, or pose ostentatiously as the ascetic man or the do-gooder. To avoid oratory, poetry, and fancy wordsmithing. Not to strut around the house in elaborate clothes or do things like that. To write letters in a simple style, like the one he himself wrote to my mother from Sinuessa. To be ready to be reconciled to those who have angered or offended me when they want to make up. To read closely and not to be satisfied with just getting the gist of it. Not to agree quickly with every garrulous talker. To have come to know the *Discourses* of Epictetus and lending me his own copy. (i. 7)

Rusticus was at least twenty years older than Marcus. The urgent, forceful brand of Stoicism conveyed by the teacher Epictetus in the *Discourses* would exercise the strongest influence on Marcus' philosophy in the *Memoranda*.[6]

The Peripatetic philosopher Claudius Severus was another one of Marcus' close friends. Severus was a consul in 146 and probably about eight years older than Marcus. Severus' son was later to marry one of Marcus' daughters. Marcus learned about the Stoics (Thrasea and the others) who opposed the tyrannies of Nero and Domitian from Severus, and thanks him for that and for

love of family, love of truth, and love of justice. It was through him that I came to know Thrasea, Helvidius, Cato, Dio, and Brutus, and got the idea of a constitution of equal laws, based on individual equality and freedom of speech, and of a monarchy which honors above all else the liberty of its subjects. From him too, consistency and uniformity in esteeming philosophy. To do good, to be eager to share with others, to be optimistic, and to trust that your friends love you. To be frank with those who met with his disapproval, and that his friends never needed to guess about what he did or didn't want, since it was always clear. (i. 14)

The philosopher Claudius Maximus was another friend of Marcus. Maximus was consul in about 144, governor of the province of Upper Pannonia from 150 to 154, and perhaps twenty years older than the prince. Marcus praises him effusively:

From Maximus: self-mastery and to be hesitant about nothing. To be cheerful in all circumstances, especially in illness. A character that was a balance of graciousness and dignity. Doing what has to be done without grumbling. Everyone's confidence that what he said was what he thought, and that what he did he did without any malice. His imperturbability and undaunted character. Never to hurry or to hesitate, or be at a loss. Neither to be downcast or obsequious, nor to be irascible or suspicious. And generosity, forgiveness, and honesty. To give the impression of someone who by nature stays on the right course rather than one who is kept on it. And the fact that no one could have ever felt patronized by him, or could regard himself as superior to him. And a pleasant demeanor. (i. 15)

The three people for whom Marcus expresses special thanks to the gods for knowing were Apollonius of Chalcedon, Quintus Junius Rusticus, and Claudius Maximus (i. 8). This suggests that, in Marcus' view, these three men—philosophers all—had the greatest impact on his life.

Sextus of Chaeronea, the nephew of the famous author Plutarch, was a teacher of philosophy whose lectures Marcus continued to attend even after becoming emperor. Marcus writes that from Sextus he learned:

> kindness, and an example of how to behave as head of the family, and what it means to live in accordance with nature. And dignity without pretense, and special consideration for friends, and tolerance for amateurs and sloppy thinkers. His ability to get along with everyone, so that his company was pleasanter than any flattery, and those who enjoyed it had the greatest respect for him. His understanding and logical method in investigating and systematizing the principles necessary for life. Not to display anger or other passions, but at the same time to be utterly free of passions and yet most loving. To praise without pomposity; to be very learned without pretension. (i. 9)

The Stoics hold that the pinnacle of self-improvement is to be free of all disturbing, violent passions, like anger, fear, hatred, envy, grief, lust, and the like. So, Marcus the philosopher gives high praise indeed to Sextus the philosopher for being both superlatively free of passions and superlatively loving. The passionlessness of the Stoic wise man does not preclude loving affection (*philostorgia*), as Marcus makes clear here.

Another friend who appears to have been a Stoic was Cinna Catulus. From him Marcus learned "not to disregard a friend's resentment, even unreasonable resentment, but to try to regain his favor; and to speak well of one's teachers whole-heartedly, as is reported of Athenodotus and Domitius, and to be genuinely fond of one's children" (i. 13).

In thirty years of marriage, Marcus and Faustina were to have no fewer than fourteen children over a period of twenty-three years. Marcus thanks the gods that his children "weren't born stupid or physically deformed" (i. 17). Of these fourteen children only six lived to be adults. Of these six adults, four of the five daughters and the one son outlived their father. The first child of Marcus and Faustina was a daughter named Domitia Faustina Aurelia born on November 30, 147. In 149 twin sons were born, but both died before the end of the year. On March 7, 150 a baby girl named Annia Aurelia Galeria Lucilla was born; she would be the first to live beyond childhood. But the first-born of Faustina and Marcus, Domitia Faustina Aurelia, died around 151. The deaths of his children were not the only losses Marcus experienced during these years. His younger sister, Annia Cornificia Faustina, died in 152 when she was no older than thirty. A few years later, probably soon after 155 and certainly by 160, Marcus' mother, Domitia Lucilla (II), died. She was not old.

Another daughter, named Annia Galeria Aurelia Faustina, was born between the death of Domitia Faustina Aurelia and 153.[7] A son was born in 152, but died by 156. In the late 150s Faustina gave birth to another son, who died before late March 158. Marcus and his wife named their next daughter, born in 159, Fadilla, after a sister of Faustina who had died many years before. In 160 another girl was born whom they named Cornificia, after Marcus' sister who had died eight years earlier. Annia Aurelia Galeria Lucilla, Annia Galeria Aurelia Faustina, Fadilla, and Cornificia would grow to be adults and marry.

Grief over the death of a child seems entirely natural and utterly appropriate to non-Stoics. But Apollonius had taught Marcus that Stoics reject grief, including grief over the loss of a son or daughter, as an irrational response to a commonplace event in nature; the Stoic strives to maintain equanimity and be "the same in all circumstances" (*Mem.* i. 8). This was evidently a lesson Marcus needed to repeat. He cautions himself not to leap from the visible impression that his son is ill to the fruitless worry that his son might die of this illness (viii. 49). Marcus instructs himself not to pray for some way to save his child from dying, since that outcome ultimately lies beyond his control, but to pray for a way to shed his fear (of his child dying), since *that* he has the power to achieve (ix. 40). Indeed, Marcus consoles himself that the true principles of Stoicism suffice to dispel all fear, for instance, the quick reminder that *all* generations of human beings, including his children, are leaves the wind blows to the ground (x. 34). Recall that Rusticus had loaned his copy of Epictetus' *Discourses* to Marcus. Presumably that was where Marcus first read the advice he would later inscribe in his *Memoranda*: "As you kiss your son good night, says Epictetus, whisper to yourself, 'Tomorrow he may die.'" The death of his child is no less natural, a Stoic father realizes, and thus no more grim, than grain being reaped (xi. 34).

On December 1, 147 Pius conferred on Marcus the tribunician power, authority over the provinces and the armies of the empire, and the right to bring one measure before the senate after every four introduced by Pius. Unfortunately, the Emperor didn't see fit to send Marcus to the provinces to gain experience with the armies. Throughout his peaceful reign, Pius acquired no military experience. He readily accepted Marcus' advice, probably increasingly so as the years passed. Certainly Pius did not easily promote anyone without consulting Marcus. Lucius, Marcus' adoptive brother, was quaestor in 153 and consul (at age twenty-three) in 154. Lucius was not a contemplative type like his brother. Lucius liked sports of all kinds, especially hunting and wrestling. Though it displeased Pius, Lucius also enjoyed without shame the circus-games and gladiatorial spectacles. It seems likely that as Pius aged, Marcus' role in ruling the empire grew, perhaps considerably so when a senior advisor of Pius died around 156. In his seventy-fifth year, Emperor Pius fell ill and quietly died on March 7, 161, the year Marcus and Lucius were consuls together. The love, admiration, and reverence Marcus felt for Pius were tremendous (i. 16; vi. 30).

THE EARLY REIGN

Marcus was reluctant to accept the responsibility of ruling the empire. Many of his predecessors had been corrupt tyrants. His education in and love of philosophy had much to do with his reluctance. In Plato's *Republic* the character of Socrates asserts that human society will have no rest from evils until philosophers rule (v. 473c–e). However, of all people, philosophers will be the least willing to rule, Plato's Socrates explains, since they desire philosophical wisdom, not political power. Yet the state ruled by philosophers will be ruled best, according to Plato, so philosophers must agree to rule, not because they want to, but for the good of all (vii. 520d). Thus, despite a sincere repugnance for imperial power, Marcus knew what duty required of him. He soberly accepted the imperial powers conferred upon him by the senate and was formally elected *pontifex maximus*, but only on the condition that his younger brother (by adoption) Lucius Commodus receive equal powers. In doing so Marcus was honoring the stated intention of Hadrian that Marcus and Lucius rule together after Pius.

The senate agreed and conferred on Lucius the *imperium* and the tribunician power, and his new name became Imperator Caesar Lucius Aurelius Verus Augustus. Marcus chose to honor Pius by taking on his surname Antoninus. The boy whom Hadrian had nicknamed Verissimus ("truest") long ago was now Imperator Caesar Marcus Aurelius Antoninus Augustus. For the first time in the history of Rome, two emperors ruled, but not as equals. Marcus had greater *auctoritas*. Marcus was consul for the first time at a younger age than Lucius. Marcus was consul three times; Lucius twice. Marcus became *pontifex maximus*, holder of the highest priesthood. Lucius was only *pontifex*. Marcus was ten years older than Lucius. Most importantly, Marcus had been exercising imperial powers helping Pius run the empire for nearly fourteen years. Lucius had spent time hunting, wrestling, and spectating at gladiatorial matches and games at the circus. From 161 until his death in 169, Lucius was his adoptive brother's co-emperor.

After receiving their powers and titles by the senate, the co-emperors went to the camp of the Praetorian Guard just outside the city. On behalf of both, Lucius addressed the troops, who hailed the pair as *imperator*. The co-emperors followed the tradition (established by the emperor Claudius) of promising the troops a donative of 20,000 sesterces per soldier, more to the officers. Considering the peaceful circumstances of their accession, the size of this bounty—equivalent to several years' salary for each guardsman—was extremely generous. In return, the soldiers swore allegiance to the co-emperors with a military oath (*sacramentum*).

Elaborate funeral ceremonies were held for Antoninus Pius. The senate agreed to deify him. His remains were laid to rest in the mausoleum of Hadrian alongside the ashes of Hadrian and the deceased children of Pius and Marcus.

Marcus formally betrothed his oldest daughter, eleven-year-old Annia Aurelia Galeria Lucilla, to Lucius, who was now thirty and, rather awkwardly, had been her uncle by adoption. When he was about seven Lucius had been betrothed to Faustina (II), who instead became Marcus' wife and Annia Lucilla's mother. Pius' fortune was willed to Faustina (II). When her husband became emperor she was three months pregnant. During her pregnancy she dreamed that she was giving birth to two serpents, one fiercer than the other. On August 31 (Caligula's birthday) 161 she gave birth to twin sons named Titus Aurelius Fulvus Antoninus and Lucius Aurelius Commodus. The astrologers cast favorable horoscopes for both. The births were celebrated on imperial coinage.

The Romans liked their new emperors, especially for their civil, unassuming behavior, leniency, and permission of free speech, including a new comedy criticizing them. Initially Marcus had the leisure to "give himself wholly to philosophy," including attending the public lectures of Sextus of Chaeronea, and "seeking the affection of the citizens" (*HA Marc.* 8. 3–4). This carefree period didn't last. In late 161 or early 162 the River Tiber flooded, destroying many buildings, drowning many animals, and bringing famine. The co-emperors attended to these disasters in person, probably making use of Rome's granaries.

Eager to challenge the new co-emperors, the Parthian king Vologases III invaded the Roman-protected kingdom of Armenia, deposed its ruler, and replaced him with a member of the Parthian royal family. The Roman governor of Cappadocia, Sedatius Severianus, led a legion into Armenia in hopes of regaining control. Instead, at Elegia near the headwaters of the Euphrates, he and his troops were trapped by the Parthian general Chosrhoes. Unable to fight their way out, Severianus committed suicide and his legion was massacred. The threat of war was brewing in Britain, and the Chatti of the Taunus Mountains crossed the empire's northern boundary, invading Upper Germany and Raetia.

Pius, having reigned in peaceful times, had provided no military experience whatsoever to his heirs Marcus and Lucius. Other than the Praetorian Guard, neither man had seen an army, much less a battle. Marcus had never visited any of the frontier provinces. Yet they had many urgent decisions to make. First, Marcus replaced one of the imperial secretaries of state, Caecilius Crescens Volusianus—a man of literary interests—with Varius Clemens, a man with a long military career. Clemens had served actively in the war in Mauretania, had been procurator, governor, and commander

in chief in Mauretania Caesariensis and Raetia, and had been procurator in three other provinces. By 162 Marcus recalled to Rome
the prefect governing Egypt, his distinguished lawyer and former
tutor Volusius Maecianus, made him a senator, appointed him prefect of the treasury, and soon thereafter consul. Statius Priscus was
assigned to replace the late Severianus as governor of Cappadocia,
despite having to travel from the opposite end of the empire in
Britain to get to his new post. In place of Priscus Marcus sent
Calpurnius Agricola to face Rome's enemies in Britain. Marcus
appointed his friend (and Fronto's son-in-law) Aufidius Victorinus
governor of Upper Germany.

Reinforcements for the eastern armies were sent. Geminius
Marcianus, commander of the Tenth legion at Vindobona (Vienna),
led detachments of the Danubian legions to Cappadocia. In addition, three entire legions were sent to the east, one from Bonn in
Lower Germany, another from Aquincum (Budapest) in Lower
Pannonia, and the third from Troesmis on the Danube, in Lower
Moesia. Though the defenses of the northern frontier were weakened by this redeployment, signs of future turmoil in central
Europe were judged to be less pressing than the war in the east. But
when the Parthian army defeated Attidius Cornelianus, the governor of Syria, the Syrians rebelled. So sometime during the winter
of 161–162 the co-emperors decided that the deteriorating situation
required one of them to lead the Roman forces in person to war
against the Parthians. The armies of the Roman frontier had not
engaged in a full-scale war commanded by the Emperor himself
since Trajan's death in 117, four years before Marcus' birth. Marcus
and Lucius decided that Lucius should go, "because he was physically robust and younger than Marcus, and better suited to military
activity" (Dio 71. 1. 3). The biographer of Lucius ascribes to Marcus
other motives for sending his brother to Parthia: to remove Lucius'
immorality from the eyes of Rome, so that he could learn frugality
abroad, to reform his character in the crucible of war, or so that
he might genuinely realize that he was an emperor (*HA Marc.* 8.9;
Verus 5.8).

Lucius would need a full staff of experienced military men. Furius
Victorinus was chosen from among the praetorian prefects. He had
served as procurator in the eastern province of Galatia as well as
serving on the Danube, in Britain, in Spain, as prefect of Egypt, and
as prefect of the Italian fleets. Victorinus brought some praetorian

guardsmen with him. The very best choice among the senators was Pontius Laelianus Larcius Sabinus. His unmatched military career began as a young tribune of the legion in Lower Germany and then Britain in 122 when Platorius Nepos went to build Hadrian's Wall. Laelianus had governed both provinces of Pannonia and in 153 had been governor of Syria. He had a reputation for being an old-fashioned disciplinarian and was given the honorific rank and title of *comes Augustorum*, "companion of the Emperors." Iallius Bassus, the recently appointed governor of Lower Moesia, was sent east as another *comes*. To replace Attidius Cornelianus as the governor of Syria, surprisingly Marcus chose his first cousin, Annius Libo, a patrician in his early thirties who must have lacked military experience and who had only been consul the previous year, 161. Lucius took with him his four favorite freedmen and his old foster-father, Nicomedes, to run the commissariat for the expeditionary force.

Lucius set off in the summer of 162. On his journey to the east coast of Italy he feasted in country houses and hunted in Apulia. Delayed by illness for a few days, Lucius continued east to Corinth and Athens with his retinue of musicians and singers. He then sailed across the Aegean, dallied his way through pleasant resort towns along the southern coast of Asia Minor, and finally arrived in Antioch, the capital of the Syrian province. Around this time Statius Priscus arrived to assume command in Cappadocia. His successes as general over the course of 163 made him something of a legend.

Back in Italy, Marcus struggled with anxiety about the distant war. A four-day getaway at a resort on the Etrurian coast failed to relax him. Marcus worked long into the night on judicial business. In Rome his public duties called for him to give more speeches. The correspondence between Fronto and Marcus continued. Fronto was particularly proud of Marcus' beautifully moving speech in the senate about an earthquake that had struck Cyzicus in Asia Minor. Fronto repeated the lesson he had imparted to his pupil twenty years before, that "Philosophy will tell you what to say, eloquence will tell you how to say it" (*De eloq.* 2.19). Before the end of 162, Faustina gave birth to another son. They named him Marcus Annius Verus, the original name of his father.

To raise the spirits of his dear friend, Fronto sent Marcus a long, carefully crafted letter detailing Rome's long military history of reversals of fortune, rebounding from setbacks to victories. When Statius Priscus captured the Armenian capital Artaxata in 163, the tide had turned to favor the Romans in the war against Parthia. Lucius had stayed mainly in Antioch, but wintered at Laodicea and spent the summer at Daphne, a resort outside Antioch. Carousing, gambling with dice, and the entertainment of actors from Rome occupied him. His passion for circus races was indulged with the latest news from Rome about his favorite chariot team, the Greens. Recall that as a young boy Marcus learned from his *educator* to rise above partisanship in sports and above cheering for any chariot team or gladiator (i. 5). In sharp contrast, Lucius carried with him all the way to Antioch a golden statue of Volucer, a horse of the Green team. Seeing little or no combat did not stop Lucius from taking the title *Armeniacus*, "conqueror of the Armenians." Lucius and his staff got to work training the Syrian troops, who had grown soft lounging at open-air cafés in Antioch during years of peace.

In Syria Lucius took a mistress named Pantheia from Smyrna, a Greek city on the Ionian coast. The satirist Lucian gushes that Pantheia was a gracious, loving, modest woman of perfect beauty with a mellifluous voice who sang wonderfully accompanied by the lyre, spoke pure Ionic Greek, had a classical Attic wit, a shrewd grasp of public affairs, and enjoyed the gifts of all the Muses. To please this incomparable, yet low-born, woman Lucius shaved off his luxurious beard. Long after Lucius had died, Marcus doubted that Pantheia was still keeping watch at her deceased lover's tomb (viii. 37).

Meanwhile, Libo disdained Lucius' authority, insisting that he was responsible to Marcus alone. After the two quarreled, Libo died. Rumor had it that Lucius had him poisoned. Lucius compounded Marcus' distress over Libo's death by marrying off Libo's widow to Lucius' freedman Agaclytus, contrary to Marcus' wishes. Years later Marcus made such marriages between a person of senatorial status and a freedman illegal by decree of the senate.

On March 7, 164 Marcus' daughter Lucilla turned fourteen and was old enough to marry Lucius. Perhaps stories of the magnificent Pantheia and a lull in military operations in the east induced Marcus to move up the wedding date. Marcus escorted Lucilla as far as Brundisium before returning to Rome to stay with Faustina and their three baby boys. Lucius' uncle, Vettulenus Civica Barbarus, led the bridal party to Ephesus, where the bridegroom met them. Marcus made Civica Barbarus a *comes Augusti*, perhaps wanting him to curb Lucius' misbehavior more effectively than Libo had. Having secured Armenia, in 164 the Romans built a new capital called Kaine Polis ("New City") to replace Artaxata. Lucius crowned as king of Armenia an Arsacid prince named Sohaemus who had been a Roman senator and consul. Lucius finally succeeded in persuading Marcus to share the title *Armeniacus*. In Rome Marcus was very active in the administration of justice. Professional jurists described him as "a most prudent and conscientiously just emperor," "most skilled in the law." The biographer in the Augustan History reports that Marcus' three major interests in the theory and practice of legislation involved the manumission (liberation) of slaves, the appointment of guardians for orphans and minors, and the selection of councillors (*decuriones*) to administer local communities throughout the provinces. His interest in the appointment of trustees and guardians may have been partly personal; his father died when Marcus was still very young. For the first time Marcus decreed that all youths could have guardians appointed to them without specific reasons being given. He always attended sessions of the senate when he was in Rome and always made proposals in person. No emperor respected the senate more than Marcus. He honored many senators of praetorian and consular rank who held no magistracy by delegating to them the settling of disputes so that they could distinguish themselves by judiciously administering the law. He was careful in his public expenditure. He prohibited libelous accusations, marking false accusers for public disgrace. Marcus banned the practice of accusing wealthy, prominent citizens of treason in order to fill the coffers of the imperial treasury. During the reigns of his predecessors Tiberius, Nero, and Domitian, these unscrupulous accusations by ambitious and greedy public informants were rampant. Marcus enacted many new measures for supporting poor children under state care (*de alimentis publicis*). He carefully managed Rome's grain supply and kept the city streets and public highways well maintained. Marcus addressed the problem of the unwillingness of the wealthy to serve on local councils (which resulted in inefficiency and corruption) with efforts to fill the local councils and by appointing senators as supervisors of the local communities beset by corruption.

The biographer sums up Marcus' rule of law as follows:

Towards the people he behaved at all times as in a free state. He was at all times extremely reasonable in restraining people from bad actions and urging them to good ones, generous in rewarding, quick to forgive, thus making bad men good, and good men very good, and he even took insults, which he had to put up with from some people, with equanimity. . . . To avoid taking an easy revenge on anyone, instead of making a praetor who had handled some cases very badly resign his office, he merely handed over the man's legal business to his colleague. The imperial treasury never affected his judgment in any lawsuits involving money. Finally, if he was firm, he was also reasonable. (*HA Marc.* 12. 4–6)

During the first eight years of his reign, many of the cases in civil law Marcus adjudicated concerned family affairs. Inheritance cases were also often litigated.

Marcus' interest in legal cases involving personal freedom and the liberation of slaves was patently philosophical. As a Stoic, Marcus embraced the philosophical ideal of cosmopolitanism, the idea that all human beings are "citizens of the universe." We are all rational beings who belong to the same universal community.[8] Since all rational persons are equally members of this one cosmos, all human beings deserve equal respect. Our kinship in rationality far transcends all our outward differences in language, race, genealogy, social rank (which depended on wealth, in Marcus' time), and sex. Moreover, our rationality is the wellspring of our freedom. Just as the earlier Roman Stoic Seneca understood that the Stoic idea of cosmopolitanism entailed real respect for those unlucky enough to be slaves, that is, legal property, Marcus was similarly enlightened. By means of jurisprudence, however, Marcus was in a much better position than Seneca (who could at best offer Stoic *advice* to Emperor Nero) to clear the path to freedom for slaves. In one inheritance case, for instance, it was unclear whether a certain man had died intestate, because in his will he had crossed out the names of his heirs and his property. He had also crossed out the name of a slave whom he had ordered to be freed. Marcus officially ruled that the slave be manumitted nonetheless, true to his belief in cosmopolitan freedom inspired by Stoicism. Throughout his reign Marcus appears to have consistently given slaves the greatest possible chance of achieving their freedom, if there had ever been any question of their masters wishing to grant it. Several other cases during this period displayed Marcus' concern for the welfare, safety, and liberty of slaves. Numerous other cases illustrate his concern over trustees and guardians. Near the end of his reign, a verdict Marcus issued in favor of a slave's manumission was to be repeatedly cited by jurists as the decisive precedent.

After his successes in Armenia, Lucius tried to negotiate with Vologases but was rebuffed by the Parthian king. In 163 The Parthians deposed the pro-Roman ruler of Osrhoene, the principality in northwestern Mesopotamia. Roman forces responded by occupying adjoining areas and in 165 pushed into Mesopotamia. By the end of 165 the Parthian war was mostly over. Credit for winning the war belongs chiefly to the subordinate generals and especially to Avidius Cassius rather than to Lucius, despite his grand boasts. In the city of Seleucia Cassius' army contracted a disease which would claim millions of lives throughout the empire for years to come. Two new legions were recruited for Marcus' forthcoming campaigns in the north.

In the fall or winter of 165 Marcus' Stoic calm was again tested when one of his twin boys, Antoninus, died at the age of four. Bereaved, Faustina took some of their children and traveled east to be with her pregnant daughter Lucilla. A few months after Fronto's wife Cratia died, Fronto's grandson, his son Victorinus' boy, died. Fronto fell into despair. Marcus tried his best to console his bereaved friend, who was embittered by his loss.

In 166 Cassius' army invaded and conquered Media, the heart of the Parthian kingdom. Lucius celebrated by taking another title, *Medicus*. Marcus accepted the title *Parthicus Maximus* won the previous year. Lucius and his entourage journeyed home, arriving perhaps in August. By then his wife Lucilla may have been pregnant again. Cassius, who was no older than thirty-five, was made consul in the spring of 166, then governor of Syria, since the major victories in the war were his. The European legions returned to their home bases.

The triumph for the victories in the east was held on October 12, 166. Marcus' sons, five-year-old Commodus and three-year-old Annius Verus, and some of his daughters joined the procession. Marcus and Lucius were awarded the "civic crown" of oak leaves "for saving the lives of fellow citizens" and received the title *pater patriae*. Traditionally, the *triumphator* (conqueror), his face painted red, carried a scepter, and wore a special costume and crown. Standing behind him in the chariot a slave whispered in his ear "remember that you are a mortal"—a particularly apt reminder for Marcus the Stoic—as the army marching behind him and the on-looking crowd cheered. After the triumph Rome's people were entertained with games in the Circus. Two illustrations of Marcus' concern for the safety and welfare of Roman citizens are reported by the biographer. First, after a boy fell from a tightrope, Marcus ordered that mattresses be laid out to protect against future accidents. Second, for their safety, he only allowed gladiators to use blunted weapons like buttoned foils. Another instance of Marcus' aversion to bloodshed involved a lion which was specially trained to eat people. Although he reluctantly granted the crowd's request to bring out the lion to be viewed, Marcus himself refused to look at the animal. Moreover, he refused to grant the lion's trainer freedom, in spite of the persistent demands of the spectators. Instead, Marcus officially proclaimed that the lion-trainer had accomplished nothing to deserve winning him his freedom. Marcus' sense of decency and desert precluded indulging spectators' enthusiasm for gore.

Unrest in the north worsened. Tribes beyond the Rhine and the Danube sought new land in which to settle, and their populations expanded into Roman territory. In late 166 or early 167 six thousand Langobardi and Ubii tribesmen invaded Pannonia. Roman forces swiftly expelled them. Eleven tribes sent Ballomarius, king of the Marcomanni, as the head envoy to make peace with Iallius Bassus, governor of Upper Pannonia.

Marcus probably wanted to travel to the northern provinces in person, but the increasing threat of the plague prevented it. It is not known whether the disease was smallpox, measles, louse-borne typhus, or the bubonic plague, but the troops returning from Mesopotamia brought it back with them and it spread throughout the empire from Persia to the Rhine and Gaul. Modern scholars have judged it to be the most serious pandemic in all of antiquity. The city of Rome was the most densely populated area in the empire and so was the hardest hit. Since they lived in barracks, Roman soldiers were the most susceptible. Thus, the plague must have been Marcus' greatest concern in 167. Hysteria gripped the populace. Marcus erected statues to the most eminent of the many thousands that died. At public expense he held funeral ceremonies for the common folk. Marcus and Lucius issued rescripts to address problems of overcrowding of cemeteries, barring the appropriation of other people's graves, and dealing with the buying and selling of sepulchers. Marcus summoned priests to perform every variety of religious rites to purify Rome. His participation in these ceremonies as *pontifex maximus* in 166 and 167 delayed his departure for the northern frontier.

Marcus had no help from Lucius after he returned from the war. Though he served as consul (a third time) in 167 for a few winter months, Lucius' recreations included banquets, orgies, cavorting with this freedmen, and being entertained by the actors, harpists, flautists, jesters, and jugglers he had brought back from Syria. Marcus had a taste of what ruling alone was like.

Fear of the pandemic inflamed hostility toward the Christians. They were considered to be haters of the human race and atheists because they refused to honor and propitiate the Roman pantheon. The failure of the Christians to participate in the religious rites of purification during this desperate time made them conspicuous targets. Anyone who hated them could easily have them arrested. The very name "Christian" was a capital crime. Yet accused Christians who recanted received a free pardon. No other accused criminals received such lenient treatment. Justin was one of those martyrs tried and executed for refusing to recant. Justin was well versed in Greek philosophy, having studied first with a Stoic, then an Aristotelian, then a Pythagorean, and then a Platonist before converting to Christianity. The prefect who presided at Justin's trial was Junius Rusticus, Marcus' chief teacher of Stoicism. It is likely that Marcus knew about the trial.

What did Marcus think of the Christians? We read: "What a soul it is that is ready, if it must be at this very moment, to be separated from the body, and be either extinguished or dispersed or remain intact! But this readiness must proceed from one's own decision, not from mere *parataxis* [like the Christians]. It has to be well-considered and serious and, in order to persuade others, without dramatics" (*Mem.* ix. 3). *Parataxis* is the Greek word for arraying troops in a battle-line. The bracketed phrase "like the Christians" may have been inserted by a later reader. If Marcus wrote it, however, then he may have meant that the Christians were not making their own individual choices to die as martyrs, but were being pressured into it by their peers in the cult, like soldiers trained to line up and get bowled over like pins. Rusticus probably died soon after the trial of Justin. About this time Claudius Severus, the son of Marcus' philosopher friend, married Marcus' daughter Annia Faustina.

In the spring of 168 the co-emperors set out for the northern frontier with their general staff, including two former governors of Pannonia whose experience would help immensely in the coming campaign. The Marcomanni, the Victuali, and tribes which had been displaced by other tribes from farther north threatened to invade unless they were allowed into Roman provinces south of the Danube. Since negotiations mended some of the treaties that had been broken, Lucius was satisfied and had resisted leaving. Roman forces had defeated the Quadi, one of the most important tribes, by the time the imperial party reached Aquileia (Venice). Marcus persuaded the greatest physician of the empire, Galen, to join them. Yet Galen was powerless to save the prefect and general Furius Victorinus and much of the army from the plague. Lucius, wanting to hunt and feast for a season, believed that he and Marcus were not needed on the front and should return to Rome. Marcus' insistence that they proceed to inspect the frontier provinces prevailed. They crossed the Alps and, for the first time in his life, Marcus was outside Italy. The co-emperors stayed at Carnuntum, the headquarters of the governor of Upper Pannonia.

Marcus reorganized the administration of northern Italy, Pannonia, and Upper Moesia to prepare for war. He was determined to engage with the barbarian tribes because he believed their retreat from Rome's huge expeditionary force was a delaying tactic. The co-emperors wintered in Aquileia in 168–169. Presumably they planned to launch an offensive in the spring, but the cold and the pandemic killed many. Galen advised them to return to Rome. On Lucius' insistence they set off in midwinter. Two days en route Lucius suffered a stroke near Altinum, where he died three days later in January 169 at age thirty-nine. Marcus, suddenly the sole emperor, brought his adoptive brother's corpse home.

A STOIC AT WAR

Funeral ceremonies were held in Rome. Marcus dutifully provided generous financial support for Lucius' relatives and freedmen.

The Northern Frontiers

Lucius was deified with the name Divus Verus. The plague had killed so many legionaries that Marcus needed huge numbers of new recruits. To replenish the legions he accepted slaves as volunteers who were freed upon enrollment, collected gladiators into special units, conscripted brigands of Dalmatia and Dardania as guerilla fighters, and hired Germanic mercenaries. This required tremendous capital outlay, yet revenues from taxes and imperial estates were sharply reduced by the plague. Marcus faced a financial crisis, but would not burden the provincials with heavier taxes. Instead, over a period of two months, he auctioned off imperial property in the Forum of Trajan. Gold, crystal, and murrine goblets, gold vases, Faustina's silk and gold-embroidered clothes, jewels, statues, and paintings by famous artists were sold. Though his wife may have resented giving up some of her jewels and dresses, the Stoic emperor had no compunction about sacrificing pretty trinkets in order to strengthen the security of the empire. Marcus trivializes luxuries: imperial garments like purple robes are merely sheep wool dyed in shellfish blood (*Mem.* vi. 13). The marble of the palace floor is nothing but hardened dirt; gold and silver are residues; clothes are animal hair (ix. 36). Marcus' more drastic measure was to mint more coinage despite his inability to increase the supply of bullion, thereby debasing the imperial currency.

Marcus also attended to Lucius' widow Lucilla and her infant daughter. Marcus decided that his nineteen-year-old daughter would marry Claudius Pompeianus, who was fifty or older. He was the son of a Syrian who had not even been a senator. But having served as governor of Lower Pannonia in 167, Pompeianus was Marcus' choice to be chief military advisor for the upcoming campaign. Both Lucilla and Faustina opposed the marriage, but no later than October 169 Pompeianus wed Lucilla. In September Marcus' younger son, Annius Verus, had a tumor removed from below his ear, but died after the surgery. He was five. Marcus mourned for five days while conducting some public business. It was almost fall when Marcus and his new son-in-law Pompeianus headed north to war. Evidently another son, Hadrianus, had been born after Annius Verus, but he must not have lived long. Of the thirteen children born to Faustina and Marcus, now only one son, Commodus, and four daughters remained. Until about 170, that is. Faustina, who was about forty, gave birth to their last child, a daughter named Vibia Aurelia Sabina.

The winter of 169–170 may have been when Marcus began writing his *Memoranda*. He was presumably camped somewhere between the Danube and its tributary the Save during his first full season in winter-quarters. In the years of warfare to come, the daily duties of commanding huge armies, issuing administrative decisions, conducting legal affairs, and dealing with the plague, far removed from Rome and the lessons in philosophy learned there years before, surely necessitated respite. We might imagine Marcus at sunset, snowflakes drifting down from the chill sky, having completed the last of the day's duties, withdrawing into his tent, lighting a lamp, taking up a pen, and freeing his mind to think about his place in the universe from the perspective of eternity. Writing down his thoughts, just for himself, about mortality, impermanence, and the power of the mind gave Marcus the therapeutic philosophical exercise that kept his intellect fit, focused, and nimble. The notes he wrote to remind himself of Stoic truths sustained him through a grim decade of bloody battles, broken treaties, deceits, desertions, disease, and death.

The Roman offensive across the Danube into barbarian territory in 170 was thwarted. Soon thereafter the Marcomanni, Quadi, and their allies, coming from Bohemia and Slovakia, slipped through the Roman lines, crossed the Alps, invaded Italy, pillaged Opitergium, and besieged Aquileia. To the east the Costoboci descended from the Carpathian region of Dacia to invade the frontier provinces of the Balkans, looting, burning, and butchering their way into Thrace, Macedonia, and Achaea (Greece). The barbarian forces destroyed the shrine of the Mysteries at Eleusis. In 171 Moorish rebels crossed the Straits of Gibraltar and invaded Baetica (southern Spain). Marcus sent his friend Aufidius Victorinus to govern both Tarraconensis and Baetica. After protracted struggles, Marcus' armies repelled the invaders.

After the first victory Marcus won in person, he accepted the salutation as *Imperator* but denied the troops' request for a donative. He told them that any bonus they got to their regular pay would be wrung from the blood of their parents and families. Cassius Dio reports that as commander in chief Marcus ruled so temperately and firmly "that even when engaged in so many and so great wars, he never did anything unworthy by way of flattery or as the result of fear" (71. 3. 3–4). The biographer remarks that, in both military and civic matters, Marcus always consulted with the experts before taking action. This was a habit Marcus admired in Antoninus Pius (*Mem.* i. 17). His devotion to philosophy, the biographer continues, made Marcus appear hard, in both his military discipline and his whole way of life. Due to this perception, people bitterly criticized him, but Marcus answered his critics in speeches and pamphlets. Marcus conscientiously heard the counsel of his many friends, but rejected their advice to abandon the war which was costing so many noblemen their lives (*HA Marc.* 22. 3–8). Late in 171 Marcus vigorously and persistently pursued diplomacy with some success. He added the Astingi and Lacringi as allies. Negotiations with the Cotini, neighbors of the Marcomanni and Quadi, ultimately failed. The Quadi, however, were soon neutralized.

The long postponed offensive into barbarian territory beyond the Danube began in 172. The Romans won some battles and lost others. Two fabulous events are recorded for 172. In one, during a thunderstorm Marcus' prayer was said to have summoned a lightning bolt that destroyed an enemy military engine. The second episode was the battle of the Rain Miracle. A large contingent of the Quadi surrounded and trapped a small Roman force broiling under the sun. Scorched by the heat, parched with thirst, wounded, and exhausted, the Roman soldiers couldn't fight, retreat, or get water. Suddenly clouds rolled in and released a downpour upon them. The Romans caught the rain in their helmets and shields, gulping it down and watering their horses. The Quadi tried to attack, but were struck by a violent hailstorm and lightning bolts. No evidence indicates that Marcus was present at the Rain Miracle, but coins minted in 173 suggest that he credited the god Hermes (Mercury) for saving the Roman troops. This evidence, coupled with the depiction of the Rain Miracle on the Aurelian Column, suggest attempts to persuade the Roman people that Marcus' reign and campaign were divinely sanctioned.[9]

Marcus defeated the powerful Marcomanni by the end of the campaign season of 172 and received the title "Germanicus" (conqueror of the Germans). That year a revolt in Egypt was quashed by Avidius Cassius, governor of Syria. Cassius received special powers over all the eastern provinces. The pro-Roman king of Armenia, Sohaemus, was deposed by Tiridates and other pro-Parthian dissidents. Martius Verus, governor of Cappadocia, restored Sohaemus. Rather than execute Tiridates, Marcus exiled him to distant Britain.

In 173 the war waged against the Quadi and other tribes dragged on as a series of small skirmishes. Marcus spent his third year in a row "at Carnuntum," the heading of the second book of the *Memoranda*. The morale of the Roman troops was low. There had been deserters since the beginning of the 170s. More trouble arose when the Quadi expelled their pro-Roman ruler and bellicose Ariogaesus seized power. Marcus put a bounty on him, dead or alive. Yet when Ariogaesus was captured, Marcus exiled him to Alexandria, in distant Egypt, instead of executing him.

The winter of 173–174 the Romans battled the Iazyges. In the early 170s in Rome Faustina was rumored to be having sexual liaisons with ballet dancers and gladiators. By the winter of 173–174 Marcus had brought Faustina and their baby girl Sabina to join him at the northern front. Whenever his military duties permitted, he carried out judicial business. Marcus closely examined details and was painstaking in administering justice for the cases on which he ruled. Due to his physical weakness, at first he could not endure the cold. He ate very little food, and only at night. During the day he could only take the medicine prescribed by Galen to treat the chronic pain in his stomach and chest (probably an ulcer). The practice of taking this medicine, *theriac* (antidote), was believed to have enabled Marcus to endure various illnesses. Rulers in antiquity took some form of antidote to build immunity from poison. Galen's *theriac* contained opium. Marcus stopped taking it because it made him drowsy, but then he suffered insomnia, so he resumed taking a regular dose as a pain-killer and sleep aid. It is possible Marcus became addicted to this medicine.

Some modern estimates put the total deaths caused by the plague as high as five million. Certainly the pandemic inflicted heavy casualties through all ranks of the army during the northern wars, dramatically reducing the number of qualified candidates for high-ranking military positions. Based on merit alone, Marcus made many poor men he knew senators. Marcus left instructions that, while absent from Rome, the entertainment of the people be funded by the wealthiest sponsors of public spectacles. Back at Rome, Commodus' education continued. By now his two sisters were probably married, Fadilla to Plautius Quintillus, Lucius' nephew, and Cornificia to Petronius Sura Mamertinus, grandson of Pius' guard prefect. Galen cured Commodus of inflamed tonsils and a severe fever.

Marcus enacted laws prohibiting riding and driving within Rome's city limits, and abolishing mixed bathing. He reformed the declining morals of married women and young nobles. Marcus customarily imposed lighter punishments for crimes than those usually inflicted by law. He himself presided at trials of distinguished men for capital offenses, and did so with complete fairness, according to the biographer.

In early spring of 175 Marcus renewed attack on the Sarmatians. His ambition was to annex the territories of the Sarmatians, Marcomanni, and Quadi to create two new provinces of the empire. But stunning news from the east arrived. Avidius Cassius, governor of Syria and essentially the ruler of the east, had revolted. He was recognized as emperor in most eastern provinces, including Egypt. The news had been sent by Martius Verus, governor of Cappadocia, who remained loyal to Marcus. Marcus was shocked and deeply disturbed by this news. Behind the scenes Faustina may have worried that illness was likely to take his life, and that if Marcus died, the thirteen-year-old Commodus would be too young to rule, and so he and Faustina would need a protector. Since she and Lucilla strongly disliked Pompeianus (the much older husband Marcus had chosen for Lucilla), and since Avidius Cassius was a man Faustina's age whom she had no doubt met years before, Faustina evidently wrote letters to Cassius to encourage him to seize the throne and take Marcus' place when he died. Interestingly, the biographer reports that Marcus regarded Faustina, who was his cousin before they married, as the source of his claim to rule. When he was advised to divorce her for infidelity, he supposedly replied that if he did, he would have to return the dowry—the empire—as well (*HA Marc.* 19. 8–9). Avidius Cassius may have received a bogus report that Marcus *had* died, proclaimed himself emperor, and only later learned that Marcus was alive, but decided to stay the course. Since Cassius was accepted as emperor in Egypt, he controlled Rome's main grain supply—a huge strategic advantage.

FATHER AND SON

The Roman senate declared Cassius a public enemy. Marcus summoned Commodus to the north to accelerate the steps needed for his succession. Marcus dispatched a special force of troops to protect Rome. At Sirmium, on July 7, 175, Commodus received the *toga virilis*, became a citizen of Rome, was commended to the army, became *princeps iuventutis*, and was proclaimed heir apparent. Before he was ready to leave Sirmium, Marcus got news that Cassius had been killed by a centurion named Antonius, just three months and six days after Cassius launched his rebellion. Martius Verus had taken over Syria and burned Cassius' correspondence, which could have incriminated Faustina and others. Cassius' head was sent to Marcus, but he refused to see it and had it buried.

Probably in early July Marcus set out to restore the loyalty of the eastern provinces accompanied by Faustina, Commodus, other family members, Helvius Pertinax, and Valerius Maximianus. En route, at a village called Halala in Cappadocia, Faustina died. She may have died of gout or due to complications of another pregnancy. She was also probably weakened by the long winter's journey. Life expectancy in antiquity was low, and Faustina had borne fourteen children. The senate deified her. Marcus renamed Halala "Faustinopolis." He was greatly distraught at her death. Once again the advice from the Stoic teacher Epictetus applied to Marcus' situation: "When kissing your wife or your child, tell yourself you're kissing a mortal human being, so when she dies you won't be so upset" (*Encheiridion* 3). Evidently Marcus had more success heeding this advice with his young children than with his wife Faustina.

In Egypt Marcus imposed light punishments like banishment upon those who had supported Cassius. Marcus negotiated new peace treaties with the kings of Parthia. On his return journey he visited Athens, home of the original Stoa.[10] There Marcus the philanthropic benefactor established teachers in every academic subject and awarded them annual salaries. These included four endowed chairs of philosophy: a Platonist, an Aristotelian, a Stoic, and an Epicurean. Marcus also visited Eleusis, where he and Commodus were initiated in the Mysteries.

After seven years away (from 169 to 176), Marcus finally returned to Rome in late fall. On November 27 Commodus was given the *imperium* at the tender age of fifteen. Marcus decided to make Commodus and his son-in-law Peducaeus Plautius Quintillus (Fadilla's husband) consuls in January 177. Ceionia Fabia, Marcus' former fiancée, wanted to marry him. Instead, Marcus took a mistress as Pius had after his wife died. After Galen correctly diagnosed and treated Marcus for an ailment (indigestion) that three other doctors had misdiagnosed, the Emperor regularly praised Galen as "first among physicians and unique among philosophers" (Galen, *On Prognosis* 11.8).

The triumph for Marcus' many victories in the northern wars was celebrated on December 23, 176. To honor the spectators, remarkably, Marcus ran beside the triumphal chariot which carried Commodus. In November the senate had voted that a triumphal arch be erected to honor their emperor. Perhaps at this time the senate also voted to begin construction of the Aurelian Column. The members of his military staff were also honored and decorated. Marcus would be acclaimed *Imperator* one more time, his tenth, in 179.

On January 1, 177 Commodus became consul and received tribunician power. Later that year Marcus gave his son all the titles, honors, and powers to be co-emperor, except for *pontifex maximus*. The sources report that Commodus liked making pottery, singing, whistling, and dancing. He also enjoyed vulgar jokes and performing as a gladiator. In one story he displayed a fiery bad temper.

Marcus' legal decisions of this time continue to show his compassion for individual slaves and efforts to ensure their liberty, regardless of the obstacles put in their way by third parties, if the slaves' masters had intended to liberate them. As a Stoic by training and by necessity of his imperial position, Marcus took civic duties very seriously. Consequently, he must have had no tolerance for individuals who flouted their duties to the state. This included the Christians, who professed complete disregard for worldly life. The Christians refused to propitiate the Roman gods and were rumored to practice cannibalism and engage in orgies. During this fearful time of war, plague, and economic hardship, they made convenient scapegoats. To publicly confess being a Christian remained a capital offense, as did refusing to recant once charged. Hostility toward the Christians flared up in Lugdunum (Lyon) and they were rounded up and accused. Some of these Christians were Roman citizens, so the governor of Gaul wrote to Marcus asking for instructions on how to treat them. Marcus instructed that any Roman citizens who recanted their Christian faith should be released, but the rest should be executed by beheading. Beheading was the form of execution a condemned Roman citizen had the privilege of receiving. The noncitizens in Lugdunum were tormented by wild animals in the amphitheater. In his reign Marcus neither initiated persecutions of the Christians, nor did he spare them from execution as a result of the course of law. Some fighting by the barbarian tribes broke out in the north. The Moors also made trouble in Spain. In 178 Marcus decreed that preference be given to a woman's children as beneficiaries of her inheritance rather than to her siblings and other relatives. This was a major advance in recognizing a woman's individual existence apart from her family. The economy improved sufficiently for Marcus to cancel all debts incurred to the state treasury over the past forty-six years. Fiscal documents concerning the years 133 through 178 were burned in the Forum. But the fighting along the Danube worsened and Marcus returned to the northern front. Commodus married Bruttia Crispina. Her father, Bruttius Praesens, had been consul in 153. One source describes Marcus as

> so outstanding for his wisdom, lenience, innocence of character and literary attainments that when he was about to set off against the Marcomanni with his son Commodus, . . . he was surrounded by a crowd of philosophers, who were protesting that he should not commit himself to the expedition and to battle, before he had expounded the difficulties and obscurities of the philosophical schools. Thus it was feared, from zeal for philosophy, that the uncertainties of war would affect his safety. And so greatly did the liberal arts flourish in his reign that I would think it the glory of the times. (Aurelius Victor, *De Caes.* 16. 9–10)

Despite this plea for him to stay, Marcus judged it necessary once again to see to the security of the north in person.

Father and son set out from Rome on the second military expedition to Germania on August 3, 178 accompanied by Pompeianus, Valerius Maximianus, Bruttius Praesens, and their staff. Marcus made countless appointments and promotions to prepare for the upcoming campaign. These appointments reflected how he valued men's merits over their background, wealth, or status. A source records Marcus saying that "It is impossible to make men exactly as one wishes them to be, but it is our duty to use them, such as they are, for any service in which they may be useful to the state" (Dio 71. 34. 4). Marcus' goal was evidently to bring the Marcomanni, Quadi, and Sarmatian Iazyges into the empire and Romanize them, not to expel or destroy them. Indeed, since the earlier campaign he had allowed many Germans to settle in the frontier provinces of Dacia, Pannonia, Upper and Lower Germania, and even Italy. Marcus' plan to create two new Roman provinces north of the Danube, Marcomannia and Sarmatia, was close to being realized when he fell gravely ill. According to the biographer, Marcus urged Commodus to complete the war for the sake of the empire, but Commodus wanted to leave to avoid being infected. When the army heard how serious the Emperor's illness was the troops were distraught, "for they loved him as none other." Seven days later, on March 17, 180, forty days before his fifty-ninth birthday, Marcus died. The exact cause of death is uncertain though the plague is likely. It is possible that his doctors euthanized him. Sources conflict about where he died, either at or near Sirmium (Sremska Mitrovica, Serbia) or at Vindobona (Vienna). The senate deified Marcus and his ashes were laid to rest in Hadrian's mausoleum in Rome.

THE THINKER

Though the *Historia Augusta* is often effusive in its praise of Marcus, it would be a mistake either to reject it out of hand as nothing but groundless propaganda serving the political agenda of its writers on the one hand, or to accept it uncritically as a completely accurate portrait of a supremely beneficent, flawless emperor on the other. Marcus Aurelius was neither a saint nor a Stoic sage. To be a sage, the early Stoics believed, was, among other things, to lack any vice, to possess all the virtues, to have no false beliefs, and to act and judge infallibly. To be a Stoic sage, therefore, was to have achieved perfection of character, to be godlike. The *Historia Augusta* reports that Marcus wanted to obliterate the Sarmatians. Marcus may have been addicted to Galen's opium-laced *theriac*. Marcus permitted brutal executions of Christians who refused to recant. Commodus' character defects[11] did not stop Marcus from making Commodus his successor. In sum, Marcus was neither an irreproachable ruler, nor a consummate philosopher, nor a flawless man. Yet it would be reckless to reject all the evidence that he was a decent man possessed of some virtues, a conscientious emperor, and a serious thinker who earnestly pursued Stoic ideals.

What was Marcus' legacy in Christendom? This question is too far ranging for this *Guide* to address. But what can be noted here is that Marcus was considered a good role model by Constantine the Great (CE 272–337), the first Roman emperor to convert to Christianity. On the arch of Constantine panels are incorporated from a monument of Marcus. Such reuse is generally considered to be a tacit claim to continuity with the great emperors of the past. Hadrian and Trajan are similarly honored on the arch. Moreover, in a panel carved by artists of Constantine's time, there is a scene on the rostra in which Constantine appears between the statues of two men who are usually taken to be Hadrian and Marcus. This, too, makes a claim to continuity with the great emperors of the past.

What was Marcus' philosophical legacy? Early Medieval thinkers typically could not read Greek. Later Medieval thinkers who could read Greek preferred to focus on Peripatetic texts, not Stoic authors. *The Passions of the Soul* is a deeply Stoic work, but it is difficult to identify the particular influence of Marcus' thought in any works of René Descartes (1596–1650). Marcus' thought was congenial to the 3rd Earl of Shaftesbury (Anthony Ashley Cooper: 1671–1713), who considered Marcus "one of the wisest and most serious of ancient authors"[12] and cited sayings of Marcus to urge readers away from pleasurable objects and toward honesty, integrity, friendship, faith, and honor.[13] Theologian, philosopher, and Cambridge Platonist Henry More (1614–1687) was particularly impressed by Marcus' conception of the rational soul and cited his sayings often in his handbook of morals titled *Enchiridion ethicum*.

Marcus' *Memoranda* had an even greater impact on Francis Hutcheson (1694–1746), especially on his concern for universal happiness. Hutcheson was a Scots-Irish philosopher who propounded a theory of a moral sense through which right action is achieved. Hutcheson studied philosophy, classics, and theology at the University of Glasgow, where he later held the Chair of Moral Philosophy. Hutcheson drew upon Marcus' thought to explain the meaning of true piety as social and humanitarian concern for all human beings. Marcus' emphasis on truth, justice, mercy, and good will to all deeply informed Hutcheson's philosophy. Hutcheson embraced Marcus' injunction to subordinate ignoble passions to the sociable passions and to the divine part of us, the rational soul, the intellect. Marcus' Stoic conception of reason and intellect was, as Hutcheson interpreted it, capable of immediate perception of virtue and vice, of good and evil. Hutcheson agreed with Marcus' sense of duty, namely, that piety should govern relations between citizens of the cosmos and the law of nature which is God's providence. Hutcheson rejected the Calvinist notion that human beings are by nature sinful. Instead, he believed, and read the *Memoranda* as affirming, that human beings are by nature affectionate, benevolent, kind, and good. Hutcheson also scolded those who charged Marcus with persecuting Christians. No one dare level such a charge, Hutcheson argued, unless he abhors *any* condemnation of *anyone* who holds different religious opinions than oneself. Four editions of Hutcheson's popular English translation of Marcus' *Memoranda* were published between 1742 and 1764.[14]

The celebrated Scottish philosopher, historian, economist, and essayist David Hume (1711–1776) saw Marcus as a believer in auguries, divinations, and admonitions from the gods in his sleep rather than as a monotheist.[15] In *The Theory of Moral Sentiments* Francis Hutcheson's student Adam Smith (1723–1790) devotes several paragraphs to Marcus' thought. Smith was repulsed by Marcus' welcome submission to all events, regardless of how painful and catastrophic they may be. Nevertheless, Marcus' philosophy had a considerable impact on the Scottish Enlightenment.

In 1863 the British poet and cultural critic Mathew Arnold (1822–1888) published a notable essay reviewing George Long's 1862 translation of Marcus' book. Arnold declared the Emperor "the most beautiful figure in history." Winners of the Nobel Prize in Literature Maurice Maeterlinck (1911), Anatole France (1921), and Joseph Brodsky (1987), as well as American novelist and journalist Theodore Dreiser (1871–1945), have been cited as authors influenced by Marcus' thought. Marcus' book is a favorite of Wen Jiabao (1942–), the sixth Premier and Party Secretary of the State Council of the People's Republic of China. Bill Clinton (1946–), the 42nd President of the United States (1993–2001), claims that during his presidency he read and reread Marcus. Yet Marcus' legacy as a thinker is poignant and ironic when we remember that he wrote his *Memoranda* not for any of us, but only for himself. Perhaps no less today than in Marcus' day, Stoic ideas remain things to remember.

CHAPTER 2

THE INFLUENCE OF HERACLITUS
AND EPICTETUS

Two of the most pronounced influences on Marcus' philosophy are the enigmatic early Greek thinker Heraclitus of Ephesus[1] (c. 535–c. 475 BCE) and the Stoic school master Epictetus (CE c. 55–c. 135). Little is known of Heraclitus' life. Most of what has been handed down about him consists of stories that seem to have been invented to portray his character as it is inferred from his writings. He is said to have written one book (papyrus roll), the structure of which is controversial, as are the interpretations of his doctrines. What remains of the book are over a hundred fragments that somewhat resemble proverbs, epigrams, or riddles. Unlike most other early philosophers, Heraclitus was an independent thinker who seems to have been self-taught.

Epictetus, which means "Acquired," was born into slavery as the son of a slave woman in the city of Hierapolis in Phrygia in central Asia Minor. His experience as a slave and lameness surely contributed to his conception of happiness as mental freedom.[2] At some point while still a slave he traveled to Rome. During the time he was owned by Nero's freedman and administrative secretary Epaphroditus, Epictetus studied with the great Stoic teacher of the day, Gaius Musonius Rufus. Later Epictetus was manumitted. He was among the philosophers expelled from Rome by the emperor Domitian, presumably in CE 89 or 92. Epictetus moved to the city of Nicopolis in Epirus[3] where he founded a school in which to teach Stoicism. The four surviving books entitled *Arrian's Discourses of Epictetus*, or simply the *Discourses*, are generally believed to be not the transcripts of the formal readings of Stoic disquisitions, but rather Epictetus' expositions of particular issues arising from those readings and responses to his students' recitations delivered to them in less formal seminars. Flavius Arrianus, a young Roman historian who attended Epictetus' lectures, evidently took notes on those lectures (*Diatribai* in Greek) which were later published as the *Discourses*.

Marcus wrote the *Memoranda* in the CE 170s, roughly seven hundred years after Heraclitus wrote his book and about four decades after Epictetus taught. Yet both Heraclitus and Epictetus made strong impressions on Marcus' thought. This chapter offers an overview of the ideas of Heraclitus and Epictetus which resonate most loudly in the *Memoranda*.

HERACLITUS

Throughout the history of the Stoa, the prophetic poet-philosopher Heraclitus was a revered and inspiring source of wisdom. He certainly inspired Marcus' own Stoicism.[4] Marcus frequently echoes, and sometimes creatively refashions, Heraclitus' ideas. Indeed, Marcus' admiration for the sage of Ephesus is explicit. Marcus calls Heraclitus, Pythagoras (c. 570–c. 490 BCE), and Socrates (469–399 BCE) "the eloquent and the wise" (vi. 47). He groups Heraclitus with Diogenes of Sinope (c. 404–323 BCE) and Socrates as philosophers who knew the what, the why, and the how, and whose minds were their own (viii. 3). Marcus also explicitly instructs himself to remember Heraclitus and then quotes five of his extant fragments (iv. 46). Elsewhere Marcus quotes another fragment and presents his interpretation of it in order to make a point about how we all collaborate in the same cosmic project (vi. 42). Heraclitus' ideas clearly inform Marcus' conceptions of the *logos*, divine law, cosmic holism and mereology, the harmony of opposites, sleep and wakefulness, forgetting and remembering, cycles of change, birth, and death, and fluidity and fire as symbols of cosmic flux. In what follows I show that Heraclitus' influence on the Emperor's philosophy is deep, wide, and in several ways remarkably subtle.

The artistic design, stylistic density, and syntactic ambiguity of Heraclitus' written words make his surviving fragments notoriously difficult to comprehend. In what follows my aim is not to devise a new interpretation of Heraclitus' philosophy but to elucidate those of his ideas which exercised Marcus in his *Memoranda*. One scholar has described the focal point of Heraclitus' philosophical reflection as "a meditation on human life and human destiny in the context of biological death."[5] As will be seen in the chapters to follow, this description also aptly characterizes Marcus Aurelius' philosophical reflection.

The divine law of logos

The concept of *logos* is fundamental to both Heraclitus' thought and Stoicism. The first and longest fragment of Heraclitus reads:

> Although this *logos* holds forever [is true], people ever fail to comprehend, both before hearing it and once they have heard. Although all things come to pass in accordance with this *logos*, people are like the untried when they try such words and works as I set forth, distinguishing each according to its nature and telling how it is. But other people are oblivious of what they do awake, just as they are forgetful of what they do asleep. (I)

What does Heraclitus understand *logos* to be? When Heraclitus uses the word *logos* it can reasonably be interpreted to refer to (a) his discourse, (b) the nature of language itself, (c) the structure of the psyche, or (d) the universal principle or cosmic law in accordance with which all things come to pass. In this fragment, he is both announcing that the account which he presents to the reader (sense (a)) is true, and that there is a universal principle which governs all things that happen (sense (d)). This universal principle is eternal. It always has been and always will be, and it is forever true. Heraclitus will show how this eternal, universal principle distinguishes each thing from one another by explaining the nature of each. Unfortunately, people don't understand this universal *logos* on their own before hearing Heraclitus report it to them. Nor do they understand the universal *logos* even after they've heard him expound it in his account, his own *logos*, to them.

Heraclitus believes that the *logos* is publicly accessible: "Although the *logos* is shared, most live as though their thinking were a private possession" (III). In this fragment Heraclitus may well be using *logos* in senses (b), (c), and (d). If so, then he could mean that language is shared by all language-users, but most people act as if how they use language is a private matter to which the public standard of correctness does not apply. He could also mean that the structure of the human mind is the same in all individuals, but most live as though their minds were sharply isolated and how they think about the world belongs exclusively to them, rather than to all thinkers equally. This interpretation is supported by the fragment "Thinking is shared by all" (XXXI) and the fragment "It belongs to all men to know themselves and to think well" (XXIX). The third sense of *logos* would suggest that all people have minds (sense (c)) that give them equal access to the eternal, universal principle steering the world (sense (d)), and this cosmic law applies to all, but most people fail to understand that *logos* which structures both all human minds and pervades the structure of the entire universe. The core idea of fragment III is the idea that the *logos* is shared and common to all people and operates in all things.

Heraclitus writes: "It is wise, listening not to me but to the *logos*, to agree that all things are one" (XXXVI). Here Heraclitus warns the reader to listen to the eternal, universal, public *logos* (sense (d)) and to attend to it, rather than to rely on a single individual's description (sense (a)) of that universal *logos*. It's possible that Heraclitus is also referring to *logos* as the nature of language itself. He might be urging us to listen to the meaning conveyed by our common language (sense (b)) as that meaning reveals the truth about the universal principle according to which things happen (sense (d)). In any case, Heraclitus asserts that it is wise to agree that all things are one. He writes: "The wise is one, knowing the plan by which it steers all things through all" (LIV). These last two fragments express the idea that there is one and only one reality, only one existing thing. This view, called monism, rejects pluralism, which is the view that there is a plurality of separate, disconnected things. Anaxagoras of Clazomenae in Ionia (c. 500–428 BCE) and Empedocles of Acragas in Sicily (c. 493–c. 433 BCE) were pluralists. Atomism, founded by Leucippus and Democritus of Abdera in Thrace (c. 460–c. 370 BCE) and later embraced by the Epicureans, is also a type of pluralism.

Heraclitus' discernment of the relationship between wholes and parts is evident when he writes: "Graspings: wholes and not wholes, convergent divergent, consonant dissonant, from all things one and from one thing all" (CXXIV). The idea is that the cosmos is in an ongoing dynamic process of parts assembling into wholes and wholes crumbling back into parts. These parts converge and unify into wholes. The wholes disintegrate and their parts scatter. From a short-sighted, narrow perspective, fragmentation, pluralism, and dissonance may appear to dominate. From the wise, long-term, deeply discerning, and global perspective, however, an over-arching, consonant monism, and rhythmic holism prevail in the macrocosm. Mindfulness of the relationship between wholes and parts exercises Marcus throughout the *Memoranda*. Chapter 3 is devoted to this theme, so here it suffices to observe that Marcus was greatly inspired by Heraclitus' suggestive remarks in fragment CXXIV.

What about monism? Marcus and the earlier Stoics follow Heraclitus in affirming *cosmic holism*, the view that the universe is a single, unified whole composed of intimately interconnected, harmoniously interrelated parts. It is wise, Heraclitus states in fragment LIV, to know the one plan by which the eternal, universal *logos* steers all the interconnected parts of the cosmos through each other. Marcus affirms cosmic holism often in his *Memoranda*. He also spells out the consequences of cosmic holism for human concerns. He sees everything as interwoven in a holy web of parts none of which are unconnected. These parts together harmoniously compose our one world. This one world has one divinity present in all things, which are made of one substance, and are ruled by one law, the *logos* that all rational beings share. Corresponding to the singularity of the world, its single holy web of parts, its single divinity, and its single ruling *logos*, Marcus adds that there is one truth describing the culmination of one process embracing the beings who share the same birth and the same *logos* (vii. 9). Marcus' belief that the holistic interconnection of all things in the cosmos is divine originates with Heraclitus. Heraclitus writes: "Speaking with understanding they must hold fast to what is shared by all, as a city holds to its law, and even more firmly. For all human laws are nourished by a divine one. It prevails as it will and suffices for all and is more than enough" (XXX). Since the universal *logos* holds forever and is true forever, it is eternal, that is, immortal. As immortal, the universal *logos* is divine. In fragment XXX Heraclitus urges solidarity among people. He urges citizens to hold fast to their common good, which ought to be preserved by civic law. All human laws, he asserts, are nourished by a divine law. This divine law is the eternal, universal, publicly accessible principle which governs all processes in nature.

Marcus reminds himself that he functions as a part of the whole—the whole city of Rome, the whole empire, the whole planet, and the whole universe. The universe produced him, and, along with everything else, he'll be restored to the *logos* from which all things are produced (iv. 14 and vii. 10). Thus, in some texts, Marcus seems to identify nature, the universe, and the *logos*. Heraclitus' conception of *logos* resonates in Marcus' entry that the *logos* knows where it stands, what it needs to do, and what it has to work with (vi. 6). Marcus notes that to a being with *logos*, an unnatural action is one that conflicts with *logos* (vii. 11), such as failing to be a straightforward, honest person (x. 32). Such a being can always use his *logos* as a resource for dealing with whatever the future brings (vii. 8) by treating all that happens to him as raw material for training his *logos* (x. 31). Indeed, a being with *logos* can make his way through anything in his path as easily as the cosmic *logos* is carried through all physical bodies in nature (x. 33; cf. vii. 55; ix. 10). Marcus warns himself that as he progresses in following the cosmic *logos* in the exercise of his own intellect's *logos*, people (his fellow citizens) will try to stand in his way, but they can't stop him from doing what is healthy and tolerating them (xi. 9; cf. iv. 51). Consequently, Marcus firmly embraces Heraclitus' injunction to preserve one's solidarity with other people.

Following Heraclitus, Marcus believes that the *logos* (law) governing nature dictates all beginnings and all endings, and he adds that this *logos* knows no evil, does no evil, and harms nothing (vi. 1). Marcus thinks that nothing harms a citizen of the cosmos except what harms the city he belongs to, and nothing harms the city except what harms its law. Fortunately, so-called mishaps and misfortunes have no power to harm the city's law (x. 33; cf. v. 22). So Marcus urges himself to strengthen his psyche, his intellect, and to conform his own *logos* to the eternal, universal *logos* steering all things in the cosmos, thereby acting as a law-abiding cosmic citizen traveling a straight path to God (x. 11a). The law of nature decrees all events in the universe, including all events which people tend to respond to with grief, anger, or fear. But since the cosmic law governs what happens to each of us, the proper response of a law-abiding cosmic citizen is not to feel grief or anger or fear about anything that happens to her. To grieve or be angry about or fear what happens to you is to be a fugitive from the law of nature (x. 25). This is how Marcus, in developing his version of Stoicism, elaborates on Heraclitus' conception of *logos*, law, and divinity.

Both Heraclitus and Marcus laud intellectual acumen. Heraclitus writes: "Thinking well is the greatest excellence and wisdom: to act and speak what is true, perceiving things according to their nature" (XXXII). Marcus strongly echoes this judgment that logical think- ing and understanding are the best of things when he asks the rhetorical question: "And is there anything preferable to thought itself—to logic, to understanding?" (v. 9; cf. iii. 6). Heraclitus' praise of speaking what is true is similarly repeated by Marcus, since he often reflects on truth and dedicates himself to truthfulness (iii. 12 especially; i. 14; v. 33; vi. 21; vii. 9; ix. 1; xi. 18). This is a subtler influ- ence of Heraclitus on Marcus' thought.

Sleeping, waking, remembering

In the last part of fragment I, Heraclitus bemoans the fact that, in a strong sense, many people don't know what they are doing. In fragment II Heraclitus writes: "Not comprehending, they hear like the deaf. The saying is their witness: absent while present." These people stumble through their days deaf to the universal *logos* and ignorant of its meaning. They are like sleepwalkers. These people also forget what they do when they are asleep. Marcus composed his account, his *logos*, the *Memoranda*, as a long set of reminders of vital lessons for living mindfully, conscientiously, wisely, and well every single day. Thus, Marcus' preoccupation with not forget- ting, with living wakefully and thoughtfully, pervades his writing. He is intent on shaking off the nightly slumber that so irresist- ibly weakens our grip on the lessons we have learned the previous day. Over time, nightly sleep gradually erases these lessons from our minds. Marcus is determined not to stumble through his day like Heraclitus' forgetful sleepwalkers. This is plain when Marcus quotes Heraclitus, although we do not know how accurately: " 'Our words and actions should not be like those of sleepers' (for we act and speak in dreams as well) . . ." (iv. 46). As we saw above, Marcus shares with Heraclitus belief in the urgency of being alert to the universal *logos* which guides all events and all processes in nature. Marcus reiterates Heraclitus' insistence on acting in accordance with knowledge of this cosmic principle. Sleep is a kind of death, Heraclitus believes (see fragment LXXXIX). Night extinguishes the reality visible in daylight, and so a person must strike up a light for himself to see at night (XC). Nighttime sleeping and dreaming isolate the person from the bright, public reality revealed by the *logos* and available to him when wakeful during daytime (cf. XCIII).

A dreamer can "touch" the dead by dreaming of deceased people he knew. But those blind to the visible *logos* and deaf to its meaning spoken by Heraclitus are sleepily unaware of the *logos* even when they are out of bed and walking around with their eyes and ears open.

For Marcus, even those oblivious to the *logos* are doing jobs assigned to them by the cosmos. He interprets Heraclitus' paradoxical fragment XCI when he explains that everyone is working on the same project. Some people do so consciously, with understanding. Others do so without knowing it. Marcus thinks this is what Heraclitus meant when he said that "those who sleep are also hard at work," since they too collaborate in what happens. Some of us work in one way, and some in others. But Marcus notes that those who complain and try to obstruct and thwart things—though it seems paradoxical—actually help in a different kind of way. The world needs them as well, he explains. So he urges himself to make up his mind and choose which group of people he will work with (vi. 42). There are two classes of people, Marcus observes here. There are those cognizant of the *logos*, who mindfully contribute to and promote the project underway in the cosmos, and there are those ignorant of and asleep to the *logos*, who try, but fail, to hinder that project. Marcus knows to which group he wants to belong.

In the very first entry of the second book of the *Memoranda*, Marcus writes out a reminder to rehearse at the start of each day. He instructs himself: When you wake up in the morning, tell yourself that the people you will encounter today will be the sleepers who try to obstruct the cosmic project because they are ignorant of the *logos* and can't tell good from evil (ii. 1). Marcus repeats a similar sort of wake-up reminder at the beginning of the fifth book:

> At dawn, when you have trouble getting out of bed, tell yourself: I have to go to work—as a human being. What do I have to complain about, if I'm going to do what I was born for—the things I was brought into the world to do? Or is *this* what I was created for? To snuggle under the blankets and stay warm? (v. 1)

Marcus rejects the rejoinder that it's nicer lazing cozily in bed because nature demands that he experience things and do his tasks as best he can. He admits that we have to sleep sometime, but insists that nature set a limit on sleeping, eating, and drinking

(v. 1). To help him sleep, Marcus took the *theriac* prescribed by his physician Galen.

In a third text about rousing in the morning, Marcus reminds himself that the cure for having trouble getting up is the right *memory*.

> When you have trouble getting out of bed in the morning, remember that your defining characteristic—what defines a human being—is to work with others. Even animals lacking *logos* know how to sleep. And it's the characteristic activity that's the more natural one—more innate and more satisfying. (viii. 12)

So although Marcus must sleep at night like everyone else, he urges himself to overcome the inertia of loafing in bed by means of a reminder. He should energetically rouse himself every morning because getting to work cooperating with others defines *what* he is—a human being. (His special job *as Marcus Aurelius* is to rule the Roman Empire.) The characteristic activity of working with others is more natural for Marcus than sleeping all day because nonrational animals sleep, but they don't collaborate to conduct the affairs of a society as complex and thickly rational as ours. Working with others is also more satisfying, Marcus thinks, than sleeping by himself. If Marcus slumbered away in the *private* little cocoon of his bed, thereby failing to promote the *public* good, he'd be one of Heraclitus' sleepwalkers trying to obstruct the project of the universe when fully dressed and wandering cluelessly around day-dreaming through their lives.

In yet another entry Marcus prompts himself, upon waking, to ask if it matters to him if others blame him for doing the right thing. No, he writes, it is irrelevant. He must not forget what loudmouths shouting praise and blame are like as they sleep, eat, fear, desire, filch, and plunder, not with hands and feet but with the most precious part of them, which can will into existence faith, modesty, truth, law, and well-being (x. 13). The blame and acclaim of others makes no difference to Marcus as he discharges his daily duties. But each morning he gets out of bed he must make a conscious effort *not to forget* this so that he will not be deterred from conscientiously performing his tasks.

Why does Marcus so often need to give himself this wake-up call to get to work doing the job he was created by the cosmos to do?

Because each night sleep can erode from our memories what we knew better the previous day. Sleep can insidiously and incrementally erase our knowledge. Marcus may have been no more forgetful than most people, but he was determined to fortify his memory by habitually writing down the *Memoranda*. When he writes: "Close to forgetting it all, close to being forgotten" (vii. 21) is he morose about his failing memory or is he calmly preparing himself for senility? In the second remark is he sad that he will soon be forgotten or is he soberly reminding himself that fame is an illusion? It isn't like Marcus to indulge in sadness because when he writes "So many who were remembered already forgotten, and those who remembered them long gone" (vii. 6) this appears to be his way of keeping a cosmic and temporal perspective that banishes any anxieties.

Perhaps Heraclitus' most puzzling fragment on sleeping and waking is: "Death is all things we see awake; all we see asleep is sleep" (LXXXIX). Kahn interprets "death is all things we see awake" to mean that all things we see around us when we are awake, all living human beings, animals, and plants, are new bodies that emerged from the material of dead, old organisms.[6] This interpretation seems plausible. Marcus often repeats and extrapolates on the importance of remembering this unending cycle of elemental transformation in order to construe events from the big picture, cosmic and temporal perspective and so preserve his equanimity.[7] In his comment on Heraclitus' fragment LXXXVIII Kahn notes that Eliot reminds us that the earth is flesh, fur, and feces.[8] This idea is suggestive of related refrains in many of Marcus' memoranda (e.g., iv. 48; v. 33; vii. 50; viii. 6; viii. 18; viii. 50; ix. 28; x. 18; x. 34; xii. 21; even vi. 13 and ix. 36). By "all we see asleep is sleep" Heraclitus suggests that the dream-state fails to disclose to us any insights about the cosmos. Dreaming is a cognitive state of awareness limited entirely to figments of our imagination that vanish the instant we awake. Sleep reveals only the illusions caused by sleep. To be aware of the *logos*, one must rouse oneself and sharply distinguish reality from the hallucinations that afflict Heraclitus' sleepwalkers. Sleeping is a kind of death. Recognizing this, Marcus writes: "Awaken and return to yourself. Now, no longer asleep, knowing they were only dreams, clear-headed again, treat everything around you as a dream" (vi. 31). What Marcus means, I think, by telling himself to treat everything around him as a dream is that physical objects are flimsy, transient specters that fool people into believing that they are lasting, concrete, tremendous treasures indispensable for living a good life. Dreams come and go, but they aren't real, and so aren't important. Similarly, physical possessions come and go, but they aren't worth clinging to, since it is the excellences of our minds that we must urgently reach for and hold onto.[9] As we will see below, Marcus follows Epictetus in judging the material resources around us as lacking intrinsic value. Material possessions function like game equipment. The point of the game is to play it well, that is, virtuously, rather than to accumulate or cling to the equipment. This is known as the Stoic doctrine of indifferents, which is discussed in Chapter 5. What is clear in vi. 31 is that Marcus is determined to leave his dreams behind, to shake off the soporific effect of Galen's *theriac*, to return to himself, to his specific tasks as a citizen of the cosmos, as a contributing member of human society, as a good emperor, and as a savvy Stoic in tune with the *logos*. Marcus is intent on recalling and being alert to Heraclitus' wisdom about waking vs. sleeping and being alive to the *logos* vs. being in a deadly dream. Heraclitus' cryptically expressed interpretations of sleeping, waking, death, life, dreaming, and remembering clearly influenced Marcus' philosophy in both subtle and powerful ways.

Harmony of opposites

Heraclitus is keen to reflect on the myriad pairs of opposites evident throughout nature. He thinks the *logos* reveals that these oppositions are in dynamic balance in our cosmos. Transformations from one opposite to its counterpart establish a common pattern of change and exchange, an endless cycle of back and forth. This cycle is symmetrical, rhythmic, necessary, and predictable to the wise. He writes: "Cold warms up, warm cools off, moist parches, dry dampens" (XLIX). Heat becomes cold and vice versa. Humidity changes into aridity and back again. Day becomes night, which becomes day. Seasons of the year unfold according to the same rolling cycle.

Heraclitus also reflects on the seemingly contrary properties displayed by the same phenomenon or the same material stuff. He writes: "The sea is the purest and foulest water: for fish drinkable and life-sustaining; for human beings undrinkable and deadly" (LXX). The same medium, the sea, is life-giving and death-bringing at the same time for different kinds of organisms. The sea is vitally valuable for fish, but of lethal disvalue to human beings. This is not a mysterious paradox, but a cosmic regularity the *logos* allows us to grasp. While human beings covet gold, Heraclitus notes that "asses prefer garbage to gold" (LXXI). Asses eat what human beings dispose of as inedible. While humans wash in clean water, "swine delight in mire more than clean water; chickens bathe in dust" (LXXII). Adults fancy themselves as engaged in serious pursuits, yet "lifetime is a child at play, moving pieces in a game. Kingship belongs to the child" (XCIV). The child is the king playing with his game pieces. Deploying armies, issuing commands, making laws, and ruling a kingdom of subjects, the king fancies himself mighty. But the child can play at being a king in a way something like life moving pieces—kings and their subjects, entire nations of peoples—in a grand, vast cosmic game.

Though inspired by Heraclitus' thinking about oppositions in nature and apparent paradoxes, Marcus takes them in a somewhat different direction. He writes:

> Honey tastes bitter to a man with jaundice. People with rabies are terrified of water. And a child's idea of beauty is a ball. Why does that upset you? Do you think falsehood is less powerful than bile or a rabid dog? (vi. 57)

Using examples similar to, but not the same as, those of Heraclitus, Marcus notes the same relativity of value identified by Heraclitus. But Marcus reassures himself not to be troubled by this relativity. Rabid people fear water, but he himself need not fear water or anything else. Many will cling to false beliefs, but that fact need not disturb him, since he can hold fast to what is true.

Heraclitus observes that "The way up and down is one and the same" (CIII). Marcus repeats this notion: "The world's cycles never change—up and down, from age to age . . ." (ix. 28). He sees this familiar cosmic cycle in the popular entertainments of his day which leave him sour: "Just as the arena and the other spectacles weary you—you've seen them all before—and the repetition grates on your nerves, so too with life. For everything, up and down, is the same, and the result of the same things" (vi. 46). Marcus seems to derive a modicum of consolation from this lesson imparted to him by the sage of Ephesus. He tells himself: "Remember Heraclitus: 'When earth dies it becomes water; water, air; air, fire; and back to the beginning'" (iv. 46). This cycling and recycling transformation of elements is the same cosmic pattern up and down, the same old thing. Marcus sees no reason whatsoever to be alarmed by bodies in nature converting from one elemental constitution to the next. Nature has always recycled its organisms back into the soil, from which new organisms spring up. "To decompose is to be recomposed. That's what nature does" (ix. 35). Dead bodies become organic matter that feeds the birth of new bodies, which in turn grow old, die, and decay. As earth dies to become water, which becomes air, which becomes fire, which becomes earth again in this elemental cycle, so too do plants die to become consumed by animals, which die to become consumed by human beings, which die to become consumed (decomposed) by microbes, which die to become plants. Death is therefore ubiquitous, eternally repeated, and indispensable for the very existence of living things. Marcus and the Stoics before him learned this lesson from Heraclitus.

Marcus adds a different twist to the Heraclitean harmony of opposites. Marcus finds it useful to survey the world of shifting opposites from a high vantage point. He writes that if you want to talk about people, you need to look down on the earth from above. From that perspective you behold entire herds of animals, whole armies of soldiers, and farms stretching to the horizon. You also see the panoply of human activities: weddings, divorces, births, deaths, and noisy courtrooms. Both desert places and all the peoples of foreign lands are surveyed. You witness holidays, days of mourning, and market days. All these myriad things are mixed together constituting a harmony of opposites (vii. 48). Marcus believes that the right way to talk about people requires inspecting the hubbub of human affairs in all their global diversity from a high mountaintop (cf. ix. 30). From such an aerie one can behold all at once the entirety of this tableaux of intermingling, variegated, ever unfolding opposites as a single, harmonized network of processes. Herds of animals are akin to herds of military troops. The cycle of marriage, divorce, sexual activity, pregnancy, child birth, ageing, and death is as old as the human race. Human beings gather and gaggle crowding law courts, while uninhabited regions surround densely populations, both in the Roman Empire and far beyond it. Some days are for festive celebrations, others are for rest and relaxation, others are for religious observances, others still are for grieving the dead, and others are for bustling commerce. Marcus' scenic overlook provides the context for perceiving these myriad, contrasting phenomena as interconnected ingredients in a symmetrically balanced, unified, harmonious whole.

Life and death are unquestionably central points of focus for Heraclitus and Marcus. Heraclitus, enigmatic as ever, writes: "Immortals are mortal, mortals immortal, living the others' death, dead in the others' life" (XCII). As we have seen, nature's process of cycle change and renewal is reversible. The elements of earth, water, air, and fire emerge, or are "born" from each other, and transform or "die" into each other. The process can go up or down, and so is the same reversible process. But all bodies, all phenomena, and all processes in nature derive their lives from the deaths of other bodies. Night is the death of day, as day is the death of night. Hot is cold's death. Cold is hot's death. Dry is wet's death (through evaporation). Wet is dry's death (through condensation or precipitation). Spring is winter's death. Summer is spring's death. Seasonal changes recur ceaselessly, and so the cycle of seasons is immortal in this respect. Yet each particular springtime is of finite duration and so is mortal, since it dies when the summertime following it is born. So Heraclitus seems to reconceive of death as any change of state in which something old gives way to something identifiably new. Reciprocally, he reconceives of birth as any change of state in which something identifiably new arises from something old.

Marcus' conception of the eternity of time and the finitude of living organisms is congruent with this Heraclitean conception of the immortality of cosmic cycles and the mortality of plants, animals, human beings, and phenomena in nature. But in the following text Marcus' focus is to bear in mind the bond tying the immortal, heavenly realm above with the mortal, earthly realm below in order to *act* properly. In iii. 13 he notes that doctors keep their scalpels and other instruments handy, for emergencies. Similarly, he must keep his philosophy ready too so he can understand heaven and earth. In everything he does, even the smallest thing, Marcus reminds himself of the chain that links them. Nothing earthly succeeds by ignoring heaven, he writes, and nothing heavenly succeeds by ignoring the earth (iii. 13). The purpose of this reminder is to inform Marcus' deliberations about how to *act*.

Should Heraclitus' fragment XCII be interpreted to be making a much more radical assertion? After all, for the traditional ancient Greek religious believer "the immortals" refers to the gods. Deathlessness is the essential characteristic of the gods, whereas mortality is what separates the human condition from the divine. So, if we ascribe to Heraclitus the incendiary view that the heavenly gods actually cease to exist and we earthly mortals transcend death and actually become deified, then the Emperor parts company with him. Marcus' piety is too firmly embedded in Stoic theology[10] and Roman conservatism to admit this Heraclitean heresy. Nevertheless, in both its style and substance, the last sentence of *Memoranda* iii. 13 bears a noticeable affinity with Heraclitus' fragment XCII.

River

One of the most famous symbols of Heraclitus' philosophy is the river. He writes: "As they step into the same rivers, other and still other waters flow upon them" (L). A river is an excellent example of the dynamic nature of reality. Indeed, a river is a wonderfully mundane object lesson in the metaphysical problem of identity. The material content of a river is constantly changing, since the waters flowing in it are ceaselessly replaced by different waters moment by moment. Yet the form of the river, its shape, doesn't change too rapidly for those who step into it to identify it as the same ribbon of flowing water. Over a longer period of time, however, a river changes its course. Its path meanders as its banks slowly and grad-ually erode. The flowing waters migrate out of their old riverbed to carve out a new riverbed. The very nature of a river is to move, shift, flow, ripple, and fluctuate in turbidity as its waters rise with new rainfall and subside during drought. Consequently, "One can-not step twice into the same river, nor can one grasp any mortal substance in a stable condition, but it scatters and again gathers; it forms and dissolves, and approaches and departs" (LI). A river is a living ribbon of tumbling water molecules, sediment, and impur-ities as well as a home for myriad fish, birds, insects, and other animals. To be more precise, what may appear to be the same single river is really multiple rivers replacing each other in rapid succes-sion, like the individual celluloid frames in a spinning reel blurring together so imperceptibly fast that they create the illusion of one, continuous movie image. For Heraclitus, rivers are emblems of the instability of all mortal substances in the cosmos.

Rivers also flow forcefully through the fundamentals of Marcus' philosophy. He describes time as a river: "Time is a river, a violent current of events, glimpsed once and already carried past us, and another follows and is gone" (iv. 43). He likens existence to a river: "Keep in mind how fast things pass by and are gone—those that are now, and those to come. Existence flows past us like a river: the 'what' is in constant flux, the 'why' has a thousand variations. Nothing is stable, not even what's right here . . ." (v. 23). The stuff around us Marcus describes as a river slipping through our fingers:

> Some things are rushing into existence, others out of it. Some of what now exists is already gone. Change and flux constantly remake the world, just as the incessant progression of time remakes eternity. We find ourselves in a river. Which of the things around us should we value when none of them can offer a firm foothold? (vi. 15)

Not only is all the furniture of world surrounding us as insubstantial and ephemeral as a river, but we ourselves are no less rivers of instability. "Human life . . . Sum Up: The body and its parts are a river, the soul a dream and mist, life is warfare and a journey far from home, lasting reputation is oblivion. . . ." (ii. 17). Marcus wrote this when he was waging war on an expedition in a foreign land, central Europe, far from home. Even there, Heraclitus' idea of cosmic fluidity profoundly shaped Marcus' thought.

Flux, fire, and fortitude

Just as Heraclitus finds flowing water representative of the instability of the cosmos, so too, fittingly, does he think that the element which water extinguishes (and so which is, in a sense, its opposite), fire, represents cosmic dynamism. "The cosmos, the same for all, no god nor human being has made, but it ever was and will be: fire ever-living, kindled in measures and in measures going out" (XXXVII). In this fragment Heraclitus seems to be asserting that the cosmos is (a) the same single universe and home for all things and all beings, (b) a self-made, or better, self-*grown* genesis of nature, and (c) identical to its eternal source, fire, which arises in proportionate measures (both locally and globally) and is reciprocally extinguished in proportionate measures (both locally and globally). Heraclitus describes the "reversals" of fire into sea (its elemental opposite), earth, and fiery lightning storms erupting from the sky (XXXVIII). When fire dies air is born from it, and when air dies water is born from it (XLI). So Heraclitus seems to envision processes of elemental birth and death and changes of state from gas (fire) to air to liquid (water) to solid. Evaporation, condensation, and sedimentation are observable phenomena corresponding to some of these theoretical shifts from one kind of element to another. Fire, however, is the eternal cosmic currency of exchange. "All things are requital for fire, and fire for all things, as goods for gold and gold for goods" (XL). As natural bodies can be consumed and destroyed by fire, so too can goods be exchanged for gold coinage, the most valuable kind of currency. Gold is also the color of the fiery ball of the sun, as it is kindled anew each dawn and goes out again each time it sets. Fire is a mysterious symbol of life and death, representing both creation and destruction. It is the one element in which no animal can live. Yet it cooks our food and keeps us warm in winter, thus sustaining human lives. It is also the instrument of funereal cremation which destroys human corpses. Fire is also the indispensable tool of the blacksmith's arts. Thus, as the stolen gift of Prometheus, it symbolizes the divine power of industry and metallurgy which separates us from nonhuman animals.

When the Stoics devised their doctrine of *ekpurōsis*, the "world-conflagration" in which the entire universe was periodically consumed by fire and then subsequently coalesced from this fire into a new universe, they may have believed that they were taking this idea from Heraclitus. However, though Marcus reports that "Heraclitus often told us the world would end in fire" (iii. 3), the Emperor shows no real interest in this doctrine of *ekpurōsis*. He repeats the idea that everything is in flux and that he too "will alter in the whirl and perish, and the world as well" (ix. 19). Yet Marcus steals fire from Heraclitus not to elucidate his own cosmological reflections, but to internalize the consumptive power of fire as a means of overcoming obstacles the cosmos throws up to block his way. Marcus reminds himself that our inward power obeys nature by adapting to whatever it faces. This inner force pursues its aims as circumstances permit, turning obstacles into fuel. "As a fire overpowers what would have quenched a lamp, what is thrown onto the conflagration is absorbed, consumed by it, and makes its flames leap still higher" (iv. 1). Marcus repeats this idea that the raw material of what the cosmos serves up in a kind of cafeteria line must be chewed up and fully digested by the Stoic's strong stomach, "as a blazing fire converts whatever is thrown on it into heat and radiance" (x. 31).

Finally, Heraclitus writes that "a human being's character is his fate" (CXIV). The idea is wonderfully straightforward. Each of us fashions the quality of his life by the kind of choices we habitually make. The kind of person we are determines what will happen to us in our lives. If we have nobility of character, we will be resilient and make the best of everything the world throws at us. If we have an ignoble character, we are doomed to be wretched. Good character creates good fortune just as poor character guarantees misfortune. Our lot in life lies in ourselves, not in the stars above. Marcus echoes this very idea when he reasons that "It can ruin your life only if it ruins your character, otherwise it cannot harm you—inside or out" (iv. 8). Heracliteans and Stoics don't believe in luck. They believe that character can conquer any so-called catastrophe. Strength of character provides precious stability amidst a cosmos forever in flux.

EPICTETUS

Epictetus' teachings were written down by his student Arrian (CE 86–160) in the *Discourses*. Only four of the original eight books of these *Discourses* published by Arrian have been preserved. Marcus' knowledge of Epictetus' *Discourses* was direct. We know this because in *Memoranda* i. 7 Marcus thanks the Roman Stoic Quintus Junius Rusticus (prefect of the city of Rome in the CE mid-160s) for not being sidetracked by Marcus' yen for sophistry and for steering him clear of oratory, poetry, and fancy language, and for introducing him to Epictetus' teachings by lending him Rusticus' own copy of the *Discourses*.

Plato's Socrates as a Stoic hero

Socrates (469–399 BCE) was a paragon of virtue in action and philosophy in practice for not only the Stoics but in different ways for the Epicureans, Skeptics, and Cyrenaics as well. Certainly Socrates' dedication to the life of reason, philosophical inquiry and self-examination, and indomitable courage, equanimity, self-mastery, and trust in divine wisdom to the end of his life when he was executed by his fellow Athenians, made him a favorite moral exemplar of the Stoics. No Stoic whose texts survive in more than fragmentary form glorifies Plato's portrayal of Socrates more than

Epictetus (CE c. 55–c. 135).[11] Epictetus repeatedly exalts Plato's Socrates as a moral paradigm throughout the *Discourses*. For his turn, Marcus too is interested in evaluating Socrates' moral character. Marcus asks how we know that Telauges (it's uncertain to whom this refers) wasn't a better man than Socrates. Marcus remarks that asking whether Socrates had a nobler death, whether he outwitted the sophists in debate, whether he displayed superior endurance spending the night out in the cold (cf. Plato's *Symposium* 220), his refusing to arrest Leon of Salamis when ordered to by the Thirty Tyrants (cf. Plato's *Apology* 32c), and whether he swaggered about the streets (cf. Aristophanes' *Clouds* 362)—none of these issues can settle the matter. All that matters, Marcus insists, is the kind of soul Socrates had. Was he satisfied to be just to people? Was he satisfied to be reverent to the gods? Did he not lose his temper unpredictably when others did evil? Did he not make himself the slave of the ignorance of other people? Did he neither treat anything assigned to him by nature as bizarre nor endure it as an intolerable burden nor let his mind be afflicted by the passions of his flesh? (vii. 66).

Marcus certainly shares Epictetus' admiration for Socrates. Marcus comments on the eloquence and wisdom of Socrates (vi 47), how he knew the what, the why, and the how, and had a mind that was his own (viii. 3). The Emperor reports the saying that Socrates was unusually temperate. Specifically, Socrates knew how to enjoy things that most people find it easy to enjoy. But Socrates also knew how to abstain from things that most people find it difficult to abstain from (i. 16). He observes that Socrates was killed by human vermin (iii. 3). Marcus is likely to be paraphrasing Epictetus' *Discourses* 2. 1. 14–15 (and compare 3. 22. 106) when he reports, with apparent approval, that Socrates[12] used to call popular beliefs (probably about death) "monsters" that frighten children (xi. 23). Marcus seems to approve of Socrates declining an invitation to come to a ruler's court "so as to avoid dying a thousand deaths" by accepting a favor he couldn't repay (xi. 25). Marcus is the sole source of a story about Socrates' wife Xanthippe taking his cloak and leaving the house, forcing Socrates to go out wearing a towel, where he encountered friends so embarrassed to see him dressed that way that they avoided him. Marcus completes this anecdote noting what Socrates said to his embarrassed friends (xi. 28). We have to imagine that Socrates must have told his friends that there is nothing embarrassing about wearing a towel when that is the only clothing circumstances provide.

Consequently, Epictetus and Marcus both follow the Stoic tradition of upholding Socrates as a sage worthy of emulation.

Epictetus' presence in the *Memoranda* is conspicuous. Marcus mentions him explicitly at vii. 19. Epictetus' paraphrase of Plato, *Sophist* 228c at *Discourses* 1. 28. 4 and 2. 22. 36 is quoted by Marcus: "Every soul is deprived of the truth against its will" (vii. 63). Justice, self-control, and kindness are other things every soul is deprived of against its will, Marcus adds, instructing himself to remember this in order to be more patient with others (vii. 63). Moreover, the last seven entries of Book xi are all quotations or paraphrases of discourses of Epictetus. In xi. 33 Marcus paraphrases *Discourses* 3. 24. 86–87, writing that "stupidity is expecting figs in winter" (cf. *Disc*. 1. 15. 7–8). In the next entry, xi. 34, Marcus paraphrases *Disc*. 3. 24. 88–91, quoting Epictetus by name who advised that, when you kiss your child good night, whisper to yourself that tomorrow your child may die. Such a practice, Marcus repeats Epictetus' analogy, is no more of an ill omen than speaking of the harvesting of grain (xi. 34). The Emperor continues his cribbing of the next section of Epictetus' *Discourses* (3. 24. 91–93) in *Memoranda* xi. 35, commenting on grapes unripe, ripened, then transformed into raisins, each transition signaling not a "not" of permanent nonexistence, but rather a "not yet" of what is to come. In his next entry Marcus quotes *Discourses* 3. 22. 105, writing that "There can be no thief of free will" (xi. 36). Marcus then reports that he (Epictetus) said that we must discover the art of assent, and in the field of impulses we must be careful that they are exercised with reservation, that they are for the common good, and that they accord with worth; and we must abstain from desire altogether and try to avoid nothing that is not up to us (xi. 37 = Epictetus fragment 27). In his next quotation the Emperor writes that it is nothing trivial at stake here, he (Epictetus) said, but whether we are insane or not (xi. 38 = Epictetus fragment 28; cf. *Disc*. 1. 22. 17–21). Marcus concludes Book xi of the *Memoranda* by relating a brief dialogue which is probably a lost section of Epictetus' *Discourses*. In this entry Socrates gets unnamed interlocutors to agree that what they want are rational, healthy minds, not irrational, sick ones; if they are working to obtain such minds, then all their squabbling is pointless (xi. 39).

In a more subtle way, Epictetus' direct, unvarnished style of calling a spade a spade seems to have influenced Marcus' method of clear-eyed scrutiny of objects in front of him. For example, Epictetus advises that with everything that delights you or is useful to you or to which you have grown attached, remember to tell yourself just what they are, starting with the smallest of things. If you're fond of a dish, say "I'm fond of a dish," so that when it breaks you won't be so upset. When kissing your wife or your child, tell yourself you're kissing a mortal human being, so when she dies you won't be so distraught (*Encheiridion* 3). Marcus adopts this same method of bald realism when inspecting what he encounters. He reminds himself always to strip bare whatever he perceives, to break it down into its component parts, and to call both the thing as a whole and its parts by their names. What is this thing made of that forces itself on my notice? How long is it designed to last? What qualities of character do I need to bring to bear on it? Is this thing due to God, due to fate, or due to a human being? Is it an inconsequential thing—like, for example, Epictetus' dish? If so, Marcus determines to do his best to treat it as it deserves (iii. 11). In the next section we will explore the unvarnished view of the body that Epictetus and Marcus share.

Mighty mind and beastly body

In iv. 41 Marcus reminds himself of what he is—what a human being is—by quoting Epictetus: "You are a little wisp of soul carrying a corpse" (Epict. fragment 26). Epictetus describes in derogatory terms the body of a cowardly worrywart. He refers to such a body as a corpse (*Disc.* 1. 9. 19; 1. 19. 9) or a carcass with a pint of paltry blood (*Disc.* 1. 9. 33–34). He says that if someone identifies himself with his body, with his flesh, bones, and sinews, rather than with the intelligence that controls the body and understands the stimuli of the body's senses, then he is a corpse (*Disc.* 4. 7. 31–32). Epictetus often refers to the body in the diminutive form *sōmation* to mean the "paltry body" or "trifling body" (*Disc.* 1. 1. 11; 3. 1. 43; 3. 6. 6; 3. 10. 5; 3. 10. 15; 3. 10. 16; 3. 18. 3; 3. 22. 33 and 101; 3. 24. 71; 4. 1. 72; 4. 1. 151, 153, 158 and 163; 4. 6. 34; 4. 7. 18; 4. 11. 13 and 23). He says that his trifling body is nothing to him, its parts are nothing to him (*Disc.* 3. 22. 21). He teaches his students that one's paltry body is not free but enslaved. The body is a slave to fever, gout, ophthalmia, dysentery, a tyrant, fire, steel, and everything physically stronger than it because it is by nature a corpse, a clod, a lump of mud (*Disc.* 3.22. 40–41; 1. 1. 11; 4. 1. 100).

Not only does Marcus share Epictetus' negative view of the body, he even mentions the same kind of threats to it listed in

Discourses 3. 22. 40. Marcus writes that no one and nothing can thwart the operations of the mind, not fire, steel, tyrant, abuse, *nothing* (viii. 41). Marcus too sees death as the end of enslavement to our bodies (vi. 28; cf. Epictetus, *Disc.* 1.9. 8–20). As Epictetus describes the body as a carcass, to Marcus it smells of the stench of decay and is as pleasant to look at as rotting meat in a bag (viii. 38). Marcus urges himself to despise his flesh since it is merely gore, bits of bone, and a tangle of nerves, veins, and arteries (ii. 2). His body is a battered crate, dirt and garbage, far inferior to his mind (iii. 3). Marcus shares Epictetus' view that the body human beings share in common with the other animals, the beasts, whereas reason and good judgment, which are our special endowment, we share in common with the gods (*Disc.* 1. 3. 3). Just as Epictetus likens the human mind to the fortress within us (*Disc.* 4. 1. 86), Marcus repeats this same image. He reminds himself that when the mind withdraws into itself and finds contentment there, the mind is invulnerable. If the mind's judgment is deliberate, well grounded in logic, and free of passions, then it is an impregnable fortress. Taking refuge there, we are safe and secure forever. To fail to recognize this fact is ignorance. To understand it but not to avail ourselves of the mind's safety ensures our misery (viii. 48; cf. iv. 49; v. 19; v. 26; vii. 16; ix. 7).

Part of what makes the human body beastly is its carnal desire for sexual gratification, which we share with the other animals. Frequently indulging one's sexual desires can lead to obsessive behavior, which enslaves the mind to those erotic impulses. Consequently, a Stoic must always avoid inappropriate sexual activity. Moreover, a Stoic needs to be cautious about sex in general. In this context we can understand why Marcus echoes Epictetus' general warning to resist indulging in sexual impulses. Marcus urges himself not to pray for certain events to happen, but to pray not to feel fear, not to desire the wrong sort of thing, and not to feel grief. He believes that the gods do care about things that are up to us, including fear, desire, and grief. He exhorts himself not to pray for some way to have sex with a woman, but to pray to stop wanting to (ix. 40).

This idea echoes a lesson about sex imparted by Epictetus. He notes that another man has a sexy wife, but you have the power not to want a sexy wife. Therefore, you have the ability to steer clear of unhealthy, insatiable appetites, covetousness, jealousy, dressing lasciviously, and becoming obsessed with seducing women (*Disc.* 4. 9. 3–7). Epictetus tells his students that they should keep their hands off what belongs to others, and that no woman but your own wife should seem beautiful to you (*Disc.* 3. 7. 21). In another lesson he tells his students about his experience of seeing an attractive woman but not saying to himself "It would be nice to have sex with her," or "Her husband is a lucky guy," because such a comment would imply that anyone would be lucky to have sex with her, even in adultery. Epictetus explains that he stopped himself from fantasizing about the woman undressing in front of him and then lying down in bed with him. He congratulates himself for refraining from indulging in this sexual fantasy. But, he explains, if the woman is willing, calls to him, winks at him, seductively fondles him and presses herself against him, and he still controls himself, quashing his lust, then that would be a worthier success to boast about than solving a tough logic puzzle (*Disc.* 2. 18. 15–18). Epictetus often mentions the importance of marital fidelity and having the strength to resist sexual temptation and adultery (*Disc.* 1. 18. 22; 2. 4. 1–2; 2. 18. 6; 3. 24. 37; *Ench.* 10; cf. 2. 16. 29).

As a married man for much of his adult life, Marcus certainly endorses Epictetus' insistence on marital fidelity. In the *Memoranda*, however, Marcus goes a step farther when he describes an orgasm in a cold, clinical light, stripped of any glamorous aura: "The sex act is something rubbing against your penis, a brief spasm, and a little cloudy liquid" (vi. 13). The bare biological realism of an ejaculation dispels the dangerous romanticizing of sex for Marcus. He and Epictetus agree that self-control, good judgment, and prudence are vital for managing all our appetites for sex, food, drink, and physical comforts. Fidelity, uprightness, decency, and dignity are immeasurably more precious than any cheap thrill could possibly be.

Recognizing what one's body and one's mind truly are is essential to knowing one's purpose in life and one's place in the world, according to the Stoics. When someone that the Stoic school master of Nicopolis regarded as unskilled at listening complained that Epictetus said nothing to him, Epictetus tells him: Whoever is ignorant of who he is, what he was born for, what kind of world he's in, and with whom he shares it, who doesn't know what things are good, and what are evil, which things are noble, and which are base, will wander around deaf and blind, thinking that he's somebody when he's really a nobody (*Disc.* 2. 24. 19). Marcus echoes a very similar chain of inferences: He who doesn't know what the world is doesn't know where he is. He who doesn't know why the world is here doesn't know who he is or what the world is. He who is ignorant of any of these things doesn't know why he in particular is here. There are plenty of such ignorant people who don't know where or who they are. Given this fact, Marcus wonders how much sense it makes to care about the applause of these ignoramuses (viii. 52). Epictetus and Marcus agree that knowledge of the nature of the world and its purpose, knowledge of what human beings are and their purpose, and knowledge of one's own personal identity are all interconnected and are all indispensable for living well.

Ignorance of good and evil, on the other hand, is the cause of wrongdoing. Epictetus teaches that he that wrongs me, wrongs himself (*Disc.* 2. 10. 26 and 4. 5. 10). Marcus reiterates this same principle, writing that he that does harm, harms himself, and he that acts unjustly, does himself an injustice by making himself bad (ix. 4). Ignorance of what is good and bad are the kind of false beliefs that cause people to act badly and thereby harm their own characters.

Epictetus says that you really meet a person only when you enter his mind, come to understand his judgments, and you reveal your own judgments to him (*Disc.* 3. 9. 12). Marcus repeats this idea, writing: "Enter into the mind of everyone, and let them enter into yours" (viii. 61). This is because it is people's judgments of truth and falsity, good and bad, right and wrong, proper and improper, beauty and ugliness, benefit and detriment, self-respect and indignity that define who they are. Epictetus teaches that "It is not things themselves that disturb people, but their judgments about those things" (*Ench.* 5). Marcus has learned this lesson well: "When you're distressed about some external event, it's not the thing itself that bothers you, but your judgment of it" (viii. 47). Because of this, the good lies not in external objects and not in the body, but within us, in the sovereign power of the mind. The mind possessed of true judgments has the real goods of tranquility, freedom to achieve its desires, invulnerability to chance events, and happiness. All these mental goods flow from maintaining correct judgments and true perceptions. Marcus writes that today he escaped from anxiety, or rather ejected it, because the anxiety arose not from outside, but from within him, from his own perceptions (ix. 13).

In all likelihood the entirety of *Memoranda* iv. 49a is a quotation from a lost section of Epictetus' *Discourses*. Marcus considers the claim that it is unfortunate that some event X has happened. No, he replies. Rather, it's fortunate that X has happened and he has remained unharmed by X. He is neither shattered by the present nor afraid of the future. After all, he reminds himself, X could have happened to anyone, but not everyone could have remained unhurt by X. Why, Marcus wonders, should he count X happening a misfortune rather than remaining unhurt by X a good fortune? Can you really call something a misfortune that doesn't violate human nature, Marcus asks. Or do you think something that's not against the will of nature can violate it? You know what its will is. Does what has happened stop you from being just, magnanimous, self-controlled, prudent, honest, straightforward, modest, free, and from having all the other qualities that allow your nature to fulfill itself? So, when something threatens to hurt you, remember this axiom: X is no misfortune, but to endure X nobly is good fortune (iv. 49a). Indeed, Marcus and Epictetus both share Heraclitus' understanding of what good fortune truly consists in. Recall that Heraclitus writes that "a human being's character is his fate" (CXIV). Marcus ends Book v writing that "true good fortune is what you make for yourself. Good fortune: good character, good intentions, and good actions." As we will see in the next section, Epictetus and Marcus agree that death does not defeat a good character.

Death's door

Epictetus' perspective on death is firmly embraced by Marcus. Epictetus holds that death is nothing other than the body separating from the soul (*Disc.* 2. 1. 17; 3. 22. 33). This event triggers a change for both body and soul, but neither is annihilated. The physical material of the deceased person's body is recycled back into the elements from which it was composed in order to accommodate the cycle of the cosmos (*Disc.* 4. 7. 15; 2. 1. 18). Epictetus compares this recycling of bodily and psychic elements to the harvesting of ears of grain, the falling of leaves,[13] fresh figs drying out, and grapes turning into raisins, all of which are changes in state managed in an orderly way by nature, not instances of destruction (*Disc.* 3. 24. 91–92). A person's consciousness does not survive this separation of body and soul and their transformations.[14] Death is thus a change of that which is not now, *not* into what is not, but into what is not *now* (*Disc.* 3. 24. 93). We were each born when the cosmos had need of us, not when we wanted to be born (*Disc.* 3. 24. 94). All plants and animals, human beings included, are temporary tenants in the cosmos, not its permanent, immortal, residents (*Disc.* 2. 6. 27). The cosmos as a whole has always recycled its parts by giving birth to them and transforming them upon their deaths. Consequently, Epictetus concludes that upon death, the restoring of the material elements of an individual within the cosmos is nothing tragic, new, or unreasonable (*Disc.* 4. 7. 15). He doubts that the cosmos is going to be upset when someone dies (*Disc.* 3. 10. 14). Epictetus' view of how we should understand death and the relationship between the plant, animal, and human parts of the cosmos and the cosmos as a whole deeply shaped Marcus' view of death and his mereology (see *Memoranda* ii. 17; iv. 14; iv. 21; iv. 36; iv. 42; iv. 48; vii. 10; vii. 25; viii. 18; ix. 3; ix. 21; x. 7; x. 34; xii. 36).

Indeed, Epictetus regards human mortality as a blessing, not a bane. He argues that just as it would be a curse for ears of corn never to be harvested, so too it would be a curse for human beings never to die (*Disc.* 2. 6. 11–13). He declares: "Is there smoke in the house? If it's not suffocating, I'll stay. If it's too much, I'll exit. Always remember and hold fast to this, the door is open" (*Disc.* 1. 25. 18; cf. 1. 9. 20, 2. 1. 19–20, 3. 13. 14, and 3. 22. 34). Marcus repeats this Open Door Policy of Epictetus when he writes "If the smoke makes me cough, I can leave" (v. 29). Thus, like Epictetus, Marcus accepts the Stoic doctrine that suicide under extreme circumstances of suffering can be morally permissible—at least for the person who is making progress in virtue. Moreover, Marcus and Epictetus both derive consolation from the fact that we are free to exercise our own judgment about what degree of suffering we will tolerate and what degree of suffering we need no longer endure. *We* have the power to decide when to exit the smoky house of life. The question is not *whether* we mortal beings will die. The question is *when and how* it is appropriate for us to exit life.

Epictetus believes that there can be a divine signal alerting us to when we are permitted to exit life. His analogy is a sailor who is on shore leave from his ship. Epictetus says that the sailor may decide to collect water when he is ashore, and along the way he may pause to collect shellfish or pick some greens. But the sailor must remember that his shore leave is temporary and he must listen for the captain's signal to return to the ship. When the captain signals the recall, the sailor must drop everything and promptly return to the ship (*Ench.* 7). Epictetus says that life is a campaign and he compares the duties of the sailor to his ship captain to the duties of the soldier on campaign to his general (*Disc.* 3. 24. 31–33). Each individual, he explains, is assigned a specific task to perform, a specific post to hold, by his commanding officer (God). You must heed the duty of a soldier and perform each task at the bidding of your general (God), if possible divining what he wishes (*Disc.* 3. 24. 34–35). This military analogy is repeated by Marcus when he instructs himself to let the spirit in him represent a man, an adult, a citizen, a Roman, and a ruler who takes up his post like a soldier and patiently awaits his recall from life (iii. 5). Marcus here embraces Epictetus' theory of roles. Each person has many natural and acquired roles to perform throughout life. We are responsible for fulfilling each of these roles or posts like dutiful soldiers until we obey the last order from our commander, God, to "retire" from active duty and die (*Disc.* 1. 29. 27–29).

Both Epictetus (*Disc.* 1. 9. 11–17) and Marcus express a passing sentiment of weariness with the many burdensome daily chores of maintenance our bodies impose on us. The Emperor tells himself to stop whatever activity he's doing for a moment long enough to ask himself whether he is afraid of dying because he'll no longer be able to do *this*—presumably banal, grubby drudgery—any more (x. 29). Marcus remarks on how tiring the cacophony we live in is. It is so tiring, in fact, that it is enough to make him invite death to come quickly (ix. 3). Such a gloomy outlook is rarely expressed in the *Memoranda*, yet it would distort his philosophy to dismiss it as an insignificant anomaly. This morbid attitude is understandable given the fact that throughout his life Marcus never enjoyed robust physical health or strength, was probably plagued with a chronic ulcer, and suffered from various illnesses in his later years.

The theater of life

A particularly vivid analogy that Epictetus uses to illustrate the Stoic's obedient role playing in life is the theater. Just as Marcus urges himself to remember, Epictetus urges his student—Arrian's reader, that is, us—to remember that each of us is an actor in a play, the plot of which is up to the playwright (God). If he wants it short, it's short; if long, long. If he casts you to act the role of a poor man, or a cripple, or a ruler, or a layman, be sure to act whatever role you have skillfully. For this is your job, Epictetus insists, to play well the dramatic part that is assigned to you, but the selection of that role is another's (*Ench.* 17). Marcus borrows this same analogy when he writes that the person who has his head on straight and is purified lacks pus, dirt, and scabs. His life is not abruptly cut short by death like an actor who stops acting and leaves the stage before the play is finished, before the plot is over (iii. 8; cf. x. 27, xi. 1). Marcus' idea seems to be that the actor does not get to decide when the play is to end but is instead responsible for playing his part and completing all his lines as scripted. A praetor who commissions a comic actor, Marcus notes, can cut the play short and dismiss the actor from the stage even if he has only acted out three of the five acts. This life will be a whole drama in three acts. For the completion of it is determined by that which put you together originally (God, Nature) and now is the cause of your dissolution. Neither was yours to determine. So exit from the stage with grace, the same grace he who dismisses you has (xii. 36).

Does this Stoic conception of accepting the roles assigned to you by God/Fate/Nature entail that all one's roles are permanently fixed by factors beyond one's control? I don't think so. The Stoics distinguish between natural and acquired relationships. Natural relationships are those we are born into, as son or daughter, a brother or sister, for example. When one's parents die, one's role as a son or daughter ends. Thus even roles assigned to us by nature can end. Acquired relationships are chosen. We choose our friends, and in so doing create the role of being a friend to certain individuals, but not to others. Evidently, Epictetus chose neither to marry nor to have his own children, though late in life he adopted a friend's child who would have otherwise been left to die and, with a woman's help, raised it. Thus, Epictetus chose the role of an adoptive father. Marcus' first fiancée, Ceionia Fabia, was chosen for him, but that engagement was dissolved when he agreed to marry Faustina instead at the request of Antoninus Pius. After Faustina died, Marcus chose to keep the role of widower, preferring to have a mistress than to marry the eager Ceionia Fabia and resume the role of husband with a second wife. Consequently, the Stoic can pursue a new role or opt out of an old role, but does so by accepting whatever the outcome regarding getting or losing a role turns out to be as "scripted" or selected by God/Fate/Nature. This is not passivity. It is adaptability.

Epictetus interprets "tragedies" to be simply the result of people wrongly judging certain events beyond their control to be bad, catastrophic, or "tragic," and to respond by making evil choices. Medea judged her husband Jason's indiscretions to be evil, and so she judged it good to kill their children to cause him grief. She failed to realize that Jason's mistakes are not evils for her, whereas to kill their children to hurt him is *her* evil mistake, resulting from her false judgment that revenge is good (*Disc.* 1. 28. 7–9). Paris wrongly judged that it was good for him to steal Helen from her husband Menelaus. Menelaus wrongly judged that he would not be better off without such a wife. The slaughter of so many people and the destruction of Troy that ensued was the result of mistaken thinking and bad decisions (*Disc.* 1. 28. 12–23). Achilles' tragedy, Epictetus explains, did not lie in the death of Patroclus, but in Achilles giving into anger, whining about losing his war prize woman Briseis to Agamemnon, and forgetting that his assigned role was to help fight a war not to indulge in romance (1. 28. 24). Epictetus holds that the *Atreus, Phoenix*, and *Hippolytus* of Euripides and the *Oedipus* of Sophocles are all simply stories about the impressions people get into their heads of what they should do. They then foolishly decide to act on these bad, poorly examined notions. Tragedies, Epictetus insists, are nothing but accounts set in verse of the ordeals of people who have chosen to value externals (1. 4. 26; cf. 2. 16. 31). Marcus and Epictetus share the same perspective on the educational value of tragedies as object lessons for how to deal stoically with startling events. Marcus thinks tragedies are useful reminders of what can and inevitably does happen. If something is pleasing on the tragic stage, he reasons, it ought not to make you angry on the greater stage of life. Tragedies serve to help you realize that tough events are things we all have to face, both stage actors in make-believe and us real people in real life (xi. 6). Indeed, Epictetus (*Disc.* 1. 6. 38–39) and Marcus (ix. 1) both think it is impious to fault nature (Zeus, the gods) for unfairly letting pains afflict the good and pleasures land in the laps of the bad.

Finally, in tracing the deep and extensive influence of the Stoic school master's teachings on Marcus, it is important to note that Epictetus recommended the address "to oneself" as a spiritual exercise (*Disc.* 3. 24. 103 and 111). For this reason it is telling that Marcus addressed his journal entries *eis heauton* ("to himself"), and this phrase appeared as the Greek title of the work in the Renaissance.

CHAPTER 3

WHOLES AND PARTS

Ontology is the study of being. Mereology, from the Greek word *meros*, meaning "part," is the branch of ontology and logic which studies the relations between parts and wholes and the relations among parts. Throughout the *Memoranda* Marcus likes to investigate a subject or object by breaking it down into its parts to reveal its nature, operation, purposes, and value. This kind of approach is analytical, since an analysis is a division of a thing into its constituent parts. Marcus' mereological analyses enable him to see beyond superficial exteriors—which can mislead careless investigators—and gain key insights into the reality of his subjects. By applying simple mereological thinking to a wide variety of subjects Marcus believes he can better understand how things are. In this chapter I show that his account of parts and wholes is so prevalent in the *Memoranda* because it elucidates what he is, what the cosmos is, how the cosmos works, why death is not harmful but necessary, and what the purposes of all rational agents are as members of the social community and citizens of the state.

SIMPLE MEREOLOGY

Why bother chopping wholes into parts? Marcus thinks that the answer to this question is very simple: We want to live a good life. He reasons that we have the potential to live a good life. If we can learn to shrug off, ignore, and overcome the things which make no difference in our lives, then this clears the way to living a good life. How do we learn to be indifferent to what makes no difference? By looking at each thing both as a whole and as parts (see xi. 16). Thus, Marcus believes that attention to wholes and parts reveals which things around us are, in fact, indifferent to a good life. This discovery, in turn, allows us to handle these "indifferents" wisely, thereby enabling us to *live* good lives.

Now what sorts of things "make no difference" to a good life? As a Stoic, Marcus believes that the only things which are truly good are things which are absolutely necessary and indispensable for a good life and unconditionally beneficial, namely, the good traits of character known as the virtues. Wisdom, courage, justice, self-control, patience, kindness, perseverance, generosity, civility, and cooperativeness are examples of virtues. Only the virtues are true goods, the Stoics argued, because only the virtues bring and secure happiness. Conversely, the only true evils are bad traits of character known as vices. Vices include ignorance, cowardice, injustice, gluttony, impatience, cruelty, complacency, selfishness, surliness, and hostility. Vices are the only things which guarantee misery. Consequently, since the virtues are the only goods and the vices are the only evils, everything else is neither strictly good nor strictly evil but ultimately indifferent. All material possessions, wealth, health, the praise or criticism of others, fame, and all such things are indifferent to one's happiness. The Stoics maintain that if one concentrates on cultivating and preserving one's own virtues, then one can take all of these "indifferents" in stride, use them appropriately as they come and go, and achieve a good life. The presence or absence of such indifferents in one's life neither improves nor diminishes how good one's life is. This is because such things in themselves make no difference to your virtues, to your good traits of character. But the virtuous person will both be careful with the indifferents that happen to be present to him, and respond attentively to those absent from him, as opportunities to exercise the virtues corresponding to those present or absent indifferents. Consequently, how one uses these indifferents counts as good if they are used well, wisely, and virtuously, or it counts as evil if they are abused, used to do harm, and used viciously. When Marcus says that one can be indifferent to the things that make no difference, the charitable interpretation is that he is speaking loosely and may not mean to depart from the more complex and sophisticated Stoic view that the things *themselves* are indifferent, though how one *uses* them matters a lot, morally speaking, as does how one deals with lacking them.

The problem many people face is that they tend to be distracted by things that in no way help to improve their characters. Many people are impressed by things that make no difference to living a good life. Marcus considers the kinds of displays that tend to impress people who are ignorant of what is truly good. Take pretty singing, for example. Many people may feel moved by pretty singing. Should they be impressed? Should they envy the singer? Should they judge the pretty song to be a good thing that makes their lives better? Marcus denies that pretty singing is a true good. Instead, he urges himself to acquire indifference to pretty singing by thinking of it as a whole with parts. What is a pretty song? It is a melody. The parts of a melody are individual notes. Marcus asks: Are we powerless against each note we hear? No, Marcus reasons, surely we need not feel swept away and emotionally overcome by each note. But then, Marcus thinks, we can understand why it is silly to be impressed by the whole melody which is composed of those individual notes. Here Marcus appears to be guilty of committing the logical fallacy of composition. He mistakenly infers that because a part lacks a property, the whole that part belongs to must similarly lack that property.

1. This individual note does (or need) not sweep us away or emotionally move us.
2. This individual note is one part of a whole melody.
3. Hence, the whole melody does (or need) not sweep us away or emotionally move us.

In his zeal to defend the Stoic doctrine of indifferents, Marcus' reasoning becomes questionable. He wishes to emphasize that what is truly worthy of our praise is neither the singer of the melody, nor the musician playing the melody, nor the composer who wrote the lyrics and the notes. None of these things merit our serious admiration. Rather, the wise person, the helpful deed, and the generous gesture are the kinds of things which we ought to praise as truly good.

Dancing is another example Marcus gives of something indifferent. A dance is another whole which can be dissected into parts. A dance is composed of a series of individual movements. No one of these movements inspires awe. No one of these movements demands our acclaim. So, Marcus rejects the logic of judging a whole to be impressive when each of its parts is unimpressive. The same holds with the pancratium,[1] he believes. Evidently Marcus does not believe that he commits the fallacy of composition or the fallacy of division in these arguments. Instead, he believes that these are cogent arguments that help him properly evaluate all such things. Since singing and dancing are kinds of entertainment, they are mere amusements and nothing to be serious about. Marcus considers sports, races, and games of all kinds to fall into this same class of unserious amusements. Virtue and what springs from it, on the other hand, are crucially different. Virtue is the one thing we must be serious about. But for all the rest, Marcus reminds himself: "Look at the individual parts and move from analysis to indifference. Apply this to the whole of life" (xi. 2).

Life is a whole. What are its parts? Life can be divided into true goods, true evils, and things neither good nor evil. Virtues are true goods. Vices are true evils. So we should pursue virtues and strive to become virtuous with the utmost urgency and diligence. Conversely, we must be ever vigilant to avoid doing anything vicious so that we do not acquire vices. But thunderstorms, tornados, lightning strikes, hurricanes, droughts, earthquakes, tsunamis, volcanic eruptions, meteorite impacts, the change of the seasons, the stock market, pandemics, famines, wars, what other people do, say, and think, and political elections do not pertain to our own virtues or vices. We can analyze each of these wholes to discover how each of its parts is indifferent to our living a good life. Thus, Marcus thinks that mereological analysis of these "indifferents" reveals that they are no obstacles to our living a good, virtuous life, and so indifference toward them is the correct attitude to take.

THE PARTS OF A PERSON

What is a human person? Marcus again employs the method of mereology to answer this question. He writes that whatever it is that he is, it is flesh, a little spirit (breath), and an intelligence (ii. 2). He then considers each of these three parts: flesh, spirit/breath (*pneuma*), and intelligence. What is flesh? Marcus describes his human flesh as "a mess of blood, pieces of bone, a woven tangle of nerves, veins, arteries" (ii. 2). These bodily elements are nothing grand, nothing special, nothing to admire.[2] So much for the first part.

What is spirit? Marcus describes it as "air, and never the same air, but vomited out and gulped in again every instant" (ii. 2). This gaseous stuff is nothing awesome, nothing exalted, nothing precious.[3] So much for the second part. Marcus considers bodily flesh and spirit/breath to share in common the feature of being components held *in trust*. He insists that he does not own them outright, but has them strictly on loan from the cosmos (xii. 3). Consequently, both bodily flesh and spirit/breath share the same subordinate, inferior status with all unthinking pieces of cosmic furniture.

Intelligence, on the other hand, is special. Why does Marcus judge intelligence to be the one precious component of what he is? He reasons that intelligence is the one and only part of himself that is precious because it alone has the power to discern how the cosmos operates (cf. ix. 15, 22, 26) and the power to think, act, and live appropriately with that knowledge. Consequently, his intelligence is the only one of his three components to which he has clear title and valid ownership (xii. 3). Indeed, it is possible that Marcus regards his intelligence as what constitutes his real self, though he neither states this explicitly nor offers a careful account of identity in the *Memoranda*. What is clear is that he conceives of his identity as intimately bound up with his intelligence rather than with his body or breath (which are merely on loan to him).

Marcus further illustrates the special power of intelligence using another kind of mereological argument in Book xii, Section 30. In this entry he notes that some things which may appear to be plural in number are actually singular. In other words, we may be fooled into perceiving the appearance of a division of parts as indicating a disunity where there is in reality a coherent and singular whole. Marcus observes that sunlight, though it may appear to be broken up by walls, mountains, and a thousand other things, is singular, not plural. The light has one source, the sun, and it remains one phenomenon. Substance, he explains, though split into a thousand forms of various shapes, is also singular, not plural. Material stuff, substance, is one kind of thing, though it can be structured in a variety of ways. So, physical substance is one thing that can be fashioned into many forms. But this is true not only of inanimate substance. Marcus also argues that life, though distributed among a thousand different natures with their individual limitations, is singular, not plural. His idea seems to be that what animates each living thing is the same, single force, principle, disposition, process, or set of dynamic operations. Similarly, Marcus reasons, intelligence, even if it seems to be divided, is unified and singular (xii. 30). This harmonizes with the Stoic view that a single spirit/breath (*pneuma*) pervades the entire cosmos and that no void exists within the cosmos. Marcus also expresses the Stoic doctrine of *sumpatheia*, which is the idea that all parts, elements, and events within the cosmos are tightly, organically interconnected and united even if they appear separate in space and time.

Marcus' notion of intelligence may puzzle us. Don't we each have *separate* minds? Doesn't each person have her own, distinct intellect, her own unique, unshared intelligence? Though this seems to be a natural way to think about intelligence, Marcus suggests that we consider how intelligence operates. Cognition is an active *power*. It is not a passive lump like matter. Marcus notes that breath and matter lack any awareness or consciousness. Matter and breath have no dynamic connection to one another beyond cohesion. Marcus believes that the power to grasp an object in thought is special and unique to intelligence (xii. 30). Moreover, since there are many different intellects, and each is intelligible to the others, Marcus reasons that intelligence is like a vast web connecting all conscious minds not only to each other, but to all intelligible objects. What binds conscious, intelligent beings (human beings) together is our shared intelligence. We will see below how, on Marcus' view, this intellectual connection and commonality among human beings establishes the goal of social living and our ethical obligations.

COSMIC HOLISM

How is the world around us to be understood? Are we surrounded by a disjointed hodgepodge of innumerable events, objects, and people? Is the world just a scattered multiplicity of things, a chaotic, fragmented welter? Marcus fundamentally rejects this conception of the world. For him, the cosmos is a whole. That is, the cosmos is one thoroughly unified, tightly organized, cohesive, and coherent whole. He describes the world as one living being with one nature and one soul. Marcus believes that every object and every event feeds into that single entity and moves with a single motion. Each and every element of the world cooperates in producing everything else. The living organism of the cosmos contains within itself the power to produce all of the parts that come to be within it. The process of production is also fed by a continuous, reciprocal process of absorption of its parts. Thus the universe continually unravels old things and spins out new things, which themselves are swallowed back into the whole and again transformed and rewoven (iv. 40).

Marcus writes that he should keep reminding himself of the way things are connected and interrelated. Presumably this is because it is all too easy for him to be fooled into thinking of the sequence of events as unrelated, disconnected, random occurrences. Consequently he urges himself to bear in mind the big picture and to keep a holistic perspective on local events. Up close, the actions of individuals and twists and turns of events may seem disjointed, capricious, or inscrutable. But from the viewpoint of the cosmic whole, all things are implicated in one another and sympathetically connected with each other. Nothing that happens occurs at random. Every event is the direct consequence of another one.[4] This causal continuity and connectedness is tight and ubiquitous, according to Marcus. He says "things push and pull on each other, and breathe together and are one" (vi. 38; he also speaks of the silent force that "pushes and pulls things" in x. 26).

The fact that everything in the cosmos is interwoven is deeply significant for Marcus. He sees this interconnection of all parts of the universe as *holy*.[5] The parts of the cosmos are themselves each composed harmoniously, and together they compose the grand symphony of the world. So, just as there is one world made up of all things, so too there is one divinity present in them all. Just as there is one substance composing the world, so too there is one law governing the whole. This law is *logos* (vii. 9).

Logos has a very rich meaning among ancient Greek and Roman philosophers. Its core meaning is "rational utterance." But because of its great semantic flexibility it can refer to (1) a single statement, (2) a collection of statements composing a speech, (3) the faculty of speech, that is the ability to use language, (4) rationality or reason, (5) an intelligible principle, ratio, or formula, or (6) a connected series of assertions composing an argument. Marcus believes that the "one law" governing the one substance that composes the one, harmoniously interconnected universe is the *logos* (the "intelligence" he described above) shared by all rational (i.e., intelligent) beings. All rational beings share the ability to understand this one divine law binding the cosmos into a single, cohesive, interconnected whole. Moreover, since the process which gives birth to all rational beings—indeed, to *all* beings and *all* things—is the same, single cosmic process, Marcus infers that there is also one truth (vii. 9). Perhaps he means by this that the nature of the cosmos as pervasively unitary, the nature of its operation as unitary, the nature of its web-like divinity as unitary, and its unitary logic altogether unite to compose a single truth.

What else is involved in this one cosmic, divine truth? Marcus explains that what is divine is full of Providence. No part of the universe is discordant or out of place relative to the whole. No event is arbitrary or haphazard. Marcus writes that even chance is not divorced from nature, because chance events are as much woven into and enfolded in the scheme of things by Providence as necessary events are.[6] Everything proceeds from Providence, according to Marcus (ii. 3). One consequence of this is that some things occur by necessity because the whole that is the world *needs* them to. In other words, the parts of the world function as they do because the whole world needs them to function those ways. Marcus reasons that whatever serves to maintain the whole of nature (the world) is *good* for every part of nature. What maintains the world? What perpetuates nature? Change. The elements change and the objects composed of elements, that is, all bodies in nature, change (ii. 3). Marcus says that nature's job is to shift things around, to transform them, to pick them up and deposit them here and there. This constant alteration is nothing new. All of it is familiar (viii. 6). This is a vitally important geological-philosophical lesson Marcus rehearses in the *Memoranda*. The world is maintained by continuous change of its constituent parts. This change occurs by necessity, as the world could not function without it. Since change is necessary for the working of the world as a whole, it follows that change must also be good for every part of nature, for every piece of the world.[7] Marcus urges himself to treat this lesson, this cosmic fact, as an axiom (ii. 3). He strives to bear this fact in mind as a starting point to guide his reflections about his situation, his circumstances, his options, his responsibilities, his choices about how to react to others, and his decisions about how to act and live.

Marcus spells out the inference from cosmic unity and holistic providence to the proper conduct of an individual more clearly in Book v, chapter 8. He begins by observing that just as a doctor is said to prescribe a certain treatment for a patient, so he should say to himself that *nature* prescribed illness for a patient. What happens to each of us is ordered by nature. What happens to us furthers our destiny. Therefore, what happens to us is never an accident, because it is assigned to us by Providence. Marcus provides a second linguistic analysis to reveal the fated nature of events. He says that when we describe things as "taking place" we're talking like builders do. Builders speak of bricks in a wall "taking their place" in the structure. This means that the bricks (the parts) fit together in an interlocking, harmonious pattern to form the wall (the whole). Events are parts which link together to form one harmonious whole, namely, fate. Marcus again emphasizes the unity of this harmony. He argues that just as the world forms a single body comprising all bodies, so fate forms a single *purpose*, comprising all purposes (v. 8).

So what should we do when we become ill or injured? Marcus applies the simile of the doctor's prescription: Just as we welcome the treatment prescribed by our doctor, we should welcome the event (in this case, the illness or injury) prescribed by nature (fate). He recognizes that the condition prescribed to us by the world may not always be pleasant, but we should embrace it nonetheless, he argues, because we want to get well, and this prescription is a step in the process of becoming well. The world prescribes this condition to us as a necessary event, after all. Since the world needs us to be ill for the moment, the good of that whole is maintained by this happening to one of its parts. Marcus says that we can accept the illness because it leads to the good health of the world and the well-being and prosperity of Zeus himself. Indeed, Marcus insists that Zeus would not have brought this event on anyone unless it brought benefit to the world as a whole (v. 8).

Marcus is consistent in his understanding of the operation of the cosmos and the law-governed, divine, providential, destined, harmonious, purposive order of events. To understand events as necessitated by fate is to conceive of them as prescribed by Zeus, which is to think of them as established by Providence. To understand events as established by Providence is to see them as destined, which is to interpret them as intended by nature. To interpret events as intended by nature is to embrace them as the manifestation of the universe's purpose. All of these are different ways of describing the same, single harmony of what happens. Marcus cannot conceive of nature bringing about something which failed to benefit what it governed. That would be like the whole deliberately harming one of its parts. Marcus' simplistic mereology excludes this possibility.

The upshot of this idea is huge. The rational thing to do is *to embrace everything that happens*, including everything that happens to us. Marcus contends that there are two reasons to embrace what happens. First, the thing is happening to *you*. The event, condition, or circumstance was prescribed for you, it was assigned to you, to *this* particular rational being, not to someone else. To embrace it is to affirm a moment in your life, to embrace a chapter in your own biography, to accept a fact about yourself, to welcome a stage in your own growth. It is easy to see how this thought promotes psychological health. Marcus seems to endorse the Stoic view that the cosmos is providentially concerned with each individual. Second, what happens to any individual—to any part—is a contributing cause of the well-being of the world—the well-being of the whole. The world is fulfilled by the events within it. The whole is actualized by what happens in it. The world as a whole operates through all the individual events occurring in its myriad parts. Consequently, even if it may seem that what happens to an individual is locally bad, that event remains globally good, good for the world, necessary for the world as a whole. For Marcus, this idea suffices to provide consolation to the local self.

Why can't the locally bad bits be excised from the world? Why can't we eliminate the unpleasant parts from the life of an individual? Marcus' answer is that this would interfere with the organic coherence of the individual's life. He holds that the whole is damaged if you cut away anything at all from its continuity. The world is a whole that needs each of its parts because it is a *living* entity with one nature and one soul (iv. 40). To cut off one thing that happens to one part of the world would be like cutting off a person's finger. The finger is a part of hand and the finger has one or more purposes in the functioning of the hand. The hand has purposes for the functioning of the rest of the body. Thus, to cut away a finger damages the integrity of the body. The purpose of the whole depends on fulfillment of the purposes of its parts. So, to want to excise certain parts of the world or to eliminate certain events in nature is to fail to recognize how doing so damages the whole world. When we reject what happens to us, when we bemoan what we regard as locally bad events, Marcus says we are hacking at the body of the whole world, we are destroying some of its necessary, life-sustaining limbs or organs. The world cannot endure, it cannot *exist*, without all of its ever-changing parts (v. 8). To want a part of the world, like an unpleasant event in one's own life, to be eradicated is to want the world to be a different whole than it is. Marcus emphatically rejects any such world-denying attitude. It makes no sense to him that we should want to reject the very nature of the whole of which we are parts.

One could object that Marcus fails to answer *why* the locally bad bits cannot be removed from the cosmos without damaging the whole. For example, why can't excess hair be cut off, why can't fingernails be clipped, and why can't a tumor be removed from the body without harming its integrity? Marcus seems committed to the position that hair and fingernails serve purposes, so to remove *all* of one's hair or *all* of every fingernail would entirely thwart their bodily purposes. But simply trimming one's hair and clipping one's fingernails does not thwart such purposes, so Marcus could not object that these kinds of excisions are harmful to the whole. The growing tumor, in contrast, threatens the survival of the whole body, so Marcus could argue that removing it benefits and pre-serves the whole rather than harming it. Nevertheless, the question remains: Why can't a good whole (e.g., the cosmos) be composed of all good parts? Marcus does not address this problem of theodicy in the *Memoranda*.

Marcus does not seem to believe dogmatically in divine providence and cosmic unity. He admits the possibility that the Epicureans, and not their opponents the Stoics, may be correct about the nature of the cosmos. As we have seen, Marcus endorses the Stoics' view that all things spring from one intelligent source (Zeus, Providence, the divine law) and form a single body (the unified, organically cohesive cosmos). If this view is correct, then Marcus reasons that each part, including each of us, should accept the actions of the whole, namely, what happens. But he entertains the possibility that there are only atoms, clumping together and splitting apart for-ever *without* any intelligent purpose or providential design (ix. 39). According to this atomic theory of the Epicureans, nature is not governed by any overarching, globally beneficial plan. Instead, invisibly small particles join together and split away from each other according to mechanistic laws completely indifferent to the good or ill of any conscious beings. Yet even if the world is an enor-mous jumble of purposeless, swarming atoms, amazingly Marcus still sees no reason to feel anxiety. In viii. 17 he offers an enthymeme which could be reconstructed like this:

1. The matter is either in his control or in the control of someone else.
2. If it's in his control, then he can handle it appropriately without blaming himself.
3. If it's in the control of someone else, then he could blame either atoms (if the Epicureans are right about how the cosmos works) or the gods (if the Stoics are right about how the cosmos works) or no one and nothing.
4. It's stupid to blame atoms (since they have no intentionality).
5. It's stupid to blame the gods (since they know best what should happen).
6. Hence, if it's in the control of someone else, then blame no one and nothing.
7. Therefore, blaming is pointless.

The unstated third possibility in the first premise is that the matter is in no one's control, in which case the cause is either atoms or the gods. But by the same logic, Marcus thinks it is stupid to blame either atoms or the gods. So, whether the Stoics or the Epicureans are right about the nature of the cosmos, there is no cause for worrying about a state of affairs that is not up to him. He can't change the fundamental nature of the universe, so there's no reason to be upset.

If Epicurean atomism is true, however, then the optimism based on belief in divine providence would be undercut. Yet even without cosmic optimism, Marcus sees no reason to feel anxiety (ix. 39). He asks himself whether he is dead or damaged or brutal or dishonest. He can't be dead if his mind is working. Since he is thinking, he need not worry that he is dead. Is he damaged? If so, then he can heal and recuperate. Is he brutal? If so, then he can choose to cease to be brutal. Is he dishonest? If so, then he can instead choose to be honest. He asks himself if he is a member of the herd or is grazing like one. If so, then he can free himself from this unthinking herd mentality and regain his good sense about how he ought to behave as an intelligent, rational member of the community. The idea seems to be that by posing these questions to himself, Marcus can determine whether he needs to repair himself in some way (by healing, shedding brutal behavior, being honest, or rising above the bestiality of the herd) or whether he has no such problems, in which case there's no reason for him to feel anxiety about anything (ix. 39). He repeats this cosmic disjunction in Book vi, chapter 4 when he writes: "Before long, all existing things will be transformed, to rise like smoke (assuming all things become one), or be dispersed in fragments" (cf. vii. 32). Here too the implication seems to be that there is no justification for anxiety, because soon all existing things, including those that one may be tempted to worry about, will be transformed. Their worrisome forms will drift away like smoke to be replaced by and recycled into new forms, or else all existing things will disintegrate into fragments. Either way, since the things we currently fret over will soon and inevitably evaporate, there is nothing to worry about, even if atoms compose the cosmos.

DEATH HARMLESSLY TRANSFORMS

In Book v, chapter 8 of the *Memoranda* we saw how Marcus uses primitive mereology to argue that to complain about what happens is to hack at the wholeness of fate and the continuity of the world. No doubt one of our favorite things to complain about is death. But Marcus believes that to complain about death is to be willfully ignorant of a fundamental process of nature at work in the whole that is the cosmos. He spells this out in Book x, chapter 7. Marcus observes that the whole is compounded by nature of individual parts, whose destruction is inevitable. Yet "destruction" here means not annihilation but *transformation*. Changeability is intrinsic to the parts of nature, so what appears to be destruction of a part is really just a relatively more dramatic alteration of the substrate into something new. Now is this process of transformation *harmful* to the parts of nature? If the process were harmful to the parts and unavoidable, then Marcus thinks that it is difficult to see how the whole could run smoothly, with parts of it passing from one state to another, all of them created only to be destroyed in different ways. But if this were the case, then either (a) Nature must set out to cause its own components harm, and predestine them to be vulnerable to this injurious process, or (b) Nature is oblivious to what goes on. Marcus believes that neither (a) nor (b) seems very plausible (x. 7). Therefore, he infers that the unavoidable process of transformation of the parts of nature is *not* harmful to those parts.

Recall that Marcus thinks that the cosmos is one substance (vii. 9), not many disconnected ones. He likens nature to a sculptor shaping wax. It takes a portion of the waxy substance and makes a horse out of it. It then melts this down and uses the same waxy material to make a tree. But just as the horse doesn't last forever, neither does the tree. So then nature melts the tree down to make a human person. But it is just as intrinsic to the person that she must unavoidably be transformed into something else as it was for the horse and the tree. Each of these organisms borne by the cosmos exists only briefly. Did it harm the horse, tree, or human being to be fabricated from the material substance that composed them? Certainly not. Well then, Marcus reasons in a symmetrical fashion, it did these things no harm to dissolve, either. Horses, trees, human beings, and all individual parts of nature are containers of the one substance making up the universe. "It does the container no harm to be put together, and none to be taken apart" (vii. 23). According to Stoic theory, benefits promote a being's nature whereas harms injure a being's nature. Mortality, Marcus contends, is an unalterable feature of the nature of living beings, and so death does not constitute a *harm* to a living being.

This is a vital lesson to be gleaned from an analysis of birth and death, of generation and destruction. Marcus consoles himself that he has functioned as a part of something, namely, a part of the cosmos. He will also vanish into that same whole which produced him, namely, the cosmos. But since he, like all other living things, will return to the same source from which he arose, his death is a restoration of cosmic-stuff back to the cosmos. This principle of perpetual cosmic recycling is the *logos*. According to this *logos*, this rule of nature, all things spring from the world, undergo continuous change, and ultimately will be restored to the world by the last kind of change, known as death (iv. 14; cf. vii. 10).

How might this cosmic recycling of its parts work, given the sheer number of living things that have arisen, generation after generation, from the earth? In Book iv, chapter 21 Marcus wonders how, if our breaths/spirits (*pneumata*) survive, the air finds room for them all. Similarly, how does the earth find room for the countless number of bodies buried in it since the beginning of time? The answer is: change, decomposition, diffusion, and absorption into the *logos* from which all things spring. Since the cosmos is composed of one substance, this same substance is ceaselessly transformed into new arrivals as each generation of living things passes away. Marcus reminds himself that we shouldn't limit our thoughts to just the mass of *buried* bodies. Rather, cosmic recycling occurs every time any living thing eats or is eaten. Consumption and digestion demonstrate daily cosmic recycling as much as death, decay, and rebirth do. All manner of foods are swallowed up in bodies, converted into flesh and blood, and transformed anew into air and fire. How do we discover the truth of this metabolic cosmic process? Through analysis of material and cause, Marcus answers (iv. 21).

Constant awareness that everything is born from change is therefore one of the most important lessons gleaned from the study of nature (iv. 36). Marcus often repeats that "there is nothing nature loves more than to alter what exists and make new things like it. All that exists is the seed of what will emerge from it" (iv. 36; cf. vii. 25). Since this is a basic, unalterable fact about nature, Marcus insists that it must be accepted. "There is nothing bad in undergoing change—or good in emerging from it" (iv. 42). What dies is not annihilated. Rather, it remains in the world transformed and dissolved as parts of the world, and as parts of *us* (viii. 18). Since this transformation is necessary, inevitable, and integral to the functioning of the whole of nature, it is *not bad.*

Marcus finds solace in tracing his own bodily transformation back through his ancestors. He matter-of-factly comments that he is made up of substance and what animates it, and that neither one can ever stop existing, any more than it began to. "Every portion of me will be reassigned as another portion of the world, and that in turn transformed into another. Ad infinitum. I was produced through one such transformation, and my parents too, and so on back. Ad infinitum" (v. 13). Marcus conceives of himself as a thread in the fabric of the universe. He thinks of himself as a temporarily existing ingredient in a cosmic stew that will be dissolved into and transformed by that stew. In this respect he is anything but alone. His parents, his grandparents, all of his ancestors, indeed, all human beings who have ever lived, indeed, all animals of every species who have ever lived, share the same fate and are equally mortal elements of the ever self-recycling, self-transforming cosmos. What is more, all plants of every species that have ever lived and all microbes that have ever existed are similarly portions of the world, arisen from the world, and transformed into other things by the world.

Another technique Marcus uses to analyze death and reveal its real nature is to conceive of death as a kind of termination. Death is a kind of ending. But what else ends? When we cease from an activity, that too is a kind of termination. When we follow a thought to its conclusion, that too is a kind of death. But neither the termination of an activity like walking nor the conclusion of a thought does us any harm (ix. 21). Marcus similarly applies mereological analysis to his life. What are the stages of his life? Childhood, boyhood, adolescence, adulthood, old age—each of these stages of life is a transformation, an ending of the previous stage, and therefore also a kind of termination, a kind of death. Was each of these transformations terrible, Marcus asks? No, they weren't (ix. 21). What about the lives and deaths of his relatives, his grandfather, mother, and adopted father? Marcus urges himself to realize how many deaths and transformations and endings he has experienced, and asks himself if they were so terrible. His answer is no. Therefore, he reasons, neither will the ending and transformation of his own life be terrible (ix. 21).

Marcus expands on this line of reasoning in Book ix, chapter 3. Death is not to be looked down on, but actually welcomed, he tells himself. Youth and old age, growth and maturity, a new set of teeth, a beard, and a first gray hair are all things required by nature (for men). Sex, pregnancy, and childbirth are all things required by nature (for many women). Our dissolution in death is thus like all the other physical changes at each stage of life. How should the thoughtful person await her death, then, according to Marcus? Neither with indifference, nor with impatience, nor with disdain. Rather, we should simply see it as one of the things that happens to us. Marcus urges himself to think about the emergence of a newborn from its mother's womb with the same anticipation he should have awaiting the hour of his soul emerging from its compartment (ix. 3). Consequently, Marcus believes that we cannot be justified in griping that our death or the death of a loved one is a terrible thing. To grumble about our deathly transformation is quite senseless (viii. 18).

What happens upon death? Marcus notes that death is the end of sense-perception. Death is the end of being controlled by our emotions. Death is the end of mental activity. Death is also the end of enslavement to our bodies, since the dead are no longer afflicted by hunger, thirst, fatigue, sickness, aches, or desires for the pleasures of the flesh (vi. 28). Our living bodies are buffeted both by external tumults of pain and by internal goads of appetites that distress us when they go unsatisfied. Though the Stoics regard these nuisances as indifferents, Marcus notes that death frees us from them. So, why do we harbor such a strong fear of death? Marcus reasonably suggests that fear of death is fear of the unknown, fear of what we may experience. But there are only two possibilities. We may experience nothing at all or something quite new. If we experience nothing, then we can experience nothing *bad*. This important insight Marcus the Stoic takes from Epicurus, earlier Stoics, and Plato's *Apology* of Socrates (40c–d). But Marcus reasons that if our experience changes upon death, then our existence will change with it, but not *cease* (viii. 58).

Given the processes of consumption, digestion, maturation, decay, and regeneration at play all around us in myriad forms, and even inside our own bodies every second (vi. 25), Marcus contends that the judgment that death is terrible betrays a ridiculous ignorance of the logic of nature and the rhythms of the cosmos. After all, stars, planets, and whole galaxies are born, change, die, and are recycled no less than everything on earth. Marcus is sensitive to this galactic perspective when he notes that all those around him, praiser and praised, rememberer and remembered, they all die soon, and the whole earth is a mere point in space (viii. 21). To his mereology of the spatial parts of nature Marcus thus pairs a mereology of time. Consider how immense the totality of time is. He describes it as a "vast abyss" (xii. 32). Then consider the miniscule fraction of that infinity of time allotted to each of us. One's entire lifespan is absorbed in an instant into eternity from this perspective of temporal holism. Consider the fraction of all substance and the fraction of all spirit allotted to each of us. Consider the fraction of the entire earth which you scramble around on. Marcus urges himself to keep all these considerations in mind to help him from treating anything as important except doing what his nature demands and accepting what nature sends to him (xii. 32). (We will examine what his nature demands of him in the next section of this chapter.)

The immensity of the whole of time, the whole of material substance, and the whole of the earth provide Marcus with a powerful reminder of how to put the tiny, fleeting moments of his own local, particular concerns that distress him into proper perspective. Anxiety about the tiniest matters of the tiniest moments is utterly banished from the viewpoint of the spatio-temporal whole. He repeats this thought succinctly elsewhere: "Remember: Matter—how tiny your share of it. Time—how brief and fleeting your allotment of it. Fate—how small a role you play in it" (v. 24). This sort of entry is aimed at easing the worries of Marcus' weary mind. When he feels the demands of the empire weighing so heavily upon him that he begins to feel overwhelmed, he can recall this sober reminder. His body is a puny particle in the enormous ocean of matter (cf. vi. 36), or, as he describes it elsewhere, "a grape seed in infinite space" (x. 17). His life is a tiny, transitory blip in the vast abyss of time. The life span of the things around us he describes as "a half twist of a corkscrew against eternity" (x. 17).

Death, then, is a commonplace necessity for all living things and always has been, Marcus insists. The death of an individual—a small part of nature—is consistent with and required for the proper functioning of the whole cosmos. Consequently, the death of the part *benefits* the whole. The death of an individual is a culmination of her mortal nature. Marcus reasons this out as follows. A given action that stops when it's supposed to is none the worse for stopping. The act achieves its goal and is done. Nothing bad occurs. Moreover, the person engaged in the act is none the worse for the act ending either. But what is a life? What are its parts? A life, Marcus suggests, can be conceived of as a succession (a whole) of actions (parts). If a life ends when it's supposed to, it's none the worse for that. No life is ever designed by nature to last forever, or even very long. That would be a biological, cosmological impossibility. Therefore, Marcus concludes, the person whose life comes to an end has no cause for complaint. Both the beginning of life (conception, then birth) and the end of life (death) are set by nature. In some cases, one's own nature determines the time and manner of death when the body expires due to the exhaustion of its organs, which we call death from old age. In other cases, nature as a whole ends an individual's life when nature's parts, shifting and changing, constantly renew the world, and keep it on schedule. Since this rearranging, recycling, and renewing of the parts of nature benefits the whole of nature, it cannot be bad. This is because nothing that benefits all things can be ugly or out of place, according to Marcus. Consequently, the end of life is not an evil because *it doesn't disgrace us.* Our mortality is not a moral failing on our part, so our deaths don't rob us of virtue. The Stoics hold that virtue, as the perfection of reason, is the only true good since it alone always benefits us. Likewise, vice, as the corruption of reason, is the only true evil since it alone always harms us. Indifferents may be used either virtuously or viciously, so in themselves they are neutral. Since the death of an organism is simply nature's transformation of one of its parts into something different, it is not an act voluntarily chosen by us. Marcus wonders why we should be ashamed of an involuntary act that injures no one. Death, then, is harmless since it involves no vice. Indeed, Marcus affirms that in a way it's a good thing, because it is scheduled by the world, promotes it, and is promoted by it. This insight into the necessity of death is a pearl of wisdom. Recognizing this wisdom, Marcus declares, is a step toward becoming godlike. It is a step following along God's path. Growth in wisdom is reason's journey toward its divine goals (xii. 23).

LIMBS OF THE SOCIAL BODY

Marcus accepts the popular ancient Greek philosophical principle that "like attracts like." He observes that all earthly things feel the pull of the earth, all wet things flow together, and all airy things must be forcibly prevented from mixing together. Fire on earth is naturally drawn upward toward the fiery sun and stars (ix. 9). Marcus holds that the principle of like to like operates not only among physical bodies, but also among things with an intelligent nature. Intellects are naturally attracted to mix and mingle with other intelligent things. Though Marcus, in company with most ancient philosophers, believes that nonhuman animals lack reason, with other Stoics he nevertheless believes that they gather in swarms and herds, nest together, and love one another in a way not unlike human love. Marcus explains that nonhuman animals have a developed bonding instinct which plants and stones lack. But intelligent, rational beings have an even greater readiness to mix and mingle with their counterparts. This is why rational beings come together to form families, friendships, and larger social groups. They also create and maintain states by means of treaties and truces (ix. 9; cf. ix. 8).

Despite this natural impulse toward association, unfortunately rational beings all too often choose conflicts and divisiveness. Marcus bemoans the fact that rational beings are the only ones that at times lose their sense of attraction, convergence, and solidarity. Yet try as they might to divorce themselves from one another, in the end rational beings cannot escape the pull to congregate. Their inborn drive to assemble with their kind is relentless and ultimately stronger than their momentary impulses of discord, division, and alienation.

"Concrete objects can pull free of the earth more easily than humans can escape humanity," Marcus insists (ix. 9). We can infer from this that Marcus would emphatically reject eremitism (the way of life of a hermit) as horribly inhuman. Moreover, it seems equally safe to infer that Marcus would consider solitary confinement to be an extremely cruel, inhumane form of punishment. Humanity is a whole. Human beings are its parts. To try to separate these parts from each other is foolishly to deny the mereology of human sociality.

Marcus' mereology of social ethics is explicit in Book vii, chapter 13. A cynical critic might consider other people to be strangers, typically hostile, self-serving competitors for power and resources, and thus potential enemies. For Marcus, however, this perspective is blind to an overriding commonality and kinship. He insists that what is rational in different beings is related, like the individual limbs of a single being. These limbs are designed to function as a unit. They are meant to work toward a shared, common goal. He thinks that this fact will be clearer if he reminds himself that he is a single limb (*melos*) of a larger, rational body. But in Greek there is a difference of only one letter between saying that he is a "limb" (*melos*) and saying that he is a "part" (*meros*). Marcus conceives of himself and all rational beings as limbs or organs of the same living body, as coordinating parts of a single organism. He then scolds himself for failing to really embrace other people as fellow parts of this rational whole. When he helps his fellows, he wonders what he is really doing. If he thinks of it only as doing the right thing, he is failing to see that helping his counterparts is really his own reward. This is because helping other rational beings helps other limbs of the *same* body. When a part of the body benefits the whole, all its parts are benefited. Whenever parts help other parts they therefore indirectly help *themselves* (vii. 13).

Sadly, sometimes people do not help each other at all. Instead they vie against each other. Sometimes people act without a sense of shame. When we encounter someone behaving shamelessly, how can we deal with that? Why do such shameless people exist? Marcus believes that a world without any shamelessness is impossible. Not all bodies enjoy perfect health all the time. Just as it is impossible for a living body never to be afflicted by illness, so too Marcus believes that a world without vice is impossible. Given this fact, he reminds himself not to ask for the impossible. He urges himself to accept the fact that there have to be shameless people in the world. There also have to be untrustworthy people and people with all the other defects of character known as vices (cf. viii. 15). When you encounter one of them, Marcus advises you to remember that the entire class of shameless, difficult, untrustworthy, deceitful, selfish people must exist. If we bear in mind that the whole class of people with a particular vice has to exist, then when we encounter one of the members of this class, we will be better able to tolerate him (ix. 42). Mindfulness about wholes and parts can therefore foster the virtue of tolerance.

In the *Memoranda* Marcus often practices how to refrain from getting upset and acting badly when he encounters difficult people. Mental preparation is vital. If he prepares his mind properly, he won't be caught off guard by nasty people and deflected from conducting himself properly. Therefore, he reminds himself that when he wakes up in the morning, he must tell himself that the people he deals with today will be meddling, ungrateful, arrogant, jealous, and surly. His advantage is that he understands why they are like this. They are like this because they fail to see the difference between good and evil. The vicious suffer from a kind of blindness. Marcus himself, however, has seen the beauty of the good and the ugliness of evil. Marcus, unlike those who are morally-blind, has recognized that the wrongdoer has a nature related to his own. Though the wrongdoer is not of the same blood or birth as Marcus, both are of the same mind (since, as we saw in Book xii, chapter 30, there is one intelligence uniting all rational beings) and both have a share of the divine, which is also unitary. Armed with this knowledge of mental kinship with all human beings, Marcus is convinced that no wrongdoers can hurt him. Shielded with the vision of the beauty of good and the ugliness of evil, Marcus is confident that no one can implicate him in ugliness. He cannot be co-opted into it. Moreover, this knowledge of good and evil and of kinship among intelligent beings frees Marcus from feeling anger or hatred toward his kin. Wrongdoers are Marcus' comrades, his counterparts, his kinfolk, and parts of the same whole as he is. "We were born to work together like feet, hands, and eyes, like the two rows of teeth, upper and lower. To obstruct each other is unnatural. To feel anger at someone, to turn your back on him: these are obstructions" (ii. 1; cf. xii. 26). To get angry at a fellow human being makes no more sense, Marcus thinks, than for your left hand to hinder your right hand or for your left eye to try to work independently of your right eye. Here part-whole social thinking is a cure for anger, hatred, and disregard of others.

For Marcus this image of coordinating, intimately synergistic body parts vividly illustrates the organic solidarity and affinity among human beings. Let's recall that Marcus saw the aftermath of many battles, and so surely witnessed the mangled bodies and grisly body parts of countless soldiers. Consider the sight of a severed hand or foot, or a decapitated head, just lying on the ground far from the body it belonged to. Marcus says that this grotesque dismemberment is what we try to do to ourselves when we rebel against what happens to us (like, e.g., being repulsed by our encounter with a wrongdoer), when we segregate ourselves from our fellow beings, or when we indulge in something selfish. In these acts we tear ourselves away from our natural state of fellowship with others. We rip ourselves away from the unity we were born to share with others. In effect, we chop off a foot and fling it far from its body when we rebuff others and remove ourselves from them (viii. 34).

But unlike the severed foot, we retain the huge advantage of the ability to graft ourselves back to the (social) body to which we belong. No other part of any other whole, when hacked off from that whole, has the power and privilege of reattaching itself. We alone are granted this by God. We can cut ourselves away from the body of nature by rejecting the challenges (i.e., events) nature assigns to us. We can cut ourselves away from the body of society by doing something selfish and shunning people. But amazingly we can also reunite with our "cousins of mind," and thereby reattach ourselves to our host, nature itself. Our special endowment, however, extends beyond even this, because God has allowed us not to be chopped off in the first place. Our intelligence enables us to correct our self-severing, to graft ourselves back onto the whole where we belong, and to resume our old position anew as a functioning *part* of an organic whole (viii. 34). Marcus regards it as a marvelous gift that we alone, of all the countless parts of the cosmos, have the power to reunite with our whole in this way.

Marcus develops this part-whole analogy further in Book ix, chapter 8. A branch cut away from the branch beside it is simultaneously cut away from the whole tree. A human being, he explains, who is separated from another human being is similarly cut away from the whole human community. But while the branch is cut off by someone else, human beings cut *themselves* off, without realizing that they are doing so, from the whole civic enterprise, which is a community founded by Zeus (God). People cut themselves off from one another through hatred and rejection. Marcus repeats the idea (viii. 34) that the gift which we have and which trees and the rest of nature lack is the ability to reattach ourselves and again become integrated parts of the whole. But in Book ix, chapter 8 he adds that if the rift is repeated too often, then it is *difficult* to reconnect and restore the severed part. Marcus states that there is a visible difference between the branch which always remained connected to its trunk from the beginning, growing with it undisturbed, and the branch which has been chopped off and grafted back to the trunk. Marcus borrows the phrase from the gardeners to describe the latter case as "one trunk, two minds" (xi. 8). When part diverges from whole, two minds pull away from each other, divide, and damage the whole *and* the part. The detachment of the part from the whole, of the individual person from the civic community, can leave a scar. Treating a fellow human being in a hateful way or rejecting a member of one's community wounds that community. Repeating such an offense is not an insurmountable harm, yet, even when healed, the community bears a scar from the frequent severing and reattachment.

How can we live without harming the community of which we are a part? Again, mereology offers helpful advice. Consider the whole of your life. A typical way to identify the parts of that whole is in units of years. The years are divided into months, weeks, days, hours, etc. One problem with this division is that it is arbitrary. But a more subtle problem is that accident, injury, or disease can abruptly terminate the arbitrary divisions of a week, month, or year. We have seen how Marcus considers developmental stages to be a more natural division of a human life: infancy, childhood, boyhood, adolescence, adulthood, old age (see ix. 21, ix. 3). But just like days and years, we have no control over these stages of maturity.

Which parts of our lives *are* up to us? Marcus reminds himself that our *actions* are units of our lives which we determine. Everyone must choose her actions. Therefore, Marcus reasons, each of us must assemble her life action by action. One builds her whole life by piecing together action after action, part by part. We must be satisfied if each of our acts achieves its intended goal, as far as it can, *because no one can prevent that from happening* (viii. 32). Though there can be external obstacles to accomplishing what we intend, Marcus recognizes that there can be no obstacles whatsoever to our behaving with justice, self-control, and good sense. If our aims are virtuous, then we cannot fail to hit *those* targets. The Stoic is like an archer. The archer musters all her skill to try to hit the target. But once the well-aimed arrow is shot from her bow, what happens to the arrow is no longer up to her. If an external factor causes the arrow to miss the target, the archer has not failed to shoot expertly. Similarly, the Stoic who does all she can to act justly and wisely succeeds in hitting her target, even if the world is not caused to improve by her virtuous "shot" (attempt).

But isn't this an empty kind of success? If an external obstacle blocks our achieving in the world what we aim at, then aren't we in reality defeated? Marcus rejects this pessimistic conception of intention and result. He insists that if you accept the obstacle and work with what you're given, then an alternative will present itself. This alternative thereby becomes another piece of what you're trying to assemble, action by action (viii. 32). So, instead of conceiving of your life as a series of arbitrary units of passing time (days, weeks, etc.), Marcus suggests that it is wiser to conceive of your life in terms of units of agency, as an edifice of individual actions built up one by one. Just, self-controlled, and sensible actions concatenate to constitute the life of a virtuous agent, a good actor on the social stage. This life, erected piece by piece of good deeds, rises to become a noble edifice.

The raw materials of this life-edifice are provided by what happens, by our circumstances, by fate, ultimately. Just as nature takes every obstacle and impediment and works around it, turning it to its own purposes, incorporating it into itself, so too a rational being, like a resourceful builder, can transform each supposed setback into raw material useable for achieving her goal (viii. 35). These "setbacks" in viii. 35 are the "alternatives" Marcus speaks of in viii. 32. Each challenging situation that presents itself to a rational being becomes an opportunity to perform an action that adds to the growing structure which constitutes her life. Rationality includes the ability to make what others call obstacles, setbacks, hardships, or even catastrophes fit into the architectural plan of our life. Not everything that happens to us will be clean, uniform slabs of pretty marble or handsome, smooth planks of burled oak. We can and often must also effectively build into our lives heaps of gravel, broken boulders, and twisted boards.

With this part-whole understanding of life, Marcus emphasizes that every one of our actions count. He tells himself that he participates in a society by his existence. Consequently, he must participate in its life through *all* of his actions. Any action not directly or indirectly aimed at a social end, a unifying goal, a solidarity-building outcome, is a disturbance to his life. This is because such an action chips away at the wholeness of his life. It weakens the structural integrity of his life-edifice. An antisocial action is thus a source of dissension, a cause of fragmentation. An antisocial action is like the man in the assembly who is a faction to himself. He is out of step with the majority when he elects to be a part standing in opposition to the will and the working of the whole (ix. 23). A part which opposes its whole is fundamentally at odds with its own purpose and in conflict with its own good. Marcus develops this idea in his political mereology.

THE BEES AND THE HIVE

Marcus believes that the source of good and bad for rational and political beings lies in actively doing, not in being acted upon. Goodness and badness for us is found not in what others do to us, but in what we do, in our own doing (ix. 16). We will examine the kind of activity that goodness consists in for rational, political beings in a few pages. But first, what is the source of bad for rational and political beings? Badness is what harms.

Now if, on Marcus' view, a human being is an organic part of the whole of humanity, then what does he understand political harm to be? What harms a citizen of a city? Marcus insists that nothing can harm a citizen except what harms the city she belongs to. Only what harms the whole—the city—can harm its part—the citizen. Yet nothing harms the city except what harms its law. Furthermore, Marcus believes, no so-called misfortune can harm the city's law. No storm, flood, drought, fire, famine, or plague can harm the law. Marcus concludes that as long as the law is safe, the city will be too. And as long as the city as a whole is safe, each of its citizens, each of its parts, will be too (x. 33). The fallacy of division again appears to mar this reasoning. Yet Marcus believes that if an act does not harm the community, then it does not harm the members of the community. Consequently, when he thinks that he has been injured, he reminds himself to apply this rule: If the community isn't injured by the deed, then neither is he (v. 22).

What if the community *has* been injured by an offense? In that case, "what injures the hive injures the bees" (vi. 54). What injures the community as a whole injures the individual citizens. Injustice injures the community, and thereby the citizens. So, what should a citizen do about an unjust, injurious offense against the community, say, for example, poisoning its water supply? Marcus insists that retaliation is inappropriate. Vindictiveness is not the right response. If the community is injured by someone, anger is not the answer. Instead, one must show the offender where he went wrong (v. 22). Anger does not correct a wrongdoer. Learning better through proper instruction does. Injustice results from ignorance.

Thought and reason, after all, are things we share with the offender. Reason is what tells both *us* what to do and what not to do and what tells all other reasoning beings, including *the offender*, what to do and what not to do. Our shared reason makes the offender and all others fellow citizens of the rational community. This rational community extends beyond the particular city in which we live. It extends beyond the state too. Indeed, the community of rational beings is as large as the entire world. All of humanity, therefore, belongs to the entire cosmos as its citizens. This is the Stoic idea of cosmopolitanism. *Politēs* is the Greek word for citizen. A cosmic citizen is thus a *cosmopolitēs*. *Polis* is the Greek word for city. The cosmic city, then, is the *cosmopolis*.

Marcus explains that it is from this *cosmopolis* which we cosmopolitans share that thought, reason, and law (justice) derive. He cannot imagine where else thought, reason, and law could come from. He reasons as follows in Book iv, chapter 4:

1. Nothing comes from nothing.
2. Nothing returns to nothing.
3. Hence, the earth composing Marcus derives from earth.
4. Hence, the water composing Marcus derives from water.
5. Hence, the air composing Marcus derives from its own source.
6. Hence, the heat and fire composing Marcus derive from their own sources.
7. Hence, thought must derive from somewhere else than earth, water, air, heat, and fire.
8. Thought is something we share.
9. If thought is something we share, then so is reason.
10. If so, then we also share the reason that tells us what to do and what not to do.
11. If so, then we also share a common law.

12. If we share a common law, then we are fellow citizens.
13. If we are fellow citizens, then we are fellow citizens of something.
14. This something is the *cosmopolis.*
15. Therefore, thought probably derives from the *cosmopolis* itself.

We have seen the persistence of Marcus' optimism in the *Memoranda.* This optimism is particularly striking in Book vi, chapter 45. There he writes that whatever happens to you is for the good of the world. The acceptance of that claim should be enough for you to embrace whatever happens to you with calm acceptance and even satisfaction. But he adds that if you look closely, you will generally notice in addition that whatever happens to a single person is for the good of others. The sense of "the good of others" which Marcus means here is not the strict Stoic sense of "good" as unconditionally beneficial—virtue is the only thing that is unconditionally beneficial, and so good in this strict sense. Rather, by "the good of others" Marcus means among the class of indifferents those indifferents which are preferred (e.g., life, health, wealth, good reputation, beauty, and the like) rather than the dispreferred indifferents (death, sickness, poverty, ill repute, ugliness, and the like) (vi. 45). The Stoics hold that it is appropriate to select a preferred indifferent over a dispreferred one if and only if doing so in no way compromises one's virtue. Sometimes, however, it is appropriate for the Stoic to select a dispreferred indifferent in order to preserve her virtue.

To review, Marcus endorses the following four principles:

A. If x does not harm the city (communal whole), then x does not harm the citizen (part).
B. If x harms the city (hive), then x harms the citizen (bee).
C. If y happens to the citizen, then y is for the good of other citizens.
D. If y happens to the citizen (individual), then y is for the good of the world.

WHAT, THEN, IS THE GOOD OF THE INDIVIDUAL CITIZEN?

Marcus investigates what his own individual good means in Book vi, chapter 44. He considers three possibilities: either (1) the gods have made decisions about him and the things that happen to him, or

(2) the gods haven't made decisions about him as an individual but they have made decisions about the general welfare, or (3) the gods make no decisions about anything. If (1), then those decisions were good decisions, he reasons, since a god couldn't make bad decisions. If the gods' decisions about him were good, then it would do neither the gods[8] nor the world good to harm him.

If (2), then whatever the gods decide about the general welfare is something which Marcus must welcome and embrace. This is because of a corollary to Principle A. Principle A is that if x does not harm the whole, then x does not harm the part. A corollary to Principle A—actually, a special case of A—would be:

A*. If z benefits the whole, then z does not harm the part.

That is why if the gods decide that z happens concerning the general welfare, then z must benefit the general welfare. And if z benefits the general welfare (whole), then z does not harm Marcus (the part). With this understanding, Marcus welcomes and embraces z (vi. 44).

What if (3) is true and the gods make no decisions at all? This would mean that the cosmos is not governed by divine providence. This notion strikes Marcus as blasphemous even to consider, because then we'd stop sacrificing to them, praying to them, swearing oaths in their names, and doing all the other religious practices we do believing the whole time that the gods are right here with us. Yet to reject it because its consequences are distasteful would be to commit a blatant fallacy. As profane as the consequences of this notion may appear to Marcus, intellectual honesty and philosophical rigor demand that he regard this notion seriously as a real possibility. So he points out that even if the gods decide nothing about our lives, he, Marcus, can still make decisions. He, Marcus, can still consider what it benefits him to do. What benefits anyone to do is what his own nature requires. Marcus' nature, he observes, is rational and civic. Consequently, he deduces that as Antoninus, that is, as a particular individual who happened to be born when, where, and into the family he was, his city and state are Rome. But as a human being, that is, as one member of a whole species of rational animals, his city and state are the world, the entire cosmos. In this way Marcus identifies himself as a citizen of the cosmic city, a *cosmopolitēs* (cosmopolitan). His conclusion is that his "good" can only mean what is good for both communities, for both Rome and the universe (vi. 44). He must work to contribute to the good of Rome locally as a Roman citizen obligated to all other Romans while at the same time working to promote the good of all human beings, globally, everywhere, as a cosmopolitan.

This is a key lesson of mereology. Each of us is simultaneously (1) a human being living in a specific locale surrounded most closely by neighbors and denizens of a city, (2) a citizen of a state, and (3) a rational being and citizen of the *cosmopolis*. In addition, each of us may be a member of different associations, clubs, social, civic, and professional groups, unions, and political parties. Each of us is also certainly a member of a family and one of a circle, or several circles, of friends. Consequently, we are parts of many different wholes at the same time. We therefore have the responsibility of fulfilling our various purposes in all of these different wholes.[9]

For Marcus, however, the first and most fundamental mereological relationship to recognize is that he is a part of the world controlled by *nature*. This is the starting point for sound mereology. Second, he reminds himself that he has a relationship with other, similar parts. It is the world (= the cosmos = nature) which assigns to each of its parts. The parts do not self-assign. Consequently, Marcus believes he has no right, as a part, to complain about what is assigned to him by the whole. In Book x, chapter 6 he explicitly states Principle A*: what benefits the whole cannot harm the parts. Marcus adds that the whole does nothing that fails to benefit it. All natures, he believes, share this trait of non-self-harm. So, he reasons, by keeping in mind the whole he forms a part of, he will accept whatever happens (x. 6).

This is the mereological lesson of cosmic naturalism. We can reconstruct Marcus' reasoning from cosmic naturalism to acceptance of events as follows:

1. Each of us is a human part of the whole that is the natural world.
2. What benefits this whole (the natural world) cannot harm the parts. [Principle A*]
3. Nothing that happens in this whole (the natural world) fails to benefit it.
4. Therefore, each of us can (or at least ought to) accept whatever happens in the natural world.

In Book xii, chapter 36 Marcus offers a supporting argument for this view. He reminds himself that he has lived as a citizen in a great city. Does he mean Rome or the *cosmopolis*? He might mean both, though it's more likely he means the *cosmopolis* (cf. vi. 44). But, Marcus wonders, does it matter whether he's lived there for five years or a hundred? What's the difference? According to its laws—the laws of generation and destruction, birth, growth, death, and regeneration—each is treated the same, so the length of a lifespan makes no difference from the perspective of the cosmos. And if, Marcus reflects, he is dismissed from the "great city" not by a tyrant or an unjust judge, but by nature, who first invited him in, why is that so terrible? (xii. 36). If the natural process of old age causes his death, why would that be awful? Death is natural, and nothing natural is evil[10] (ii. 17). Neither the fact, nor the time, nor the place of his creation and birth, nor the duration of his lifespan, was determined by him. As a part of the whole (nature), created *by* that whole, Marcus urges himself to exit life with grace, accepting his death along with whatever else happens in the world (xii. 36).

What of Marcus' relationship to other parts? Because other people are just as much parts of the same whole that he is, Marcus infers that he must do nothing selfish. He must instead aim to join his counterparts. He must direct his every action toward what benefits everyone and to avoid what doesn't benefit the whole.[11] If he does all that, he reasons that his life should go smoothly. His life will go as you might expect a citizen's life to go, a citizen whose actions serve his fellow citizens and who embraces the decree of the community (x. 6). Here we arrive at the kind of activity that goodness (virtue) consists in for rational, political beings. The good for rational and political beings is to collaborate with each other, to *actively* serve their fellow citizens, to strive to benefit the *whole* community in *all* of their actions, and to do nothing selfish or in any way harmful to their community. To spurn, neglect, or abandon one's fellows, to foster discord, or to feed dissension within the city or state is directly contrary to the purpose of the rational, political cosmopolitan. Ontologically, it is bad mereology.

CHAPTER 4

TIME, TRANSIENCE, AND ETERNITY

Reflections on time, impermanence, and forgetting figure prominently in the *Memoranda*. Marcus repeatedly reminds himself of facts about the past, present, and future in order to vanquish worries and fears, preserve his peace of mind, and remain focused on what really matters in deciding on actions. He is a keen observer of patterns of flux, change, generation, destruction, renewal, and the ability to see events from a big picture perspective. He also often reminds himself that even the more memorable figures in history and their accomplishments, along with he himself and everyone else, will sooner or later be forgotten. Such observations provide Marcus philosophically grounded solace and equanimity. In this chapter we will see that his ideas about and arguments concerning time are central to his philosophy because Marcus believes that the proper understanding of time, transience, and eternity yields wisdom for living well.

THE RUSHING RIVER OF EXISTENCE

Marcus uses his powers of observation to draw valuable lessons about the nature of reality. Even the most ordinary unfolding of events, which people routinely take for granted without any further thought, afford Marcus the opportunity to learn something vital. Consider a bunch of grapes. What could be more commonplace? What happens to grapes? They come into existence unripe. Slowly and gradually they grow and ripen, changing in color and increasing in sweetness. As time passes they gradually shrivel, dry, and turn into raisins. This phenomenon couldn't be more familiar. Yet it reveals a theme that we rarely reflect on and even more rarely apply to our own lives when wrestling with the woes and worries that seem to spring up on us daily. All the things in the world around us are in constant transition, like the grapes. The grapes on the vine don't suddenly wink out of existence. They slowly transform. They gradually mutate. Marcus reminds himself not to think in terms of what is not, but rather in terms of what is not *yet* (xi. 35). Thus, reflection on the ripening grapes becoming raisins teaches him the lesson of *patience*. Events will unfold when it is their time. Impatience tends to seduce us into being pessimists about the blessings that the future can deliver. The impatient person tastes an unripe grape and hastily judges that all grapes are sour and bad to eat. The patient observer of the changing grapes knows better.

One of Marcus' favorite images for illustrating the nature of time is a river. Likening the nature of reality to a river was famously put on the philosophical map centuries before by Heraclitus of Ephesus (c. 535–c. 475 BCE).[1] Marcus writes that "time is a river, a violent current of events, glimpsed once and already carried past us, and another follows and is gone" (iv. 43). Note that the river of time is always dynamic. This river never freezes. The current of events moves not just constantly but violently, according to Marcus. We glimpse a temporal slice, but only for a moment. The next moment that slice is swept away and followed by a new slice, which itself is swept away. No state of existence is permanent. No condition endures. No circumstance lasts.[2]

Marcus emphasizes how rapidly things change. They are here one minute and gone the next. He tells himself to keep in mind how fast things pass by and are gone. Which things does he mean? He means both all those things that are now and all those things that will come to be. Existence flows past us like a river, Marcus explains. What exists is in constant flux. Why things are as they are has a thousand variations. Stability, Marcus insists, is an illusion. Not even what is right here in front of us is, in reality, stable or static. Look to the past. Marcus says that the infinity of the past gapes before us as an invisibly deep chasm. We cannot even grasp in thought the enormity of the past. It stretches beyond our imagination, beyond years, beyond decades, beyond lifetimes, beyond centuries, and beyond millennia. What about the future? The infinity of the future too gapes before us. It too is a chasm whose depths we cannot see. From this perspective of infinite past and infinite future, Marcus wonders who would feel self-important. Who would feel distress? Who would feel indignation? Marcus reasons that it would take an idiot to feel self-importance, distress, or indignation about *anything*. After all, how long is the cause of these feelings going to last compared to the depthless chasm of future and past? Nothing that irritates us in the present will last (v. 23). That is because nothing that irritates us *can* last. And that is because nothing that comes to be in the world can last. Marcus understands that all things that exist now and all things that will exist in the future share the same fate: to be swallowed up by an infinite, ever growing, past. He argues that this understanding demonstrates the idiocy of feeling proud, troubled, indignant, or irritated by anything or anyone. These emotions make no sense to the person wise to fact that existence is in constant flux and all that appears will vanish. Everything is temporary and transient.

Is this an obvious, trivial truth? Marcus doesn't think so. He finds it necessary to repeat this truth as a refrain again and again. Why? Perhaps it is because this truth is so easy for us to forget. It is all too easy to be fooled into believing that something, whether pleasant or painful, will last a long time. To guard against this false belief Marcus reminds himself that some things are rushing into existence, while others are rushing out of it. Moreover, some of what now exists is already gone. This process is nothing to be sad about. It is simply a fact to accept and to remember. The world is not, never has been, and never will be a static, stable place. Change and flux are the causes which constantly recreate the world, according to Marcus. Change and flux ceaselessly remake the cosmos just as the never-ending progression of time remakes eternity. The progression of time transforms the infinite future into the infinite past. Thus, Marcus writes that we find ourselves in an ever-flowing river. We are swept along in its current without an anchor. Given this undeniable reality, Marcus asks which of the things around us should we value when none of them can offer a firm foothold? Money? Power? Fame? Pleasure? Other people? All of these things are swept away in the current along with us. If we encounter a sparrow, shall we get attached to it? As soon as we glimpse it, it flies off and is gone.

What of life itself? Can we cling to life itself as our durable flotation device? The blood in our bodies sustains our vitality. Yet we survive only as long as our heart keeps pumping away and circulating that blood. So our lifeblood must keep moving to keep us alive. The blood itself is a flowing river. Our breathing in of air sustains our vitality. Inhaling air oxygenates our blood, sustaining our metabolic functions. But we also must exhale for the process of respiration to continue and keep us alive. So breathing too is a process, a rhythm of flux and change. When we die we expel the breath we drew in at birth. From the perspective of eternity, we were born just yesterday or the day before. It is a sobering thought that each breath we exhale could be our last gasp (vi. 15; cf. vii. 25, viii. 6). Marcus concludes that life itself is just as temporary as everything else in the river of time. We ourselves are just as transient, mutable, and impermanent as everything else rushing into and out of existence.

Marcus observes that all bodies, including our own, are carried through existence as through rushing rapids. All bodies, including our own, are sprung from nature and cooperate with it. Both living, organic bodies and mineral formations cooperate with nature, Marcus suggests, as our arms and legs cooperate with each other. Nature coordinates its geological and biological forms, recycling them all. The same applies to human beings. Marcus notes that time has swallowed up Chrysippus (c. 279–c. 206 BCE), the most brilliant of the early Stoics, the great Socrates (469–399 BCE), and Epictetus (CE c. 55–c. 135), the slave turned masterful teacher of Stoicism, many times over. These famous philosophers were swallowed up by time just like everyone and everything else in their day (vii. 19). All is swept away and drowned in the rushing currents of the cosmos.

These currents never stop. Therefore, the cosmic cycles of change never change. The cycles themselves run continuously. The pattern of generation, destruction, and transformation, from age to age, endures. Marcus wonders what causes events to occur in the world. He reasons that either the world's intelligence wills each thing individually or the world's intelligence exercised its will once and for all with all else following as a consequence of that first cause. If the world's intelligence wills each thing, then we should accept its will manifested in each event, Marcus reasons. On the other hand, if the world's intelligence exercised its will once and for all, then we shouldn't worry about the entire causal sequence consequent to that one initial act of will (ix. 28).

Marcus considers a corresponding twin possibility for the material constitution of the cosmos. Either the Epicureans are correct and the world is composed of an infinite number of atoms or the cosmos is a unity. Monists believe that what is real is unitary, that only one thing or object exists. So Marcus reasons that either pluralism (in the form of atomism) is true or monism is true. What, then, are the causal mechanisms at work in atomism and monism? If monism is true, Marcus seems to think that God is what causes events to occur in this unified cosmos. If this is so, then events are steered by divine providence and all is well. But if atoms exist, then the cause of their motions is ultimately arbitrary. If this is so, Marcus tells himself not to imitate this arbitrariness (ix. 28). Whether atoms exist or a unity exists, Marcus knows that the earth will cover us all and then be transformed in turn. The transformed earth will also change, and change again, ad infinitum. The process of transformation goes on forever. So Marcus instructs himself to think about the waves of change and alteration, which endlessly break, rippling continuously across the infinite ocean of time. In this eternal context, he urges himself to see the brief mortality of human beings for what it is (ix. 28).

Human mortality is a brief flash of foam swallowed up by an endlessly changing ocean that repeatedly churns up new blobs of foam before swallowing them too. This reminder dispels obsessing over the minute annoyances of daily life. For Marcus it is a sobering thought but not a depressing one. It is a wise and healthy insight, not a sad one. He reminds himself that before long he will be no one and nowhere, like all the things he sees now and all the people now living. All share the same destiny: to change, to be transformed, and to perish. This cosmic cycle of generation, destruction, and transformation is necessary so that new things can be born (xii. 21). All that exists now arises from what used to exist. All that will exist will arise from what exists now but won't exist soon.

Does Marcus' philosophy of time lead to nihilism, the view that nothing matters? To the contrary, as we saw in Chapter 3, Marcus believes that fulfilling our roles well as parts of the cosmic whole matters a great deal. This is because, as I will show in Chapter 5, whether we strive for virtue or not matters. Indeed, Marcus is convinced that nothing could matter more than our character as persons, the condition of our minds, and our conduct.

In one *Memorandum* Marcus seems to endorse the possibility mentioned in Book ix, chapter 28 that the world's intelligence exercises its will once and for all, and that all events occur as a consequence. In Book x, chapter 5 Marcus writes that whatever happens to him has been waiting to happen since the beginning of time. He writes that the twining strands of fate wove both of them together: his own existence and the things that happen to him (x. 5). This kind of reflection seems consonant with his inclination to affirm cosmic unity. Given the holistic connectedness of all events within the world, Marcus considers his existence to be similarly tied together to each thing that happens to him. The idea seems to be that none of the events in his life are accidental, arbitrary, or eliminable. Whatever happens to him fits with the plan of the cosmos. Both his birth and all subsequent things that happen to him are equally fated. Could this belief be false? Given Book ix, chapter 28 and many other texts, Marcus clearly believes that it is possible that the world is composed of atoms and not governed by Providence, and so might not be governed by fate. For this reason, perhaps his reflection in x. 5 functions more to strengthen his psychological resolve to embrace each thing that happens to him and incorporate it deliberately into his plan of life. This interpretation would square well with the comments on v. 8 and viii. 32 in the previous chapter.

Though it might seem as if Marcus' orientation to time is too often with the distant reaches of eternity, he is actually just as thoughtful about the microcosm as he is about the macrocosm. He thinks about how much is going on inside of him every second. He considers the countless minute events and processes going on in his soul (mind) and in his body. Nearly two millennia before the development of modern biochemistry, Marcus has some inkling of the countless catabolic and anabolic changes going on inside his body every microsecond. Given this, he asks himself why it should astonish him that so much more—everything that happens in that all-embracing unity, the world—is happening simultaneously (vi. 25). Not only is his heart pumping blood and his lungs breathing in and out, but the electro-chemical processes occurring in his brain and nervous system and the micro-processes of growth, maturation, digestion, reproduction, and the activities of his immune system together add up to a dizzying array of biochemical events teeming throughout his body from moment to moment. Multiply this amazing physiological pyrotechnic display by all the animals, insects, plants, and microorganisms on this planet, and one's mind boggles. Then add to this the geological, atmospheric, and oceanic processes occurring at the same time on our planet and all other planets in our galaxy. Multiply all these physical events by the number of astronomical events in the planets, moons, asteroids, comets, stars, and quasars in all other galaxies, and we must be even more astonished. The rushing river of existence is unimaginably vast with an unimaginably enormous number of events flashing simultaneously throughout it every moment.

ALL THAT HAPPENS HAPPENED BEFORE

As astonishing as the macrocosmic swarm of things rushing into and out of existence every moment plainly is, Marcus sees no novelty in it. He writes that if you've seen the present, then you've seen everything. You've seen everything as it has been since the beginning of time. You've seen everything as it will be forever into the future. This immense cosmic parade of events in the present is the same substance and the same form as it has always been. All of it is familiar (vi. 37; cf. iv. 32). Nothing is new under the sun, as they say. Indeed, not even the sun is new, since there have been many stars like it since the beginning of time. Look at the past, Marcus instructs himself. Look at empire succeeding empire, and from that, extrapolate the future: the same thing. Obviously, he writes, there is no escape from the rhythm of events. Does it make sense, knowing this, to be greedy for a longer and still longer life? No. Marcus assures himself that observing life for forty years is as good as a thousand. He asks himself: Would you really see anything new? (vii. 49). He doesn't believe so. That is why the present, according to Marcus, gives us a sufficiently representative glimpse of the kinds of things that happen throughout the whole of eternity.

This "same old thing" perspective is very important to remember. Marcus says that it is essential to bear in mind at all times what things are like, from the planting of the seed to the quickening of life, and from the quickening of life to the cessation of life. He thinks it is crucial to bear in mind where the parts come from and where they return to (xii. 24). Another thing essential to remember is that if you were suddenly lifted up and could see life and its great variety from a vast height, and at the same time you could see all the things around you, in and beyond the sky, Marcus says that you would see how pointless it is. No matter how often you saw it all from this cosmic perspective, he emphasizes that it would be *the same*: the same life forms, the same life span. Because of this, Marcus concludes that arrogance about anything in one's life is ludicrous (xii. 24). Whatever we might feel arrogant about shrinks to a vanishing point when viewed objectively from this lofty cosmic perspective. He means that arrogance, pride, fear, worry, anger, and greed are all pointless, whereas truthfulness, wisdom, and the other virtues are the point.[3]

Looking at life from the "same old thing" cosmic perspective rids us of arrogance. Other noxious traits of character can also be cured by reflecting on the fact that nothing is truly novel. Marcus writes that everything that happens is as simple and familiar as the rose in spring and the fruit in summer. Disease, death, blasphemy, and conspiracy are all equally familiar and equally banal. So too, Marcus remarks, is everything that makes stupid people happy or angry (viii. 44). People are stupid to get worked up over what is so ordinary and so often repeated. Stupid people forget what the wise remember: "that whatever happens has always happened, and always will, and is happening at this very moment, everywhere. Just like this" (xii. 26). What does he mean by this? Does he mean that the sequence of events experienced by every single person is identical to the sequence of events of an earlier time, down to the smallest detail? This would be a strictly circular conception of time. But this does not seem to be Marcus' view. Rather, he seems to believe that history is an account of very similar patterns of events. He urges himself to bear in mind constantly that all of what he is experiencing around him has happened before. He adds that it will all happen again following the same plot from beginning to end with the identical staging (x. 27). This theatrical metaphor suggests that the same basic *kind* of drama has unfolded before and will do so again. He prompts himself to recall, as he knows them firsthand or from history, the court of Hadrian (CE 117–138), the court of his adoptive father Antoninus (CE 138–161), and the courts of Philip II of Macedon (359–336 BCE), Alexander the Great (336–323 BCE), and Croesus, King of Lydia (560–546 BCE). All these courts are just the same, Marcus states. Only the people are different (x. 27). So it would appear that what he means is that though the names and unimportant details of the lives of these rulers differ, all the important features of their reigns—the intrigues, the ambitious gambits, the scandals, plots, negotiations, maneuvers, and political machinations—all these significant features were indistinguishable. The idea is that though the actors on the stage don't all look identical, the dramatic roles they play, the staging of the drama, the lines of the script they utter, and the plotline which unfolds all remain the same from one season's production to the next. This view of history, according to which history repeats itself in all its important features, helps explain why Marcus believes that if you've seen the present, then you've seen everything (vi. 37). The course of human events is as familiar and predictable as ever.

TIME QUICKLY ERASES

When reading the *Memoranda* one can get the impression of an emperor Aurelius weary of squabbling, petty sycophants buzzing around him in his court. As a balm to these irritations, the philosopher Marcus recalls the large-scale perspective of time. He thinks about the people which those around him want to ingratiate themselves with to advance their self-interest. He considers the results of their actions and the things they do in the process. He then puts all this ugly scrambling about into perspective by recalling how quickly all this will be erased in time and how much has been erased already (vi. 59). The folly of people who wrestle over puny baubles and fear trifling things results from their blindness to what time does to those baubles and scary trivialities. Marcus reflects on how their minds work and the things they long for and fear. He explains that events are like piles of sand. Each drift is soon hidden by the next (vii. 34). Each event, no matter how grand or grave it seems when it occurs, is soon covered over and erased by the sands of time.

A firm grasp of the truth that time erases all things is a potent cure for emotional maladies. In Book x, chapter 34 Marcus writes that if he has immersed himself in principles of truth like this one, the briefest, most random reminder is enough to dispel all his fear and pain. From Homer's *Iliad* he quotes the famous line (6. 147 ff.) that the generations of men are like leaves the wind blows to the ground. He reminds himself that his children too are short-lived, fragile leaves. (Eight of them died in childhood.[4]) Other leaves are applauding him loyally and heaping praise upon him. What reason is there to swell up with pride when applauded and praised by *leaves*? Still other leaves are turning around and cursing him, sneering at and mocking him from a safe distance. What reason is there to get angry or feel pained by the cursing and mocking of *leaves*? If he has a glorious reputation handed down to subsequent generations, this reputation is handed down by leaves to new leaves! All of these generations of human beings "spring up in the spring-time" and the wind—time—blows them all away. The tree of the cosmos puts forth others to replace the ones blown away. New leaves sprout every spring to replace the old leaves swept away every fall. None of us leaves have much time, Marcus muses. And yet he scolds himself for acting as if things were eternal by fearing and longing for them as if they last forever. Before long, darkness, that is, death, will descend upon him, and whoever buries him will be mourned in his turn (x. 34). The leaves that fall to the ground decompose to become soil upon which next season's leaves will fall and decay into soil. The soil erodes away as well. Nothing lasts. Time erases all.

Marcus' "big picture" strategy frees him from being gripped by silly, immediate fears, worries, appetites, and desires. He urges himself to have constant awareness of all time and space to keep what leaps up in front of him in perspective. He strives to have continual awareness of the size and life span of the things around us. From the "big picture" perspective, how big a deal are the things around us right now? They are a grape seed in infinite space, Marcus believes. How long are they around? They last no more than a half twist of a corkscrew against eternity (x. 17). Marcus rehearses this lesson to keep from getting upset by what happens and to stop obsessing over tiny things that are not, in reality, terribly important.

What about the Roman Empire? What about his legacy as the ruler of this gigantic empire of millions of people stretching around the entire Mediterranean basin? What about the demands of today's royal court upon him? Aren't these things enormously and urgently important? Marcus consistently situates such questions in a wider perspective. Asia and Europe, he writes, are distant recesses of the universe. The ocean is a drop of water. The present is a split second in eternity. Though what leaps up at him in the present moment may seem hugely significant and of lasting importance, it is in reality miniscule, transitory, and ultimately insignificant in the context of eternity (vi. 36).

This "big picture" perspective saves Marcus from blowing out of proportion whatever is immediately before him. It protects him from exaggerating the impact and import of what he is dealing with in the present. It also prevents him from amplifying the significance of his own life. He reflects on the fraction of infinity, of that bound-less abyss of time, allotted to each of us. This eternal abyss absorbs into itself the tiny fraction of each of our lifetimes in an instant. Marcus contemplates the fraction of all substance and all spirit in the universe which we constitute. How vanishingly small we are! He considers the fraction of the whole earth we travel about on. The bodies, lives, and locales we live in are much smaller in relation to the earth than the tiniest insects are in relation to us. Marcus instructs himself to keep all that in mind and not to treat anything as important except doing what his nature demands and accepting what Nature sends him (xii. 32).

Marcus uses the "big picture" reminder to separate what is trivial and distracting from what he should focus his thoughts on. He tells himself that he can discard most of the junk that clutters his mind—the trifling things that exist only there—and clear out space for himself by doing three things. First, he can comprehend the scale of the world, as he does in xii. 32, vi. 36, and x. 17. Second, he can contemplate infinite time (eternity) as he does in many of the texts examined in this chapter. Third, he can think of the *speed* with which things change: each part of everything, the narrow space between our birth and death, the infinite time before, and the equally unbounded time that follows (ix. 32; cf. xii. 7). From the perspective of eternity, those alive now enjoy no advantage over those who are long dead. This is because *all* mortal beings are absorbed into eternity. Who lived and died before whom couldn't matter less inasmuch as all reach the very same destination and share exactly the same fate.

Marcus reminds himself that all that he sees will soon have vanished, and those who see it vanish will vanish themselves, and the ones who reached old age will have no advantage over the untimely dead (ix. 33; cf. vii. 6). An octogenarian ends up just as dead and gone as someone who died in infancy. Eternity swallows up all. Marcus detects some irony in our often desperate efforts to prolong our lives by seeking medical help. The vast majority of people take death so seriously that for them it looms as the worst, most dreadful thing of all. Yet for Marcus, death is so commonplace, routine, and predictable that it is banal. In Book iv, chapter 48 he tells himself not to let himself forget how many doctors have died after furrowing their brows when leaning over so many deathbeds. Though a doctor may outlive many of her patients, she and all other doctors will die, too. Marcus instructs himself not to forget how many astrologers, after pompous forecasts about the deaths of others, will die, too.

How many philosophers, Marcus asks himself, have died after endless discourses on death and immortality? He is acutely aware that he too will share this same fate with all other philosophers. How many warriors, he recalls, after inflicting thousands of casualties themselves, have died? Marcus may well have seen with his own eyes thousands of warriors die during his military campaigns. How many tyrants, he wonders, have died after so horribly abusing the power of life and death over their subjects, as if they were themselves immortal? (iv. 48).

But these are just a few different groups of individuals who have witnessed many deaths. Marcus tells himself not to forget how many entire cities have met their end. He mentions Helike, a Greek city on the northern coast of the Peloponnese destroyed on a winter night by an earthquake and tidal wave in 373 BCE. He also mentions the Roman cities of Pompeii and Herculaneum, destroyed by the violent eruption of Mount Vesuvius in CE 79, without bothering to list countless others. He adds to these cities erased before he was born all the cities he himself knows of which met their end in his own lifetime. He remembers one who laid out another person for burial, and was buried himself, and then the person who buried him—all three deceased and buried in the same short space of time (iv. 48). Marcus writes: "In short, know this: Human lives are brief and trivial. Yesterday a blob of semen; tomorrow embalming fluid, ash. To pass through this brief life as nature demands. To give it up without complaint" (iv. 48). Time quickly erases everything that comes to exist. How silly is it to complain about this fact which is repeated constantly before our eyes every day, week, and month?

Human beings are just as transient and short-lived in the infinite sweep of time as fruit is. Accepting our human mortality and shortness of life should be no more difficult than accepting the ripening of fruit falling from a tree because the very same kind of impermanence is manifested in both cases. Time quickly erases *everything*. Marcus urges himself to pass through his brief life as nature demands and to give up his life without complaint like an olive that ripens and falls from its mother tree, praising and thanking the tree it grew on (iv. 48; cf. iv. 19). He strives to achieve a similar kind of acceptance of his own necessary mortality by recognizing his own organic relationship to the world which bore him as his mother. Indeed, Marcus wants to muster an attitude of gratitude toward the cosmos for bringing him into existence. Does it make sense for him to complain about no longer being a blob of semen? Of course not. Nor does it make sense for him to complain that his body will soon become a corpse and molder. The brevity of human lives is uncontestable and just as commonplace as the brevity of all other things. However, Marcus also asserts in iv. 48 that human lives are *trivial*. Does he mean that everything in human life is trivial? If so, does he think that everything is trivial? In the next section we will see how he answers "no" to these last two questions.

THE GIFT OF THE PRESENT

Chapter 3 examined Marcus' method of dividing things into parts. Time, of course, also divides into parts: past, present, and future. Marcus carefully elaborates on the differences among these three parts of time. In Book vi, chapter 32 he begins his remarks on time by observing that he is composed of two parts, a body and a soul. He asserts that things that happen to the body are meaningless, because the body has no consciousness, no intelligence. Hence, the body cannot discriminate among the things that happen to it, so those things lack meaning. Consequently, he reasons, nothing has meaning to his mind except its own actions. Only the mind's own actions are within its own control. Now, which of the mind's actions matter? Marcus argues that only the mind's immediate actions matter. That is because its past and future actions are not under its control. Therefore, the mind's past and future actions are as meaningless (to his mind) as whatever happens to his body (vi. 32). This is how Marcus reasons to the conclusion that the present occupies the privileged place in the proper understanding of time.

What about the future? Marcus tells himself to forget the future, because when and if it comes, he will have the same resources to draw on in order to deal with it. He will have the same *logos*, the same rational ability, to cope with whatever happens (vii. 8). What does Marcus mean when he says "if the future comes"? He probably means that it is possible that he will die soon, before *he* experiences events yet to occur. Since he will have the same *logos* for dealing with whatever the future may bring him, he infers that there is no point in worrying about the future. The future is out of his control, so he won't waste his mental energy fretting about it.

What about the past? Mindfulness of certain elements of the past can yield vital lessons for living well in the present. However, many aspects of the past have nothing to do with these vital lessons. Dwelling on past events by regretting them, wishing they had occurred differently, or fearing how they will affect the future is definitely contrary to *logos*. Marcus tells himself that everything he is trying to reach, by taking the long way around, he could have right now, this very moment. If he would only stop thwarting his own attempts to achieve wisdom and the other virtues, for example, he could achieve them. He believes that if he would only (a) let go of the past—that is, forget about past events that in no way enable him to better himself in the present, and (b) entrust the future to Providence, then he could (c) focus intently on guiding the present toward reverence, justice, wisdom, and the other virtues (xii. 1). Therefore, the correct understanding of the three parts of time is this: (1) Use the past only to draw lessons about the world, yourself, and other people which help you gain wisdom and promote the virtues; let go of wanting to change the past in any way. (2) Don't worry about the future, since your *logos* equips you with the resources for handling whatever the future brings; entrust the future to Providence and embrace whatever will happen, confident that you can deal with it virtuously. (3) Concentrate on doing what is under your control now by exercising reverence, justice, wisdom, and all the virtues in your *present* circumstances.

Marcus often prods himself not to postpone making progress cultivating virtue. He writes: "This is what you deserve. You could be good today. But instead you choose tomorrow" (viii. 22a). He urges himself to strengthen his virtues now, without any further delay. This is what he means when he commands himself to limit himself to the present (vii. 29). Worrying about the future and regretting the past badly interfere with focusing on being virtuous in the present. He writes that if he can cut free of distracting impressions that cling to his mind and can free his mind from the future and the past, then he can make himself, as Empedocles says, "a sphere rejoicing in its perfect stillness." Such a mental repose is unhampered by worries, fears, regrets, and all such disruptive mental afflictions. This contented mental stillness will allow him to concentrate on living what can be lived, which means living in the present and doing what is up to him to do. If he frees himself from psychological captivity to the future and the past, then he can spend the time he has left in tranquility, kindness, and at peace with the spirit within him (xii. 3). These are no small blessings. If he can live and act virtuously in the present undisturbed by debilitating thoughts about the future and the past, then he will enjoy mental serenity for the rest of his happy life.

This is why Marcus instructs himself to give himself a gift: the present moment (viii. 44). In this reminder he observes that people who vie for posthumous fame forget that future generations of people will be just as annoying and just as mortal as the people alive today. This text is reminiscent of x. 34, in which Marcus recalls the Homeric metaphor that human beings are leaves the wind blows to the ground. What does it matter to you, Marcus asks himself and anyone hungry for posthumous fame, if future people say x or think y about you? (viii. 44). The desire for fame rests on the false belief that what future people will think about you matters. Marcus cautions against misplaced cravings about the future. The present is a gift because proper understanding of it frees us to live well, to live a good life, with wisdom, peace of mind, kindness toward others, and reverence toward the gods. We can neither alter the past nor change the future. But we can embrace the present as the one and only precious opportunity to live "what can be lived," as he says in xii. 3. To him the present is a chance for the exercise of rational virtue, that is, civic virtue (vii. 68). Consequently, the true, objective understanding of time is vital for living what can be lived and exercising rational virtue.[5]

In another, particularly urgent entry, Marcus calls for objective judgment, right now, at this very moment. He calls for unselfish action, right now, at this very moment. He calls for willing acceptance, right now, at this very moment, of all external events. He writes that these three things, objective judgment (proper understanding, wisdom), unselfish action (cooperation, justice, beneficence, kindness), and willing acceptance of all external events (cosmic holism) are all that he needs (ix. 6). Notice that objective judgment, unselfish action, and acceptance of all external events are all things Marcus has the power to secure for himself immediately, in the present. Armed with these three mental resources, he would be self-sufficient.

The first chapter of Book x opens with Marcus writing a note to his soul. He asks it whether it is ever going to achieve goodness. Is his soul ever going to be simple, whole, and naked, as plain to see as the body containing it? Will it know what an affectionate and loving disposition would feel like? Will it ever be fulfilled, ever stop lusting and longing for people and things to enjoy? Will it ever stop wanting more *time* to enjoy these people and things? Will it ever stop pining for some other place or country with more temperate weather to live in? Will it ever stop hankering for people easier to get along with? The alternative to this boundless array of dissatisfactions is instead to be satisfied with what his soul has, and to accept *the present*—all of it. If his soul can accept all of the present, then it would thereby convince itself (him) that everything is the gift of the gods, that things are good and always will be, whatever the gods decide and have in store for the preservation of that perfect entity, the cosmos, which is good, just, and beautiful. If he can accept the totality of the present, he can convince himself that this beneficial cosmos creates all things, connects and embraces them, and gathers in their separated fragments to create more like them (x. 1). To accept the gift of the present consequently enables Marcus to persuade himself that everything that exists and everything that happens is a divine gift for him to embrace. In x. 1 Marcus questions his soul to try to get it to accept this belief and to stand as a fellow citizen with gods and human beings, blaming no one for anything and deserving no one's criticism.

Some texts clearly show Marcus' frustration with himself, specifically with his failure to sustain nobility of character. One can imagine him sighing when he writes: "Yes, keep on degrading yourself, soul" (ii. 6), as if he were exasperated with a naughty child. But he reminds himself that soon his chance at dignity will be gone. He reminds himself that everyone gets one life. Since Marcus was in his fifties when he wrote the *Memoranda*, he recognizes that, given his weak constitution and chronic ailments, his life is almost used up. But instead of treating himself with respect, he scolds himself for having entrusted his own happiness to the souls of others (ii. 6). When he worries about his reputation, about what others think and say about him, he is foolishly entrusting his happiness to the souls of others. When he wants things from other people, he is foolishly entrusting his happiness to them. Self-respect is the way to secure dignity. The respect of others is beyond his control. Hence, it is urgent that Marcus redouble his efforts to achieve self-respect and preserve his dignity right away, before he dies and it is too late. If he fails to achieve virtue in the one and only life he has, he will have only himself to blame.

The clock is running. Marcus instructs himself to remember how long he has been putting off energetically striving for virtue. He reminds himself how many extensions the gods gave him, and yet he didn't use them. He writes that at some point he has to recognize what world it is that he belongs to, what power rules it, and from what source he springs. This is the lesson of cosmic holism discussed in the previous chapter. Marcus reminds himself that there is a limit to the time assigned to him, and if he doesn't use it to free himself it will be gone and will never return (ii. 4; cf. iv. 17). From what must he free himself? His captors are false beliefs about the past and the future, complacency about improving his moral character, laziness, weakness of resolve, selfishness, and forgetting what he has learned. His failure to work mightily to achieve virtue will be nobody's fault but his own. Like everyone else, the length of his life is limited. What will he do with the precious little time he has? What will he make of himself before he is dead and gone?

Would Marcus be justified in resenting the brief time the cosmos has assigned to him? He argues that this resentment makes no more sense than resenting the limit of the weight of his body. He reasons that it doesn't bother him that he weighs only x or y pounds and not three hundred. So why should it bother him, he wonders, that he has only x or y years to live and not more? He accepts the limits placed on his body's weight and size. Therefore, Marcus concludes, he should also accept the limits placed on his time (vi. 49). This is a clever argument. If he accepts the limit placed on one property of his body, say, its weight, then consistency dictates that he should also accept the limit placed on another property of his body, say, its size. But lifespan is simply the limit placed on his body's property of duration. Therefore, reason compels him to accept the limit on how long his body will last. This temporal limit, however, in no way restricts his *ability* to progress in virtue, though it does restrict the length of time in which to exercise that ability. Before he expires, he has the gift of the present in which to achieve that goal.

We have seen that Marcus thinks it essential never to forget the crucial differences between past, present, and future. Misunderstanding the future is particularly dangerous. False beliefs about the future can become the soil from which debilitating fears grow. Marcus is fully aware of the power of imagination. That's why he orders himself not to let his imagination be crushed by life as a whole. He tells himself not to try to picture everything bad that could possibly happen.[6] This kind of pessimism-mongering is extremely harmful. Instead, he urges himself to stick with the situation at hand. He should ask himself, "Why is this situation so unbearable?" He should ask himself "Why can't I endure this?" He thinks he will be embarrassed to answer and he can then remind himself that past and future have no power over him (viii. 36). This is a keen insight. The thought that we have no power over the past or the future may make us feel powerless as we are swept along in the river of time. Yet here Marcus empowers himself by remembering that the past and the future equally have no power over *him*. Only the present, he recognizes, has power over him. But even that, he insists, can be minimized by simply marking off its limits. The idea seems to be that if Marcus is presently experiencing an ugly, or unpleasant situation that seems bad, then he can recall that, like any event or situation, this one cannot last indefinitely. What if his mind tries to claim that it can't hold out against *that* brief, transient situation? Well then, Marcus writes, he must heap shame upon such a cowardly, pathetic mind, so weak in resolve (viii. 36). When a present event seems bad and difficult to endure, Marcus optimistically believes that if we can remember that it won't last, we can find the strength to endure it. We know, after all, that time erases everything. So, soon enough this seemingly bad event will also be swept away. Time will then offer us the gift of a new present.

YOU CAN'T LOSE WHAT YOU DON'T HAVE

Marcus believes that knowing what to remember and what to forget is essential to living wisely. The multitude of things and people constantly swirling around us can be powerful distractions. Any one or combination of them threatens to provoke in us anxiety, anger, fear, and misery. To defend himself against these constant threats, Marcus writes the *Memoranda* to rehearse what he needs to remember and what he is better off forgetting. For him, this philosophical exercise is a kind of meditative practice for achieving the wisdom sufficient for living well. A good example of this is found in Book iii, chapter 10. There Marcus tells himself to forget everything else and to keep hold of and remember this one truth: Each of us lives only now, in this brief instant. The rest of our life has been lived already, or is impossible to see because it lies in the unknowable future. The span we live is small, as small as the corner of the earth in which we live it. Our lifespan and earthly neighborhood are as small as even the greatest renown, passed down from mouth to mouth by short-lived stick figures. These short-lived stick figures are ignorant alike of themselves and those long dead (iii. 10). Why? Because they fail to grasp how very short their lives are and how fleeting are all the things they so frantically pursue and avoid. They are ignorant of their transient natures and how they belong to the world as temporary, tiny parts of an ever-changing, self-recycling whole. Marcus describes them as "stick figures" to emphasize their fragility and impermanence. They are also ignorant of—oblivious to—the long dead. Why do they think they will be remembered once they themselves are long dead too? When he writes: "Close to forgetting it all, close to being forgotten" (vii. 21), Marcus seems to be recognizing that as he continues to age and approach his death, his own memories will begin to slip away. Once he dies, he too will begin to be forgotten by those who survive him. The "stick figures" wrongly believe that they, unlike all those before them, will be remembered after they die. But Marcus points out that even the greatest renown fades away gradually after each generation and disappears in eternity. The lesson is: Live now, in this brief, present moment. It is all any of us have. Don't forget how small and short our lives are. Don't forget how small the stage is upon which we live it. Don't think that fame lasts.

Like all Stoics, Marcus rejects anger as a noxious emotion triggered by (or consisting in) false judgment. To be angry, the Stoics believe, is to victimize oneself by committing a mental error. Marcus writes that to be angry at something means that you have forgotten. In Book xii, chapter 26 Marcus details a number of things that one has forgotten when one is angry. For the purpose of this chapter, however, my focus is on the last three things he states that are forgotten. He writes that to be angry is to have forgotten first (a) that nothing belongs to anyone. Children, body, and life itself all come from the same source, the cosmos itself (xii. 26). Our bodies, our children, our lives, all people, and all "possessions," meaning all objects, belong to the universe. The parts belong to the whole. None of the parts belong to each other. Second, to be angry is to have forgotten (b) that it's all how you choose to see things. Anger is a decision. It results from (or is) an evaluation selected, a judgment opted for. Finally, Marcus writes that to be angry is to have forgotten (c) that the present is all we have to live in, and it is all we have to lose (xii. 26).

How does (c) relate to being angry? The idea seems to be that responding to some happening with anger requires that we forget that the incident slides rapidly into the past. For this reason, to decide (in the present) to be angry is foolish, since the thing we are angry about has passed. We can instead choose to see the event as past and gone, and consequently irrelevant to what we should do now, in the present. Why try to live in the past by choosing to be angry *now* about what happened *then*? Marcus advises the angry person to get over it. Since the present is all we have to live in, let's make the best of it. Is being angry a good way to be? Is it a productive, beneficial way to live? No, of course not. We spoil the present by making ourselves angry. We ruin the present by filling it with this horribly ugly, violent, and dangerous emotion. It makes no sense to Marcus to waste a moment of his life being angry. He knows better because he knows his life is too short for that. Since the present is all we have, the present is all we can lose. If we choose to lose it to anger, we are foolish. Anger and happiness are incompatible.

Marcus believes it is extremely important to bear in mind the fact that the present is the only miniscule fragment of all eternity which we have. Consequently, he offers another argument to establish this fact in Book ii, chapter 14. He relies on the "big picture" perspective of eternity as an objective guide for understanding longevity and death. Marcus observes that even if you're going to live three thousand more years, or ten times that, you must remember that you cannot lose another life than the one you're living now, or live another one than the one you're losing. The longest life therefore amounts to the same as the shortest. Thus, the present is the same for everyone. Hence, the loss of the present is the same for everyone. But your past life is already gone, no matter how many years you've lived. So, Marcus reasons, it should be clear that a brief instant is all that is lost when you lose the present. For you can't lose either the past or the future. The past is gone. The future isn't here. How, then, could you lose what you don't have? (ii. 14). The upshot is that no one loses more than anyone else by dying. Marcus' elegant argument can be reconstructed as follows:

1. Either you have the past, or you have the future, or you have the present (unless you are dead, in which case there is no you and no possible having).
2. You don't have the past.

3. You don't have the future.
4. Hence, you only have the present. [From 1, 2, 3]
5. You can't lose what you don't have. You can only lose what you have.
6. Hence, you can't lose the past or the future. [From 2, 3, 5]
7. Hence, you can only lose the present. [From 4, 5]
8. The present, which is a brief instant, is the same for everyone.
9. Therefore, you and everyone else can only lose a brief instant by dying. [From 7, 8]

This argument yields two lessons for Marcus. First, he must remember that everything has always been the same, and keeps recurring. Hence, it makes no difference whether he sees the same things recur in a hundred years, in two hundred years, or in an infinite period. Second, he must remember that the longest-lived and those who will die soonest lose the same thing. The present is all that anyone can give up, since that is all anyone can have. What you do not have, you cannot lose (ii. 14).

This is a fascinating argument because it directly attacks the notion that death is an enormous loss. Intuitively, I may think that when I die, I lose my entire life, and that would be an enormous loss. But if I think of my entire life as my entire lifespan, Marcus shows that this is a mistake. If, say, I die at the age of seventy, my death does not erase those seventy years. Those seventy years have already elapsed on the day after my seventieth birthday. All those years of living are behind me in the past. It is *time* that erased them. Those years are long gone. I don't have any of them. All I have is the present moment. Logically, therefore, the present is the only thing I can possibly lose. So, from this perspective, my only real chance is the present moment. If I don't live in this moment, I'm not really living at all at any time. Try as I may foolishly want to, I can't actually succeed in clinging to the past because it is already gone. Death, therefore, does not erase my past life. My past life has already disappeared under the piles of temporal sand. Death only eliminates my present living moment. This same logic applies to everyone of every age.

For Marcus, these considerations help alleviate the fear of death. Fear is just as toxic to living a good life as anger is. So again Marcus follows his Stoic predecessors by marshalling arguments against fear. Since death is commonly believed to be one of the most fearful things of all, Marcus employs argumentative tactics to defeat this fear. Fortunately, this is not difficult to do. He writes that a trite but effective tactic against the fear of death is to think of the list of people who had to be pried away from life. What did they gain by dying old? In the end, they all sleep six feet under the ground (iv. 50).

Marcus recalls that the father of medicine, Hippocrates (c. 460–c. 370 BCE), cured many illnesses and then fell ill and died. The Chaldaeans (Babylonians), who were well-reputed astrologers, predicted the deaths of many others, Marcus says, and in due course their own hour of death arrived. Alexander the Great (356–323 BCE), Pompey the Great (106–48 BCE), and Julius Caesar (100–44 BCE), who destroyed so many cities and cut down so many thousands of foot soldiers and cavalrymen in battle, also departed this life. Heraclitus (c. 535–c. 475 BCE), Marcus notes, often told us that the world would end by being consumed in fire, but it was moisture that did him in when he died smeared in cow shit. Democritus of Abdera (c. 460–c. 370 BCE), the influential pre-Socratic philosopher who formulated the atomic theory, was killed by ordinary vermin, Marcus reports, while Socrates (469–399 BCE) was killed by the human kind (iii. 3).

In Book vi, chapter 47 Marcus tells himself to keep in mind that all sorts of people have died, all professions and all nationalities. He lists the eloquent and the wise—Heraclitus (again), Pythagoras of Samos (c. 570–c. 495 BCE), and Socrates (again). He lists the heroes of old, the soldiers and kings who followed them, the Greek mathematician and astronomer Eudoxus of Cnidus (c. 408–c. 347 BCE), the Greek mathematician, geographer, astronomer, and founder of trigonometry Hipparchus (c. 190–c. 120 BCE), and the mathematician, scientist, engineer, and inventor Archimedes of Syracuse (c. 287–c. 212 BCE). Marcus adds the smart, the generous, the hardworking, the cunning, the selfish, and even the satirist Menippus of Gadara (early third century BCE) and his fellow Cynic philosophers, who laughed at the whole brief, fragile business of life. All these people, Marcus soberly observes, have been underground for a long time now, and we have to go there too, where all of them have already gone (vi. 47; cf. vi. 56).

In Book viii, chapter 25 Marcus recalls his father, Marcus Annius Verus, dying (sometime between CE 130 and 135) and leaving behind his mother Lucilla, then Lucilla dying (sometime between CE 155 and 161). Marcus lists his teacher Claudius Maximus (the second century CE Roman consul, Governor of Upper Pannonia and later

Governor of North Africa) leaving Maximus' wife Secunda, and Secunda dying after that. He lists his mother-in-law Annia Galeria Faustina (c. CE 100–140), leaving her husband Titus Aurelius Antoninus Pius (CE 86–161; the Roman emperor who adopted Marcus in 138 at the age of sixteen; Marcus married their daughter). Then Antoninus died. So with all of them, Marcus writes: The rhetorician Hadrian, leaving the rhetorician Celer (who taught Marcus), and Celer too (viii. 25). In Book viii, chapter 31 Marcus adds to this growing list Gaius Julius Caesar Augustus (63 BCE–CE 14), the first ruler of the Roman Empire, and his court: his wife, daughter, grandsons, stepsons, sister, Marcus Vipsanius Agrippa (c. 63–12 BCE; Augustus' son-in-law, defense minister, and lieutenant), the relatives, servants, friends, Areius Didymus (first century BCE – first century CE; the Stoic philosopher highly esteemed by Augustus), Gaius Cilnius Maecenas (70–8 BCE; Augustus' lieutenant and minister of the arts), the doctors, the sacrificial priests—this whole court, dead. These are only some of the very many dead and buried in tombs. Marcus reflects on the line written on tombs: "last surviving descendant." What does this inscription reveal about the ancestors of the deceased? It betrays their anxiety that there be a successor to continue the family lineage. But someone has to be the last, Marcus declares. And when the last descendant of the family line expires, there, too, is the death of a whole house and the family name dies with it (viii. 31).

Where have they gone, Marcus asks, the brilliant, the insightful ones, the proud? His answer is that all of them were short-lived creatures, all are long dead. Some of them not remembered at all, some become legends, some lost even to legend (viii. 25). Marcus names a number of other people in the *Memoranda* that historians today cannot identify with certainty. This fact underscores Marcus' point that many people remembered by a few for a brief while in Marcus' time have by our time long since been "lost even to legend." All of these people, Marcus writes, buried their contemporaries and were buried in turn. Clearly, then, we must remember that our lifetime is so brief. Each of us lives it out in these circumstances, among these people, in this body. This is nothing to get excited about. Why? Because Marcus considers the abyss of time past and the infinite future. From this eternal perspective, what's the difference between three days of life or three generations? (iv. 50; cf. ix. 37). The wisdom Marcus gleans from this question is that it is ridiculous to be angry, fearful, anxious, or proud of one's fame, or to feel self-important.

Time is the great vanquisher of all human arrogance. Marcus' lengthy recitation of the many people he has known in person, the many of those he has loved, the many figures of history he has learned about, and the multitudes he never knew at all, all of whom have died, serves to keep his mind focused sharply on living in the present. The present is the only thing he has and the only thing he can lose. So he resolves to make a gift of the present to himself and to frequently remind himself of the urgency to treat the present as the slender, fleeting chance for doing good that it is. Why are so many reminders necessary? Because it is so very easy, day in and day out, in our hurly-burly lives, to forget this vitally important wisdom about time, transience, and eternity.

CHAPTER 5

VIRTUES, VICES, AND JUNK

Though the *Memoranda* may seem to take the form of a scattered set
of disjointed musings, the ideas Marcus rehearses in those entries
are in fact systematic and interconnected. In this final chapter I
will try to illustrate the method by which Marcus moves from an
analysis of the substance, source, purpose, and durability of each
thing to a determination of its value. I will explain why he judges
commonly prized things like wealth, luxuries, sex, fine food, and
status to be cheap, fleeting trash. On the basis of this determination
of value, Marcus establishes his account of the virtues as the only
true goods, which is the orthodox Stoic position. The role that philosophy plays in the cultivation of the virtues, the task of goodness,
perfection of character, justice and reverence, and dealing with the
shortcomings of others will be examined in turn. Explicating these
topics in an orderly way reveals that Marcus' philosophy is more
conceptually systematic than it may appear.

DETERMINE ITS NATURE, SUBSTANCE, CAUSE, PURPOSE, AND DURATION

Marcus believes that to understand how to approach and deal with
a thing, he must first understand what it is made of (xii. 11a). So he
asks himself: What is this thing, most fundamentally? What is its
nature and substance? What is its reason for being? What is it doing
in the world? How long is this thing going to exist? (viii. 11). Where
does this thing come from? What is its source? What does it change
into? What is it like when it is transformed? (xi. 17). Marcus believes
that if he can puzzle out its origin, fundamental nature, and type
of substance, as well as the reason for its existence, the causes of its

transformations, and the length of time it exists, he will have a thorough understanding of the thing under scrutiny. This clear-sighted analysis will allow him to see things as they are: their substance, cause, and purpose (xii. 10). He repeats that at all times he must look at the thing itself, the thing behind the appearance, and unpack it by analysis: its cause, substance, purpose, and the length of time it exists (xii. 18). To know how to deal with something, to know what to do with it, he must identify its purpose and examine what makes it what it is. Its concrete form may veil its real purpose, so he must ignore that and then calculate the length of time that such a thing was meant to last (ix. 25). Using this analytical method, Marcus can identify what the thing is, where it is from, why it is, how it operates, what it is for, and how long it will last. Unfortunately, many obstacles interfere with gaining this circumspect analytical understanding. Exaggerated, melodramatic behavior, combat, and confusion can swirl up around us, blinding us to understanding individual things. Laziness and servility also stand in the way. Every day these impediments threaten to block Marcus from applying his sacred principles. He reminds himself that his actions and perceptions need to aim: (i) at accomplishing practical ends, (ii) at the exercise of thought, (iii) at maintaining a confidence founded on understanding. His confidence must not be swagger, but rather an unobtrusive confidence hidden in plain sight. He believes that he can let himself enjoy straightforwardness and seriousness and he can achieve this unobtrusive confidence by means of a strong understanding of individual things. He must grasp their nature and substance, their place in the world, their life span, and their composition. He must also understand who can possess them and whose they are to give and to receive (x. 9). If Marcus can achieve this multi-faceted understanding of an individual thing, then he can handle it with complete confidence.

STUPID, PALTRY, DECAYING, PUTRID, FILTHY, VILE, CONTEMPTIBLE, WORTHLESS JUNK

What does Marcus notice when he observes the things around him? He sees the speed with which all of them vanish, both the objects in the world and the memory of them in time.[1] What is the real nature of the things our senses experience? What things, in particular, entice us with pleasure (e.g., candy) or frighten us with pain (e.g., excessive heat or cold) or are loudly trumpeted by pride (e.g., popular acclaim)? By using our intellectual powers to identify what these things are made of, their substance, cause, purpose, and duration, Marcus thinks that we can see how stupid, contemptible, grimy, decaying, and dead they are (ii. 12). What about those people whose opinions and voices constitute "fame"? Marcus understands that popularity among these people really amounts to nothing. What about dying? What is it, really? Marcus writes that if you look at dying in the abstract and break down your imaginary ideas of it by logical analysis, you will realize that it is nothing but a *necessary* process of nature, which only a child can fear (ii. 12).[2]

What are the things around us made of? What are the features of the bodies of human beings and all other animals? Liquid, dust, bones, and filth, Marcus observes with disgust. These are the material components hidden underneath our clothes and beneath our skin. What about the beautiful marble adorning the floors of lavish palaces? What is marble, really? Marcus looks hard at marble and sees it as hardened dirt. What about sparkling gold and silver plates, goblets, and coins? Gold and silver, Marcus soberly observes, are just residues mined from the ground. What about sumptuous woolen garments? These clothes are *hair*. What about a fancy purple robe? Purple dye is shellfish blood, Marcus baldly states. All these material things that people herald as the finest amenities and most desirable luxuries are made of the same disgusting, changeable stuff. The same is true of our living breath, Marcus writes, because it too is transformed from one thing to another (ix. 36). Yet people strive mightily to obtain such expensive furnishings, clothing, and jewelry. People douse their bodies with pricy perfumes to mask their funk. But when Marcus scrutinizes these coveted items, he sees that all of these objects in the visible world and the whole of life aimed at amassing them are like what you see in the baths—oil, sweat, filth, greasy water, all of it disgusting (viii. 24). They are "known by long experience, limited in life span, debased in substance—all of it" (ix. 14). Their vile, repulsive substance is now exactly as it was before, in the time of those we buried long ago (ix. 14).

A kind of learned blindness prevents us from seeing that most of what we frantically desire every day is, at bottom, disgusting. Food is an excellent example. When we are hungry, we can deceive ourselves into seeing the morsels in front of us as nothing but deliciously edible. But Marcus expresses the sensibility of vegetarians when he describes the experience of the scales falling from his eyes when looking at the "meal" on his table. He writes that it is like seeing roasted meat and other dishes in front of you and suddenly realizing: This is a *dead fish*. That is a *dead bird*. That over there is a *dead pig* (vi. 13). We try to conceal the nature of what we eat by calling it bacon, ham, or pork, but it is really rotting flesh from a dead pig. Roasted meat is cooked carcass. Meat eaters eat corpses.

What about alcohol? Marcus has a similarly deflationary view of wine. Fine, aged bottles of wine cost hundreds (of dollars or Euros). The rarest finest vintages cost more. But what is this noble vintage, really? It is grape juice, Marcus reports (vi. 13). Fermented and aged in oaken casks, perhaps, but ultimately grape juice. Is a bottle of grape juice worth hundreds? Is it a tragedy to drop and break such a bottle, really?

What about those regal, purple robes? Those robes are sheep wool dyed with shellfish blood (vi. 13). Does knowing that the gorgeous purple color comes from the blood of a crustacean increase or decrease the splendor of wrapping those robes around you? Does knowing that the fabric was shorn from the belly and the back of a ruminant quadruped increase or decrease the thrill of feeling the fabric against your skin?

Marcus has a similarly deflationary, unromantic analysis of sex. We romanticize the sex act by calling it "making love," but a clinical look at the "act of love" is revealing. Marcus writes that, for a man, sex is something rubbing against your penis, a brief spasm, and a little cloudy liquid (vi. 13). That's it. An orgasm is friction on a body part akin to a section of bowel, a seizure, and the discharge of mucus-like fluid. With this strategy, Marcus shatters the rosy-colored lenses through which we prefer to view the things we so intensely desire. He insists on seeing these pleasures for what they really are. By latching onto things and piercing through them, Marcus can reveal what they really are. He insists that this is what we need to do all the time. All through our lives, when things lay claim to our trust, we need to lay them bare and see how pointless they are (vi. 13). To be happy, do we need houses with marble floors and gold and silver furnishings to live in? Marcus thinks not. Do we need meat to give meaning to our lives? Marcus thinks not. Do we need expensive wine to better our lives? Marcus thinks not. Do we need stylish clothes to live well? Marcus thinks not. Do we need sex to lead fulfilling lives? Marcus thinks not. He lays these things bare, removing their hype to reveal their naked reality. In this way he strips away the deceptive aura, the overblown reputation, that encrusts these superfluous, ultimately "pointless" things (vi. 13). Pride is a master of deception, Marcus warns himself (and us). When you think you're occupied in the weightiest business, that's when pride has you in its spell (vi. 13). He rejects the notion that fancy food, fancy drink, fancy clothes, sexual activity, or sex appeal are weighty, important things to be proud of. All such things are actually worthless junk.

It is difficult to discern this, however. We are habituated—brainwashed—by others to regard such things as hugely desirable, true goods. Such things are not what they may seem, and we can all too easily be taken in by their glitzy appearances and the high esteem most people hold them in. Since their appearances can change quickly, even moment to moment, the real natures of these things can easily be disguised in a mysterious complexity. Marcus writes that things are wrapped in such a veil of mystery that many good philosophers have found it impossible to make sense of them. Even the Stoics, Marcus admits, have trouble piercing this veil of mystery. Consequently, any assessment we make of them is subject to alteration, just as we are ourselves (v. 10). This is because the appearances of things are ephemeral and we ourselves are in flux and change. When Marcus looks closely at them, he sees how impermanent they are and how meaningless. Why are these things meaningless? Because they are things that any pervert, whore, or thief can own (v. 10). Marcus then looks at the way the people around him behave. He laments that even the best of them are hard to put up with sometimes. Moreover, he has to put up with himself—his struggles getting out of bed (v. 1 and viii. 12), weakness, arrogance, and procrastination (cf. viii. 22). So, given that things are so mysteriously veiled from our understanding, given how impermanent and trivial they are, given that they can be owned by depraved people, and given the difficulty of putting up with the misbehavior of people around us and with our own shortcomings, Marcus writes that things are in such deep darkness, in such a sewer, in the flux of material, of time, of motion and things moved, that he doesn't know what there is to value or to work for (v. 10). But he quickly banishes this dark doubt. He says that we need to comfort ourselves, wait for death and the subsequent dissolution of our bodies, and not get impatient in the meantime (v. 10). How do we comfort ourselves? Marcus believes we (he) can take refuge in two thoughts: (a) Nothing can happen to him that isn't natural; (b) he can keep from doing anything that God and his own spirit don't approve. No one can force him to act against what God wants. No one can force him to do what his own spirit rejects (v. 10).

This requires interpretation. First, how can Marcus take refuge in the thought (fact) that nothing can happen to him that isn't natural? This idea is thoroughly Stoic. Whatever happens to him occurs in the flow of cause and effect in Nature. Whatever cosmic process affects Marcus, he can embrace it as the result of the necessary operation of natural laws. In Chapter 3 we examined Marcus' belief that he is an individual part of an organic, cosmic whole. So, whatever happens to him fits logically into the cosmic plan of the whole universe. Therefore, nothing can happen to him that is out of place in the scheme of nature. Second, he can avoid anything that is contrary to divine will by conforming his own spirit (will) to what God approves of. Basically, Marcus means that he can choose to act piously and reverently, and no one can prevent this. No one can stop him from keeping his spirit, his mind, his decisions, and his actions pure and holy. What about waiting for the dissolution of his body? Even if meat, wine, purple robes, marble, gold, silver, sex, and fame are all stupid, paltry, decaying, dead, grimy, contemptible junk, isn't his *body*, at least, valuable?

ASHES, BONES, AND SMOKE

In Book iii, chapter 3, Marcus likens life to a sea voyage. He writes that he boarded, he set sail, and he has made the passage on this voyage. Now that he is facing death, it is time for him to disembark. Surprisingly, this is the one text in the *Memoranda* in which Marcus plainly allows for the possibility that his "disembarking" might be to another life. If so, he reassures himself, there is nowhere without gods on that side, either. On the other hand, if he disembarks to nothingness, then he will no longer have to put up with pain and pleasure, or go on dancing attendance on this battered crate, his body. Marcus asserts that his body is far inferior to that which serves it. The one is mind and spirit, the other, the body, is earth and *garbage* (iii. 3). Here Marcus describes his body as a "battered crate." Its substance he calls "garbage." He repudiates pleasure and pain as dangerously annoying distractions to the superior part of him, his mind and spirit. Marcus is clearly tired of having to pay so much attention to his "battered crate." He looks forward to no longer being forced to expend mental energies serving bodily demands. Given this weariness with the relentless demands of his body, it's likely that Marcus refers to his body when he describes "the stench of decay, rotting meat in a bag. Look at it clearly, if you can" (viii. 38). The battered crate of his body is not valuable. Its mental-spiritual *contents* are. But the foulness of the crate is explicit when he describes its disgusting, decaying stink. What is his body, really? It is rotting meat—flesh, bones, blood, and guts—in a bag of skin. But it is tough to bring himself to look clearly at the disgusting bag of guts that is his body.

For Marcus, Epictetus, and earlier Stoics the mind is all important. Success in living the good life depends on it. Marcus focuses on how the mind conducts itself. "It all depends on that. All the rest is within its power, or beyond its control—corpses and smoke" (xii. 33). Things outside the mind's control are dead flesh, corpses, and as insubstantial and quick to dissipate as smoke. But human lives themselves are just as insubstantial and quick to dissipate. Marcus instructs himself, when he sees someone alive today, to see in his place his dead counterpart from years ago. When Marcus looks at himself, he tells himself to see any of the emperors. Everyone else is the same, equally interchangeable from the perspective of the cosmos. Then, Marcus writes, let it hit you. Where are all these people now? Nowhere or wherever, he replies. "That way you'll see human life for what it is. Smoke. Nothing. Especially when you recall that once things alter they cease to exist through all the endless years to come. Then why such turmoil?" (x. 31). Marcus describes human life as smoke that vanishes into nothing, as all things in human life morph and perish in the fullness of time. Human lives and human bodies undergo rapid decay, and this has always been so. Given the fleeting, insubstantial nature of human lives, to be perturbed by what happens is senseless. Agitation, panic, and turmoil are unwarranted.

Is anger *ever* an appropriate response? Marcus thinks not, in agreement with earlier Stoics. He reminds himself to constantly review the list of those who felt intense anger at something: the most famous, the most unfortunate, the most hated, the most whatever. He then asks himself: "Where is all that now? Smoke, dust, legend . . . or not even a legend" (xii. 27). All his predecessors who flew into a rage died and were buried. All the bodies of those who were angry have crumbled into dust or were cremated and floated away as smoke. Only fragile memories of some of them survive as legend today. The lesson: What we choose to be angry about is trivial and will soon vanish like smoke. The ordinary things we want so passionately—wealth, physical comforts, prestige, fame—are equally trivial (xii. 27).

In short, Marcus writes, he must know this: Human lives are brief and trivial. Yesterday a human life was a blob of semen. Tomorrow it will be embalming fluid and ash (iv. 48). His deflationary strategy sharply undercuts all human arrogance. Vanity about one's body is blatantly ridiculous, given how brief and trivial the life of that body is. All human bodies quickly molder into ashes in the grave. Indeed, vanity and pride about anything are equally foolish. Why? Because, Marcus writes, soon you'll be ashes or bones. You'll be a mere name, at most, and even that is just a sound, an echo. The things we want in life—wealth, status, power, glory, toys, entertainments, pleasure—are empty, stale, and trivial, Marcus insists. We are like dogs snarling at each other, fighting over scraps of meat, posturing for social dominance. We are like quarreling children who laugh and then burst into tears a moment later (v. 33). Marcus laments that trust, shame, justice, and truth are, quoting the Greek poet Hesiod (c. 700 BCE), *Works and Days* line 197, "gone from the earth and only found in heaven." Here Marcus' reflections turn particularly gloomy. He wonders why he is still here. Sensory objects are shifting and unstable. Our senses are dim and easily deceived. The soul itself is a decoction of the blood. Fame in a world like this is worthless. And so, Marcus writes, he should wait for his demise patiently. Death will be either annihilation or metamorphosis. And until that time comes, what should he do? Honor and revere the gods, treat human beings as they deserve, be tolerant with others and strict with himself. He must remember that nothing belongs to him but his flesh and blood, and nothing else is under his control (v. 33). And since his flesh and blood will soon become ashes and dust, his body is as "empty, stale, and trivial" as what most people crave. Rather than slumping into nihilism, however, his deflationary strategy leads Marcus to prescribe a rigorous set of goals to achieve in action: honor and reverence to the gods, just treatment of human beings, tolerance of the conduct of others, and strictness with himself. Using his body to strive to achieve these ethical goals is one of the few things under his control. Everything outside his mental life, in contrast, is beyond his control.

Non-Stoics routinely classify both objects of desire and certain kinds of events beyond their control as good, and objects of avoidance and other kinds of events as bad. For example, finding money on the sidewalk or getting a raise at her job a non-Stoic judges as good. Hail damaging her automobile a non-Stoic judges as bad. Accordingly, the non-Stoic takes things she doesn't control and defines them as "good" or "bad." Naturally, then, when the "bad" things, like hail stones making lots of little dents in her automobile, happen, or the "good" ones don't, like not getting a raise, the non-Stoic blames the gods (or fate) and dislikes those people she *decides* to make responsible, e.g., her supervisor). But, Marcus observes, much of our bad behavior stems from trying to apply these faulty criteria of "good" and "bad." In contrast, if we limited "good" and "bad" to our *own* actions, which are under *our* control, then we would have no cause to challenge the gods (fate), or to treat other people as enemies (vi. 41). We would no longer blame the gods or anyone else because we would be masters of our own good and bad things. Good and bad would be under our control, not subject to factors beyond our control.

Non-Stoics are so entangled in the hurly-burly of what is going on around them in their immediate surroundings that they make their happiness depend on people and events that are decidedly *beyond* their control. They chase what is before their noses, oblivious to the global and eternal perspectives. Marcus rises above this blinkered perspective because he recognizes the importance of seeing human affairs from above. He observes the thousands of animal herds, the rituals, the voyages on calm or stormy seas, the different ways we come into the world, share it with one another, and leave it. As we have seen, he often considers the lives led once by others, long ago in the past, the lives to be led by others after him in the future, and the lives led even now in the present in foreign lands. Marcus notes how many people don't even know his name, even though he rules a vast empire! He reflects on how many others will soon have forgotten his name. Beyond that, he ponders how many people offer him praise now, and tomorrow, perhaps, contempt. He reaffirms that to be remembered is worthless, just as fame is worthless, just as everything beyond our control is worthless (ix. 30). Our bodies, our clothes, our vehicles, our residences, all our material possessions,

the praise and contempt of others, and our reputations are all ultimately worthless ashes, bones, and smoke: Here today, gone and
forgotten tomorrow.

WHAT IN US SHOULD WE PRIZE?

Given the relentless, far-reaching onslaught of Marcus' deflationary strategy, does *anything* remain that is not worthless? Yes, indeed
there does. As we saw above, in Book v, chapter 33, while patiently
awaiting our deaths, Marcus sets four targets to aim at: (1) to honor
and revere the gods; (2) to treat human beings as they deserve, that
is, with justice; (3) to be tolerant of others, that is, to be gentle with
them when they err; and (4) to be strict with himself, that is, to
urgently strive to perfect his moral character. He summarizes these
goals when he writes that the only thing that isn't worthless is to
live this life out truthfully and rightly and to be patient with those
who don't (vi. 47).

Notice that this ethical goal is under his control. This goal per-
tains to how he conducts his mind, not what happens to his body or
to any other material thing. The body, as we saw, Marcus regards
as "rotting meat in a bag," disgusting blood and bones, doomed to
become ashes, dust, and smoke. So, to the question: "What is it in
ourselves that we should prize?" Marcus answers using a process
of elimination. Transpiration is a biological process human beings
perform, but even plants do that. Consequently, that can't be what
is special in us and so can't be what we should value. Respiration is
another biological process human beings perform, but even beasts
and wild animals breathe. Hence, that can't be what we should prize
in ourselves. Being struck by passing thoughts is not very admirable, so Marcus rules this out too. Being jerked like a puppet by your
own impulses is nothing exalted, so that too is ruled out. Moving
in herds is popular among human beings, cattle, sheep, and other
gregarious animals. Most people follow others, tending to do what
most people do. So, herd behavior isn't precious. Neither is eating
and relieving yourself afterwards (vi. 16). What is to be prized, then,
Marcus wonders. What about the applause of an audience? No, this
is no more valuable than the clacking of their tongues. The clapping
of hands and clacking of tongues is all that public praise amounts
to, and such noise is quite worthless. So, Marcus reasons, we throw
out other people's recognition. What's left for us to prize? Marcus

writes that he thinks it is to do *what we were designed for*. That, he observes, is the goal of all trades, all arts, and what each of them aims at: that the thing they create should do what it was designed to do. The nurseryman who cares for the vines, the horse trainer, and the dog breeder all aim at this same goal. All of them seek to teach and educate. Therefore, Marcus argues, the teaching and education in us are what we should prize.[3] Marcus writes that if he holds on to that, he won't be tempted to aim at anything else (vi. 16). Why? Because he will have what is truly precious and, recognizing everything else as stupid, paltry, decaying, putrid, filthy, vile, contemptible, worthless junk, he won't be tempted by any of it.

This is the Stoic's logic, but Marcus is surrounded by non-Stoics. Every day they all go crazy for all the stupid, paltry, decaying, putrid, filthy, vile, contemptible, worthless junk. So, what if Marcus can't stop prizing a lot of other things besides teaching and education? Then, he realizes, he will never be free, independent, or imperturbable. Why? Because he will always be envious and jealous, afraid that people might come and take all the material (junk) away from him. He will never have independence of will or peace of mind because he will be incessantly plotting against those who have the material possessions, which are the things he prizes. People who need those things, Marcus remarks, are bound to be a mess and bound to take out their frustrations on the gods. In contrast, to respect his own mind and to prize it will give him a unique kind of self-satisfaction. This is because respecting and cherishing his own mind will leave him well integrated with his community and in tune with the gods as well. He will secure harmony with the gods because he will be embracing what they allot him, and what they ordain (vi. 16).

Marcus believes that we all have a fundamental choice to make about what we will value, and as a consequence, what we will pursue in our lives. Having detailed the disgusting, vile, worthless nature of material objects of desire, physical pleasures, fame, and the like, only one kind of thing remains as a candidate for what is good: the virtues as excellences of the mind. Thus, he instructs himself, if, at some point in his life, he should encounter anything better than justice, honesty, self-control, and courage, then he had better embrace it and enjoy it to the full. If he comes across anything better than a mind satisfied that it has succeeded in enabling him to act rationally, and satisfied to accept what is beyond its control—if he finds anything better than that, then he ought to embrace it without reservations, because it must be an extraordinary thing indeed (iii. 6). However, Marcus reasons, if nothing presents itself that is superior to the spirit that lives within—the one that has subordinated individual desires to itself, that discriminates among impressions, that has broken free of physical temptations, and subordinated itself to the gods, and looks out for the welfare of human beings—if he finds that there is nothing more important or valuable than this exalted, self-disciplined, fate-embracing, philanthropic spirit, then he ought not to make room for anything but it. He must not make room for anything that might lead him astray, tempt him off the road to virtue, and leave him unable to devote himself completely to achieving the goodness that is uniquely his. Marcus writes that it would be wrong for anything to stand between him and attaining goodness as a rational being and a citizen (iii. 6). His membership as a rational citizen of the universe (a cosmopolitan) is his unique goodness.[4]

Obstacles that threaten to stand between us and attaining this goodness include the applause of the crowd, high office, wealth, and self-indulgence. All of these might seem to be compatible with goodness for a while. But any one of them has the power suddenly to control us and sweep us away. So, Marcus directs himself to make his choice straightforwardly, once and for all, and to stick to it. He must choose what is best. But isn't what is best what benefits *him*? If it benefits him as a rational being, then yes, he should follow through with it. But if it benefits him just as an animal, merely serving a biological function, then he must say so and stand his ground, cleaving to what serves his *rational* nature, without making a show of it. He cautions himself to just make sure he has done his homework first (iii. 6). Presumably he means that he must learn about what his animal nature *really* requires to sustain itself so he can limit himself to that. Thereby he can avoid falling prey to pleasures of the flesh, wealth, high office, the adulation of the crowd, etc. that in no way promote his goodness as a rational being or as a citizen of both Rome and the whole cosmos.

THE TASK OF PHILOSOPHY

Philosophy is, of course, the tool which Marcus uses to do mereological analyses of persons, the cosmos, death, and communities (see Chapter 3), to understand time and transience (see Chapter 4), and to investigate the nature, substance, origin, cause, transformations, purpose, and duration of objects (see above). Philosophy is also what reveals to Marcus what his nature demands and, accordingly, how to live. Consequently, philosophy plays a vital role in attaining goodness. In this section we will examine Marcus' comments in the *Memoranda* about philosophy to illustrate how he conceives of its important task.

In Book ix, chapter 29 Marcus observes that the design of the world is like a flood, sweeping all before it.[5] He describes the foolishness of the little men busy with affairs of state, and with philosophy—or what they think of as philosophy. Their political frippery and pseudo-philosophy is nothing but phlegm and mucus, according to Marcus. What then?, he wonders. He tells himself to get a move on, if he has it in him, and do what nature demands. Moreover, he mustn't worry about whether anyone will give him credit for it. Marcus tells himself not to go expecting Plato's *Republic*, because the *polis* (political community) which the character of Socrates describes in Plato's dialogue the *Republic* was an ideal state, unrealizable in reality. In contrast, Marcus instructs himself to be satisfied with even the smallest progress (ix. 29) in bettering Rome and its provinces, and to treat the outcome of his attempts to rule wisely and justly as unimportant. Why? Because only Marcus' *attempts* to rule well are under his control. How those attempts play out in the incredibly complex scheme of the enormous Roman Empire is quite beyond his control. Marcus wonders who can change the minds of his subjects. Without that change, his attempts to rule well reduce to his subjects' groaning, slavery, and pretense of obedience. Whether other rulers knew nature's will and made themselves its student is for them to say. But, Marcus notes, no one forced him to model himself after them. Marcus writes that the task of philosophy is modest and straightforward (ix. 29). Studying philosophy instills modesty and straightforwardness in your character.

Humility is an important virtue for Marcus. He links it to a proper understanding of nature, the task before him, truthfulness, and kindness. He writes that the first step is not to be anxious, because nature controls it all. Marcus reminds himself that, like all those before him, before long he'll be no one, nowhere. The second step is to concentrate on what he has to do, to fix his eyes on it. He must remind himself what nature demands of people. He must remember what nature demands of him. Then, he must do it, without hesitation, and speak the truth as he sees it, but with kindness and humility, and without hypocrisy (viii. 5). So, rather than being angry or passionately wanting trivial things, Marcus remarks on how much more philosophical it would be to take what we're given and show uprightness, self-control, and obedience to God, without making a production of it. He writes that there is nothing more insufferable than people who boast about their own humility (xii. 27). Consequently, Marcus is intent upon obeying God (by taking what he is given) and being self-controlled and upright, while speaking truthfully, with kindness and humility, without hypocrisy, and without boasting about any of his virtues. This is a "more philosophical" way to be than to lose your temper or chase trivial things.

How does philosophy inculcate the traits of modesty and humility? Marcus reminds himself that another encouragement to humility is that he can't claim to have lived his whole life as a philosopher. Indeed, he can't even claim to have lived his whole adulthood as a philosopher. He says that he can see for himself how far he is from philosophy, how short of its ideals he has approached. Many others can see his failing too. Marcus scolds himself, calling himself "tainted." It is not so easy now to have a reputation as a philosopher, Marcus notes. His position as the Emperor, he believes, is an obstacle as well. So he knows how things stand. He tells himself to forget what others think of him. He must be satisfied if he can live the rest of his life, however short, as his nature demands. He must focus on that and not let anything distract him. Marcus writes that he has wandered all over—presumably meaning in his studies, activities, and travels—and finally realized that he never found what he was after: how to live. Neither in syllogisms, nor in money, nor fame, nor self-indulgence, nor anywhere else, did he discover how to live. Where, then, is it to be found? In doing what human nature requires, Marcus concludes. How does he do this? Through first principles, which should govern his intentions and his actions. Which principles are these? Those having to do with good and evil. What has Stoic philosophy taught him about good and evil? That nothing is good except what leads to fairness, self-control, courage, free will, and the virtues of character. Similarly, that nothing is bad except what does the opposite (viii. 1). Pride, arrogance, self-conceit, greed, and self-indulgence are all examples of bad traits of character. Philosophy rids us of these vices.

Marcus considers his position as emperor to be an obstacle to attaining fairness, self-control, courage, and the other virtues. Why? Because the tremendous power of the office invites corruption. Wary of this, Marcus is determined to escape the indelible stain of "imperialization" (vi. 30). He is vigilant to avoid allowing his character to be stained by the megalomania that can so easily infect the emperor of Rome. Marcus recognizes the danger of being *captured* by delusions of omnipotence, because from his knowledge of previous emperors, he knows it happens. So he urges himself to make sure he remains straightforward, upright, reverent, serious, unadorned, an ally of justice, pious, kind, affectionate, and doing his duty with resolve. He encourages himself to fight to be the person philosophy tried to make him (vi. 30). Philosophy, then, can protect Marcus from being imprisoned by the vices of imperialization. Philosophy teaches him to revere the gods and watch over human beings. Our lives are short, he repeats here and often throughout the *Memoranda*. The only rewards of our existence here, Marcus states, are an unstained character and unselfish acts (vi. 30). Clearly in this text there is no hint of a possibility of reward in an afterlife. Keeping one's character unstained and acting unselfishly are the *only* rewards Marcus countenances. But doesn't time sweep away our lives, reducing our moral accomplishments to dust along with everything else in the cosmos? For Marcus, purity of character and the virtues are the only things which time doesn't show to be transient, worthless junk. Though our lives are eventually swept away by the rushing river of existence, the achievement of goodness cannot be trivialized by anything. Philosophy teaches us that striving for goodness is under our control, though most everything else is not. Virtue matters immensely, even though the lives of the virtuous don't last.

Marcus thinks that the task of philosophy is modest and straightforward (ix. 29), moreover, philosophy's job includes cultivating the virtues of modesty and straightforwardness in the philosopher. Learning the lessons of philosophy (about mereology, time, *logos*, ethics, etc.) results in improvement of character. Marcus wants to develop his character so that no one can say truthfully that Marcus is not a straightforward or honest person. He wants it to be the case that anyone who thinks that about him believes a falsehood. But Marcus fully recognizes that the responsibility for his moral character is all his. No one can stop him from being honest or straightforward. He needs simply to resolve not to go on living if he isn't. It would be contrary to the *logos*, Marcus writes, to fail to be honest or straightforward and to go on living nevertheless (x. 32). Cultivating our virtues and being virtuous is entirely up to us. Therefore, there can be no excuse for failing to be good.

This isn't to say that cultivating our virtues is easy. There will be plenty of hurdles and pitfalls along the road of moral progress. Not every day will be full of virtuous deeds. Consequently, Marcus advises himself not to feel exasperated, or defeated, or despondent because his days aren't packed with wise and moral actions. Instead, he must get back up when he fails and celebrate behaving like a human—however imperfectly—and fully embrace the pursuit that he has embarked on. Marcus explains that he should not think of philosophy as his instructor, but as the sponge and egg white that relieve ophthalmia, as a soothing ointment, a warm lotion (v. 9). He conceives of philosophy as a kind of therapy or remedy for healing a kind of mental illness. He writes that he ought not to show off his obedience to the *logos*, as if he was preening himself to impress others, but rather he should rest in the *logos* (v. 9). Interestingly, Marcus chooses the analogy of inflammation of the eye as the condition which philosophy treats, since *seeing* things for what they truly are is a fair way to conceive of what philosophy does. Philosophy is therefore like a cure for being partially blind to reality.

The motivation to see things for what they really are is a basic impulse of *logos* (reason). Our nature as rational beings impels us to get things right. Consequently, Marcus tells himself to remember that philosophy requires only what his nature (as a logical being) already demands. The pursuit of things (e.g., pleasures) not sanctioned by *logos* is something unnatural. But pleasures can trap us by *appearing* to be preferable to what our rational nature dictates. So, Marcus asks himself: Wouldn't magnanimity or freedom or honesty or prudence or piety be preferable to any such pleasures? He asks himself if there is anything preferable to thought itself, to logic, or to understanding. Their surefootedness and fluent stillness (v. 9), Marcus thinks, make them far more reliable, more dignified, and more admirable than anything else. These treasures of the mind, these dependable virtues of character, surpass any cheap, fleeting gratifications of the body or accolades from others. Philosophy serves to train our rational nature and strengthen our minds so we can attain the virtues of straightforwardness, modesty, honesty, prudence, piety, wisdom, fairness, self-control, courage, uprightness, reverence, seriousness, justice, kindness, fondness, magnanimity, and freedom that bring peace of mind.

GOODNESS IS YOUR JOB: PERFECT YOUR CHARACTER

A point in aesthetics helps Marcus elaborate on the nature of the virtues. He contends that beautiful things of any kind are beautiful in themselves and sufficient to themselves. Praise is extraneous. The object of praise remains what it was—no better and no worse. Marcus also applies this principle to "beautiful" things in ordinary life, like physical objects and artworks. He asks whether anything genuinely beautiful needs supplementing. His answer: No, no more than does justice or truth or kindness or humility. Are any of these improved by being praised or damaged by contempt? Is an emerald suddenly flawed if no one admires it? Is gold or ivory or purple less beautiful if lauded by no one? (iv. 20). Marcus thinks not. He is a value realist. Lyres, knives, flowers, and bushes (iv. 20), like emeralds, gold, and ivory, are all intrinsically valuable, inherently beautiful. Indeed, Marcus even detects charm and attractiveness in cases of "Nature's inadvertence." He describes the examples of loaves of bread splitting open on top while baking in the oven and ripening figs beginning to burst. The shadow of decay in olives about to fall from the tree gives them a peculiar beauty. Stalks of wheat bending under their own weight, the furrowed brow of the lion, and the flecks of foam on the boar's mouth are all things a deeper sensitivity to nature reveal to be beautiful (iii. 2; cf. vi. 36a). The virtues too are no less beautiful, no less good, when not praised by others.

Marcus reminds himself not to be distracted from his pursuit of virtue by the opinions or actions of others. After all, non-Stoics will find Stoicism to be dubious or will reject it outright. Non-Stoics, believing that pleasure, wealth, high office, fame, or some other such thing beyond their control is truly good will reject Marcus' commitment to virtue and resort to vicious behavior when it helps their chances of winning what they believe to be good. But no matter what anyone says or does, Marcus insists that his task is to be good. He again uses the examples of emerald or gold or purple when he imagines one of these colors repeating to itself, "No matter what anyone says or does, my task is to be emerald, my color undiminished" (vii. 15). Marcus sees his task as a rational human being, as a citizen of the universe, to be good. He refuses to let anyone deter him from accomplishing this task. He describes his profession as goodness. This profession is to be achieved only by thought about the world and about the nature of people (xi. 5), more specifically, correct thought about the world and the nature of people (cf. iii. 9). Marcus writes that *salvation* is to see each thing for what it is, to grasp its nature and its purpose. His overriding goal is to do only what is right and say only what is true, without holding back. What else could it be, he wonders, to live life fully? To live life fully is to pay out goodness like the rings of a chain, without the slightest gap between each good deed (xii. 29). If Marcus can achieve this unbroken series of good acts, he can realize the life of the good man. What is the good person like? It is someone content with what nature assigns him, and satisfied with being just and kind himself (iv. 25). Marcus is impatient to become such a man. He urges himself to stop talking about what the good man is like, and just be one (x. 16).

How do we determine whether something really benefits us? Marcus says never regard something as doing you good if it makes you betray a trust, or lose your sense of shame, or makes you show hatred, suspicion, ill will, or hypocrisy, or a desire for things best done behind closed doors. Goodness can be attained if you can privilege your own mind, your guiding spirit, and your reverence for its powers. These things should keep you clear of dramatics, of wailing and gnashing of teeth (iii. 7). Cherishing your mind and respecting its powers will save you from disappointment, frustration, resentment, envy, and grief. Marcus writes that he won't need solitude or a cast of thousands, either. Above all, dedicating himself to the fitness of his mind will make him free of fear and desire. Moreover, how long his body will contain the soul that inhabits it will not cause him a moment's worry. If it's time for him to go, he should leave willingly, as he would to accomplish anything that can be done with grace and honor. Marcus must concentrate on this, his whole life long: for his mind to be in the right state, the state a rational, civic mind should be in (iii. 7).

Happiness is all about developing good character, according to Marcus and the Stoics. If things beyond our control bring us well-being, as non-Stoics believe, then well-being ultimately depends on good luck. Therefore, Marcus reasons, either well-being is good luck or it is good character (vii. 17). He holds that something can ruin your life only if it ruins your character. If it can't ruin your character, then it cannot harm you, either inside or out (iv. 8). But why does Marcus believe, as he seems to in this last remark in iv. 8, that if an assault on your body doesn't ruin your character, then it cannot harm you even on the *outside*? Wouldn't damage to your body be undeniably harmful? Marcus sharply divides what affects the body from what affects the mind (or soul). He reasons that either pain affects the body, which is the body's problem, or it affects the soul. But the soul, Marcus insists, can choose not to be affected, preserving its own serenity and its own tranquility. All our decisions, urges, desires, and aversions lie within, according to Marcus. No evil can touch them (viii. 28). The idea seems to be that pain affecting the body need not be allowed by the mind to affect the mind. Some people, with sufficient mental discipline and training, have elevated their pain thresholds so high that by strength of mind they can conquer the pain in their bodies. Marcus seems to endorse this notion of "mind over matter." Such mastery of pain is admittedly difficult to achieve. Marcus had to wrestle with chronic chest and stomach pain, and so he tried as best he could to master his own pains.

The goal for Marcus is to perfect his character. What is perfection of character? To live your last day, every day, without frenzy, sloth, or pretense (vii. 69). The mind of the person with a perfected character is a mind that has been set straight and purified. This mind has no pus, no dirt, and no scabs, Marcus writes (iii. 8). It is a mind that has been healed of all filthy, ugly scars of character. Such a person's life is not cut short by death, like an actor who stops before the play is done, the plot wound up (iii. 8). Marcus seems to mean that the life of a good person is *complete*. The person has attained integrity of character, rather than having made some progress toward goodness, but still falling short of getting there. The goal Marcus aims for is neither servility nor arrogance, neither cringing nor disdain, neither excuses nor evasions (iii. 8).

Marcus is a tough critic of his own moral progress. He scrutinizes his strengths and weaknesses closely. Even though he may have become a better wrestler, he criticizes himself for not having become a better citizen, a better person, a better resource in tight places, or a better forgiver of faults (vii. 52). He notes that no one could ever accuse him of being quick-witted. He admits this, but responds that there are plenty of other things he can't claim he hasn't got in him. Marcus prods himself to practice the virtues he *can* show: honesty, gravity, endurance, austerity, resignation, abstinence, patience, sincerity, moderation, seriousness, and high-mindedness. Don't you see, he writes to himself, how much you have to offer, besides excuses like "can't"? And yet, he laments, he still settles for less. Or is it some inborn condition, he wonders, that makes him whiny, grasping, and servile? Is it some innate disorder that makes him complain about his body and curry favor and show off and leaves him so turbulent inside? No, he replies. He could have broken free of these character defects a long way back. And then he would have been only a little slow on the uptake. Marcus insists that he needs to work on that slow-wittedness too. It is not something to be ignored, let alone to be prized (v. 5). Slow-wittedness remains a character flaw.

JUSTICE AND REVERENCE, INJUSTICE AND BLASPHEMY

Marcus regards justice as *his* responsibility, not an expectation imposed on others. Thus, in addition to cultivating indifference to external events, since they are beyond his control, he is committed to justice in his own acts. What does this mean? Justice for Marcus means that his thought and action result in the common good, which is what he was born to do (ix. 31). He pairs acceptance of what happens in nature with commitment to the common good because both are dictated by divine will. Marcus wants to be the man who has stripped away concern about his body and has realized that at some point soon he will have to abandon humankind and leave all this behind. He writes that this person has dedicated himself to serving justice in all he does, and serving nature in all that happens. What people say or think about him, or how they treat him, isn't something he worries about. He asks himself only these two questions: Is what he's doing now the right thing to be doing? Does he accept and welcome what he's been assigned? He has stripped away all other occupations, all other tasks. He wants only to travel a straight path to God, by way of law (x. 11a). From this perspective, living the good life is remarkably simple: Do the right thing right now, accept and welcome what nature assigns to you, namely, what happens. The former is required by justice. The latter is what it means to revere the divine. As we saw in Chapter 4, Marcus concentrates not on the past or future, but the present. He instructs himself to guide the present toward reverence and justice. Reverence is necessary so he will accept what he is allotted. Nature intended the event, circumstance, or situation for him, and intended him for it. Justice is necessary so that he will speak the truth, frankly and without evasions, and act both as he should, and as other people deserve. Marcus urges himself not to let anything deter him in enacting reverence and justice, neither other people's behavior, nor his own misperceptions, nor what people will say, nor the feelings of his body. He wants to let the affected part take care of those feelings. And if, when it's time to depart, he shunts everything aside except his mind and the divinity within, if it isn't ceasing to live that he is afraid of but never beginning to live properly, then, Marcus believes, he will be worthy of the world that made him. By attaining this concentrated focus on his mind, on the divinity within him, and fearing not death but living improperly, he will no longer be an alien in his own land. He will no longer be shocked by everyday events, as if they were unheard-of aberrations. He will no longer be at the mercy of this or that (xii. 1). Therefore, justice and reverence will have brought with them true belonging to the cosmos in which he is a citizen, true imperturbability, and true invulnerability of spirit.

Justice and reverence, therefore, are not traits separable from equanimity, calmness, fearlessness, self-possession, and invulnerability. Marcus follows the earlier Stoics in affirming the doctrine of the unity of the virtues: to have one virtue, one must have them all. He again links reverence of the divine, understood as obedience to nature, to justice when he writes that when a slave runs away from his master, we call him a fugitive slave. But the law of nature is a master too, and to break it is to become a fugitive. To feel grief, anger, or fear, Marcus reasons, is to try to escape from something decreed by the ruler of all things (God), now or in the past or in the future. And that ruler is law, which governs what happens to each of us. To feel grief or anger or fear, Marcus concludes, is to become a fugitive from justice (x. 25). The law of nature equally governs the material elements. Marcus writes that his spirit and the fire within him are by their nature pulled upward. The elements of earth and water in him are by their nature pulled downward. Hence, he observes, even the elements obey the natural world when they are ordered and compelled because they occupy their stations until the signal to abandon them arrives. So, Marcus wonders, why should his intellect be the only one dissenting from nature's orders?

Why should his intellect be the only one complaining about the station to which it is posted? Nothing is being forced on it, Marcus thinks, other than what its own nature requires. Yet it refuses to comply and sets off in the opposite direction by heading toward what is wrong and self-indulgent, toward anger, fear, and pain. This is when the mind revolts against nature. For the mind to complain about anything that happens is for it to desert its post. It was created to show reverence, that is, respect for the divine, no less than to act justly. That too is an element of coexistence and a prerequisite for justice (xi. 20). In this text Marcus parses reverence as respect for the divine, and respect for the divine is a prerequisite for justice. For the mind to do what is wrong and self-indulgent, for it to be angry, fearful, or distressed, is for the mind to revolt against nature, to disobey it, and thus to disrespect the divine. Therefore, for the mind to do wrong, to self-indulge, to fear, or be angry, is for the mind to act unjustly.

Since Marcus closely connects reverence with justice, logic requires him to connect blasphemy with injustice. He does so explicitly. How does Marcus conceive of injustice? He endorses Socrates' idea,[6] championed by the Stoics, that to do harm (to another) is to do yourself harm. To do an injustice is to do yourself an injustice. Doing injustice, therefore, degrades you (ix. 4). Marcus also thinks you can commit injustice by doing nothing, by an act of omission (ix. 5).

In Book ix, chapter 1, Marcus presents a series of arguments on different kinds of conduct that are blasphemous. He first argues that injustice is a kind of blasphemy.

Argument A

1. Nature designed rational beings for each other's sake: to help, not harm, one another, as they deserve.
2. To harm another who doesn't deserve it is to commit injustice.
3. To commit injustice is to transgress nature's will. [From 1]
4. To transgress nature's will is to blaspheme against the oldest of the gods.
5. Therefore, injustice is a kind of blasphemy. [From 3, 4]

Having held that injustice is a kind of blasphemy, Marcus proceeds to argue that to lie is to blaspheme. He distinguishes between deliberate and involuntary lying. Regarding the former, he reasons as follows:

Argument B

1. "Nature" means the nature of that which is.
2. That which is and that which is the case are closely linked.
3. Hence, nature is synonymous with truth—the source of all true things. [From 2]
4. To lie deliberately is to commit deceit, that is, to violate truth.
5. To commit deceit is to commit injustice.
6. Hence, to lie deliberately is to commit injustice. [From 4, 5]
7. Injustice is a kind of blasphemy. [Conclusion of Argument A]
8. Therefore, to lie deliberately is to blaspheme. [From 6, 7]

Marcus argues that lying involuntarily is blasphemous in this way:

Argument C

1. Anyone who deviates toward what is opposed to the truth is in conflict with the way the world is structured.
2. The involuntary liar deviates toward what is opposed to the truth.
3. Hence, the involuntary liar is in conflict with the way the world is structured. [From 1, 2]
4. Nature gave the involuntary liar the resources to distinguish between true and false.
5. The involuntary liar neglected these resources and now can't tell the difference between true and false.
6. Hence, the involuntary liar disrupts the harmony and order of nature. [From 3]
7. Therefore, to lie involuntarily (i.e., without realizing it) is to blaspheme. [From 6]

Marcus then takes aim in Book ix, chapter 1 at the common twin beliefs that pleasure is to be pursued as a true good that contributes to one's happiness, and that pain is to be avoided as a true evil that reduces one's happiness. Stoics reject these twin beliefs.

Argument D

1. Someone who pursues pleasure as good and flees pain as evil constantly reproaches nature by complaining that nature doesn't treat the good and bad as they deserve, but often lets the

bad enjoy pleasure and the things that produce it, and makes the good suffer pain and the things that produce pain.
2. To reproach nature is to blaspheme.
3. The world being as it is, to fear pain (flee it as evil) is to fear something that's bound to happen.
4. Something that is bound to happen is nature's will.
5. Hence, to fear pain is to fear nature's will. [From 3, 4]
6. To fear nature's will is to blaspheme.
7. Hence, to fear pain is to blaspheme. [From 5, 6]
8. If you pursue pleasure, then you can hardly avoid wrongdoing.
9. To do wrong is to blaspheme.
10. Hence, to pursue pleasure is to blaspheme. [From 8, 9]
11. Therefore, to pursue pleasure as good and flee from pain as evil is to blaspheme. [From 1, 2, 7, 10]

Arguments A, B, C, and D prepare the way for Marcus' argument for the Stoic theory of indifferents in Book ix, chapter 1. According to the Stoics, the goal is to live in agreement with nature or to follow nature. For human beings, this means living in agreement with *logos* (reason), since *logos* is our special endowment. The perfection of *logos* is the state of the mind known as virtue. Consequently, the Stoics hold that the virtues and what promotes them are the only true goods, because only these things are necessary and sufficient for happiness. Similarly, the Stoics hold that the vices and what contributes to them are the only true evils, because only these things necessarily result in misery. All other things are "indifferents," according to this ethical theory, because obtaining or losing them does not necessitate either our happiness or our misery.

For example, when eating is appropriate and would not be vicious under the circumstances, wisdom (a virtue) directs a Stoic to eat, and she eats. But neither the food itself, nor the pleasure of eating it, nor the healthy operation of the body produced by digesting it, is good, strictly speaking, because none of these things contributes to the Stoic's happiness. Only the virtues and what promotes them do that. Food is not necessary for happiness, because the lack of food in no way detracts from the Stoic's virtue. A hungry Stoic can still be wise, just, courageous, self-controlled, kind, friendly, magnanimous, reverent, dutiful, etc. Consequently, the Stoics deny that food, life, pleasure, wealth, good reputation, political power, liberty, fame, beauty, and health are true goods. When virtue recommends these things, then the Stoic selects them as preferable to their opposites. But sometimes virtue requires the Stoic to select one of their opposites. This is why hunger, death, pain, poverty, bad reputation, political disenfranchisement, slavery, anonymity, ugliness, and illness are ordinarily not preferable, but are not true evils. On some occasions, the appropriate thing to do may be to select one of these things precisely in order to preserve one's virtue by, say, protecting a friend, caring for one's child, defending one's country, or fulfilling some other social or familial role one is responsible for.

Marcus makes his case for the Stoic theory of indifferent by arguing that some things *nature* is indifferent to, because if it privileged one over the other it would hardly have created both. For example, life and death, beauty and ugliness, pleasure and pain, abundance and famine, floods and droughts, are all things created by nature. So, Marcus reasons, if we want to follow nature, to be of one mind with it, we need to share its indifference. To privilege pleasure over pain, life over death, or fame over anonymity is clearly blasphemous, Marcus contends, because nature certainly doesn't. When Marcus says that nature is indifferent to them, he means that they happen indifferently. Life and death, pleasure and pain, and all the rest happen at different times, to the things that exist and the things that come into being after them, through some ancient decree of Providence. This is the decree by which from some initial starting point Providence embarked on the creation that we know, by laying down the principles of what was to come and determining the generative forces, namely, existence and change and their successive stages (ix. 1).

We can reconstruct Marcus' argument for the Stoics' theory of indifferents (in ix. 1) as follows:

Argument E

1. Either nature privileges pleasure over pain, life over death, fame over anonymity, health over illness, etc. or nature is indifferent to these pairs of opposites.
2. If nature privileged pleasure over pain, life over death, fame over anonymity, health over illness, etc. then nature would not have created both of all such pairs of opposites.

3. Nature did create both of all such pairs of opposites.
4. Hence, nature does not privilege pleasure over pain, life over death, fame over anonymity, health over illness, etc. [From 2, 3, by *modus tollens*]
5. Pleasure and pain, life and death, fame and anonymity, health and illness, etc. happen indifferently, at different times, to the things that exist now and the things that will exist after them in the future.
6. Hence, nature is indifferent to all such pairs of opposites. [From 1, 4, by *disjunctive syllogism* and from 5]
7. If we want to follow nature and be of one mind with it, then we should share nature's indifference to all such pairs of opposites.
8. If we privilege pleasure over pain, life over death, fame over anonymity, health over illness, etc., then we do not share nature's indifference to all such pairs of opposites.
9. If we do not share nature's indifference to all such pairs of opposites, then we do not want to follow nature and be of one mind with it.
10. Either we want to follow nature and be of one mind with it or we want to blaspheme against nature.
11. We do not want to blaspheme against nature.
12. Hence, we want to follow nature and be of one mind with it. [From 10, 11, by *disjunctive syllogism*]
13. Therefore, we should share nature's indifference to pleasure and pain, life and death, fame and anonymity, health and illness, and all such pairs of opposites. [From 7, 12, by *modus ponens*]

Since Providence decrees nature's indifference to pleasure and pain, life and death, etc., to fail to share nature's indifference is to defy Providence itself. Defying Providence is clearly blasphemous and clearly unjust disobedience to its divine decree. So, by means of this clever chain of reasoning in Book ix, chapter 1, Marcus logically connects blasphemy with injustice, just as he connects reverence with justice.

THE SELF-CLEANING SPRING AND
THE ALL-CONSUMING FIRE

Though Marcus is adept at constructing careful, discursive arguments for Stoic doctrines, he is also skilled at using poetry to illustrate his Stoic ideas. For modern readers, those of a more literary bent may find the latter more appealing. Those exercised by logic, on the other hand, may find the former more convincing. But as far as we can tell, Marcus wrote the *Memoranda* only for himself, for his own philosophical edification, personal consolation, and therapy. Plainly, then, Marcus found writing both deductive arguments and imaginative metaphors to be effective "reminders" in his life.

One of his favorite images to describe the goodness always available to the soul (mind, self) is a spring of bubbling water. He writes: "Dig deep; the water—goodness—is down there. And as long as you keep digging, it will keep bubbling up" (vii. 59). For Marcus, the cleansing power of water symbolizes his own ability to make his soul clean, fit, and good. He instructs himself to wash himself clean with the virtue of simplicity, with the virtue of humility, and with the mindset of indifference to everything but right and wrong. He instructs himself to care for other human beings and to follow God (vii. 31). In this text the virtues of simplicity and humility, and the state of mind that is indifferent to all but right and wrong, wash away the grimy residue left behind on him by indifferents like his body's aches and pains, sumptuous meals, lavish clothes, glittering jewelry, the cheers, jeers, fawning, and scheming of others, and worries about things beyond his control.

Fame is an indifferent Marcus often targets in the *Memoranda*. In one text, he asks himself: What is "eternal" fame? Emptiness, he replies. What, then, he wonders, should we work for? Only this: proper understanding, unselfish action, truthful speech, and a resolve to accept whatever happens as necessary and familiar, flowing like water from that same source and spring (iv. 33). The same source and spring which produces the mental blessings of proper understanding, unselfish action, and truthful speech supplies Marcus with the resolve to accept whatever happens as necessary and familiar, as the inevitable process of change and transformation in all of nature and as decreed by Providence. In effect, Marcus urges himself to drink in whatever happens as the water that sustains his soul with life and vigor from the "spring" of the cosmos.

The most detailed image of the inexhaustible spring of virtue is found in Book viii, chapter 51 where Marcus lists traps to avoid. He seeks neither carelessness in his actions, nor confusion in his words, nor imprecision in his thoughts, nor over-activity. He prohibits himself from retreating into his own soul or trying to escape it. Since Marcus has many responsibilities to others he must engage with those around him every day. That's why he forbids himself from withdrawing into his own soul and shutting out the rest of the world. But what if others cut him with knives, shower him with curses, or even kill him? Why, Marcus wonders, would that somehow cut his mind off from clearness, sanity, self-control, and justice? (viii. 51; cf. xi. 15). In a similar text he says his goal is to live life in peace, immune to all compulsion. Let others scream whatever they want. Let animals tear apart the soft flesh covering him. How would any of that stop him, he wonders, from keeping his mind calm, reliably sizing up what's around him, and being ready to make good use of whatever happens? He wants his power of judgment to be able to look the event in the eye and say, "This is what you really are, regardless of what you may look like." His adaptability can add, "You're just what I was looking for" (vii. 68). The impossibility of vanquishing the virtues of a sound mind is illustrated with a vivid image. Imagine, Marcus writes, a man standing by a spring of clear, sweet water and cursing it, while the fresh water keeps on bubbling up. The man can shovel mud or dung into it, and the stream will carry it away, wash itself clean, remaining unstained by the futile attempts to pollute it. This is the kind of unpollutable, self-cleaning mind that Marcus strives to have: a mind that is not a cistern but a perpetual spring. How can he attain such a mind? By working to win his freedom from all external forces beyond his control, hour by hour, through patience, honesty, humility, and the exercise of all the virtues (viii. 51).

A second elemental image Marcus uses to describe the invincible mind is a blazing fire. Isn't it enough, Marcus asks himself, to live his brief life rightly? He thinks he's missing the raw material, namely, the opportunities. What is any of this but training for his *logos*, in life observed accurately and scientifically? Marcus urges himself to keep at it until it's fully digested. As a strong stomach digests whatever it eats, and as a blazing fire takes whatever you throw on it and makes it light and flame, so too Marcus strives to train his *logos* to convert everything that happens to him into good actions and right living (x. 31). Our *logos* (reason) has this extraordinary power to deal with whatever comes its way. Marcus writes that our inward power, a rigorously trained, rationally empowered mind, when it obeys nature, reacts to events by accommodating itself to what it faces, to what is possible. This mind needs no specific material. It pursues its own aims as circumstances allow. It turns obstacles into fuel as a fire overwhelms what would have quenched a lamp. What's thrown on top of the conflagration is absorbed, consumed by it, and makes it burn still higher (iv. 1).

The well-trained mind is not only unharmed by so-called obstacles, it is actually *strengthened* by all challenges that confront it. More than simply enduring what occurs, such a mind obeys nature by embracing what happens to it. The inner strength and resilience of the virtuous mind radiate continuously from it. Thus, Marcus also likens the virtuous mind to a lamp. The lamp, he writes, shines until it is put out, without losing its gleam. Marcus wonders why truth, justice, self-control, and the other virtues all gutter out so early in him (xii. 15; cf. viii. 57). The virtues of the burnished mind shine out steadily, like a beacon.

In stark contrast, evil is a plague, according to Marcus. He calls evil a mental cancer that attacks one's humanity. Biological diseases only threaten one's life, which is not a huge concern since there is no escape from one's mortality. Consequently, Marcus thinks that good luck would be to exit life without encountering dishonesty, hypocrisy, self-indulgence, or pride (ix. 2). Human beings being what they are, however, no one is this lucky. Yet Marcus denies that the existence of evil harms the *world*, just as he denies that an individual act of evil harms the *victim*. Only one person, the agent committing the evil act, is harmed by that act, and he can stop being harmed as soon as he decides to (viii. 55). Therefore, each has the power to inoculate herself against the plague which assaults her humanity by never doing evil.

WHAT IS OWED TO OTHERS

Marcus is keenly aware that the process of cultivating virtues of character is long and challenging. Stumbles and slips along the way are inevitable, but they need not signal defeat. So, when Marcus needs encouragement for the ongoing task of improving his character, he instructs himself to think of the qualities the people around him have: this one's energy, that one's modesty, another's generosity, and so on. Nothing, he believes, is as encouraging as when the virtues are visibly embodied in the people around us, when we're practically showered with them. Therefore, Marcus reasons, it's good to keep this in mind (vi. 48). This is a significant point in the *Memoranda* because in many texts Marcus complains about the misbehavior, foolishness, pettiness, shortsightedness, selfishness, obsequiousness, hostility, and other moral failings of the people around him. Recognition of the positive qualities of his fellow citizens reveals Marcus' gratitude to those who facilitate his own moral progress by displaying their virtuous character traits for him to model. Indeed, Book i of the *Memoranda* contains seventeen entries which recount, in roughly chronological order, what Marcus has learned in his life from various people. Marcus lists the blessings and character-building lessons he received from his grandfather (Marcus Annius Verus, died CE 138), his biological father (Marcus Annius Verus, died between CE 130 and 135),[7] his mother (Lucilla), his great-grandfather (Lucius Catilius Severus), his teachers (Diognetus, Apollonius, Sextus of Chaeronea, Alexander of Cotiaeum), his mentors (Cinna Catulus, Claudius Maximus, Quintus Junius Rusticus, Gnaeus Claudius Severus), and his letter-writing correspondent (Marcus Cornelius Fronto). The last two entries, however, are the longest. In entry sixteen Marcus details the virtues modeled by his adoptive father (Titus Aurelius Antoninus Pius, Roman emperor CE 138–161). In entry seventeen Marcus expresses gratitude to the gods, detailing the many blessings they gave him. Most scholars think that the short sketch of Antoninus Pius in Book vi, chapter 30 was an initial draft for the longer memoir in i. 16. Be that as it may, for our purposes it will suffice to look at vi. 30.

The prime (human) model of ethical conduct for Marcus was without a doubt his adoptive father Antoninus Pius. Marcus explicitly reminds himself always to take Antoninus as his model. Marcus recalls his energy in doing what was rational, his steadiness in any situation, his sense of reverence, calm expression, gentleness, and modesty. Marcus recalls Antoninus' eagerness to grasp things and how he never let things go before he was certain he had examined them thoroughly and understood them perfectly. Marcus remembers the way Antoninus put up with unfair criticism without returning it, how he couldn't be hurried, and how he wouldn't listen to slander. Antoninus was never one to carp, or be easily flustered, or overly suspicious, or pretentious. He was content with the basics in living quarters, bedding, clothes, food, and servants. Marcus recalls how hard Antoninus worked, how much he put up with, and his ability to work straight through till dusk because of his simple diet. His constancy and reliability as a friend, his tolerance of people who openly questioned his views, his delight at seeing his ideas improved on, and his piety, without a trace of superstition, are all admired by Marcus. He identifies all these excellences of his late adoptive father to emulate so that when his own time comes, Marcus' conscience will be as clear as Antoninus' (vi. 30). Therefore, given Book i, Book vi, chapter 30, and Book vi, chapter 48, one supremely important thing that Marcus believes is owed to others is abiding gratitude to the people who embodied virtues for Marcus to model, thus serving as precious moral teachers.

All too often, however, other people fail to serve as models of virtue for Marcus. Indeed, others often enough criticize Marcus for doing the right thing. So, he instructs himself, when he wakes he should ask himself: Does it make any difference to him if other people blame him for doing what is right? No, he replies, it makes no difference. The false opinions of others are indifferents, naturally. He reminds himself what the people who are so loud in praise or blame of others are like as they sleep and eat, how they behave, their fears, desires, thefts, and plunders perpetrated not physically but by what should be highest in them—the right mind that creates, when it chooses, loyalty, humility, truth, law, and inner well-being (x. 13). Marcus echoes his distaste for how others act when they eat, sleep, copulate, defecate, command, exult, rage, and thunder from on high (x. 19).

Marcus must remind himself that how (badly) others act is ultimately beyond his control. "You can hold your breath until you turn blue, but they'll still go on doing it" (viii. 4). Though ruler of an enormous empire, even Marcus, in the end, lacks the power to make others act well or stop them from acting badly. This is because the wills of other people are as independent of his as their breath and bodies. We may exist for the sake of one another, but our will rules its own domain. Otherwise, Marcus notes, the harm they do would cause harm to him. But God did not intend for his happiness to rest with someone else in that way (viii. 56). Consequently, when a bad action occurs, there are only two possibilities. Either the misdeed is in one's own control or it's in someone else's control. If it's in his control, Marcus asks himself, why does he do it? If it's in someone else's control, then who is he blaming? Atoms?[8] The gods? Marcus reasons that it would be stupid to blame either atoms or the gods.

Blame no one, he decides. He should instead set people straight, if he can. If he can't, he should just repair the damage. But what if he can't do that either? Then blaming people doesn't get him anywhere. Therefore, Marcus concludes that he must rid himself of all pointless actions, including blaming (viii. 17).

Marcus draws a lesson from the wrestling ring. There, he writes, our opponents can gouge us with their nails or butt us with their heads and leave a bruise, but we don't denounce them for it or get upset with them or regard them from then on as violent types. Rather, we just keep an eye on them after that. We are wary not out of hatred or suspicion. We are simply keeping a friendly distance. We need to do that in other areas, whenever people misbehave around us and oppose our actions. We need to excuse them and, without suspicion or hatred, keep our distance (vi. 20). Marcus warns himself that as he advances in the *logos* (i.e., in achieving a sound mind, good judgment, consistent reason), people will stand in his way. Yet, he reminds himself, they can't keep him from doing what's healthy. So, he mustn't let them stop him from putting up with them either. He must take care on both counts. He needs not just sound judgments and solid actions. He needs *tolerance* too for those who try to obstruct him or give him trouble in other ways. Anger is a failure to be tolerant. Hence, anger is weakness just as much as breaking down and giving up the struggle. Marcus argues that both the man who breaks and runs, and the one who lets himself be alienated from his fellow humans, are deserters (xi. 9). Therefore, both the person who withdraws from and ignores others and the person who gets angry with and hostile toward others desert the "army" of humankind. Here Marcus' idea is that human beings are allies. We are fellow comrades on the same side, the same team.

Consequently, Marcus reasons that what we owe others includes: (1) never to blame them, (2) to keep a watchful, friendly distance from them, when necessary, if they are in a position to injure us, (3) never to be suspicious of or hateful toward them, (4) to tolerate them (and never be angry with them), and (5) never to abandon them. Surely, though, it is very tough to maintain such constant equanimity in the face of the misdeeds of others. That's why Marcus writes that when faced with people's bad behavior, he must remember to turn around and ask when *he* has acted like that. When did he see money or pleasure or social position as a good? His anger will subside, Marcus reassures himself, as soon as he recognizes that wrongdoers acted under compulsion. What else could they do when so compelled? The only alternative for him is to remove the compulsion, if he can (x. 30). If he can't, then there's still no reason to get angry with himself or anyone else. Consequently, Marcus owes it to others (6) to recall when he himself committed the same misdeeds that they did, and (7) to remember that they acted under compulsion when they behaved badly.

Understanding the poor behavior of others requires putting oneself in their place, trying to get inside their heads, Marcus explains. When you face someone's insults, hatred, or whatever, look at his soul. Get inside him. Look at what sort of person he is. You'll find, Marcus thinks, that you don't need to strain to impress him. But you do have to wish him well. He's your closest relative. The gods assist him just as they do you, by signs and dreams and every other way, to get the things he wants (ix. 27). In other words, the gods help all members of the human team. Marcus must wish all his teammates well, both those that falter and do badly and those that perform well. Why? Because whether everyone knows it or not, Marcus insists that people exist for one another. Therefore, he can instruct or endure them (viii. 59). Presumably, he believes he ought first to try to instruct them. Failing that, he must endure them. Marcus urges himself to do his best to convince them to do better. If he does not succeed and justice requires it, then he must act on his own. If he is met with force, then he should fall back on acceptance and peaceableness. He should use the setback to practice other virtues. Marcus reminds himself that our efforts are subject to circumstances, and he wasn't aiming to do the impossible. What he was aiming to do was to *try*. Since whether he tries or not is entirely under his control, *making* the attempt counts as succeeding. He was setting out to try, so he accomplished what was possible for *him* to accomplish (vi. 50). Whether others are convinced to do better by what Marcus says depends on them, not him.

Finally, Marcus believes that he needs to teach himself to be at one with the things ordained for him. Moreover, the people among whom his lot has fallen Marcus tells himself to love sincerely (vi. 39). Loving those around him, literal philanthropy, makes good sense to Marcus since the cosmos has provided him with *their* company. Treating the people who share his life lovingly is in his power.[9]

To summarize, then, what does Marcus think he owes (we owe) to others?

A. Gratitude to those who embody virtues for us to model and who blessed us with good lessons, i.e., lessons in goodness.
B. Never to blame others.
C. To keep a watchful, friendly distance from those who have tried to injure us in the past.
D. Never to be suspicious of, angry with, or hate others.
E. Never to abandon others.
F. When others misbehave, to recall when we ourselves committed the same misdeeds that they did.
G. To remember that those who act badly act under compulsion; to understand the motives (reasons) that compel them.
H. To try to instruct those who act badly and convince them to do better.
I. To tolerate (endure) others at all times, even when they don't learn to do better.
J. To wish everyone well as our closest kin and fellow cosmic citizens.
K. To sincerely love those who share our lives with us.

These duties owed to others are a far cry from being indifferent to human beings. Marcus' concern for others is, I contend, abundantly evident throughout the *Memoranda*. Though he follows earlier Stoics in endorsing the ethical theory of the virtues (and what promotes them) as the only real goods, the vices (and what promotes them) as the only real evils, and everything nonmoral as indifferent, Marcus is definitely not indifferent to the well-being of other people. Marcus is indifferent to the trivial junk cluttered around us, including money, expensive clothes, fancy food (especially meat), pricey alcohol, gaudy baubles, lavish décor, prestigious offices, anything "prestigious," toys people amuse themselves with, self-indulgent gratification, cheers, jeers, and fame. He is anything but indifferent to *people*. Marcus fully appreciates that *all* people exist for one another (viii. 59), not to fight over junk.

EPILOGUE: THE SOUL OF A STOIC

Stoicism may well be the most demanding and least compromising of all ancient philosophies, but a case can be made that it is also the most noble. Marcus learned it as the philosophy befitting an educated person, the philosophy for shaping the Emperor responsible to millions of people inside the Roman Empire and, to some degree, millions more outside it. But he wrote the *Memoranda* not as a handy *How to Rule an Empire for Dummies.* He wrote it as an exercise to make himself a better, wiser, more helpful, more magnanimous, more humble, and more genuinely loving human being. His philosophy aims at crafting a sane, sober, sound soul, that is, the soul of a Stoic.

What are the characteristics of this rational soul? Self-perception, self-examination, and the power to make of itself whatever it wants. It reaps its own harvest, unlike plants and animals, whose yield is gathered in by others. It reaches its intended goal, no matter where the limit of its life is set. Marcus writes that it is not like dancing and theater, where the performance is incomplete if it's broken off in the middle. Rather, at any point, no matter which one you pick, the rational soul has fulfilled its mission. It has completed its work. Such a soul can say, "I have what I came for." It surveys the world and the empty space around it, and the way it is all put together. It delves into the endlessness of time to extend its grasp and comprehension of the periodic births and rebirths that the world goes through. It knows that those who come after us will see nothing different, that those who came before us saw no more than we do, and that anyone with forty years behind him and eyes in his head has seen both past and future alike (xi. 1). Yet the rational soul is not detached from people, indifferent to humanity, remotely and disinterestedly surveying the universe from the isolated perch of eternity. The other characteristics which Marcus ascribes to the rational soul are affection for its neighbors, truthfulness, and humility. It does not place anything above itself, and neither does law. For Marcus, there is no difference here between the *logos* of rationality and that of justice (xi. 1).

Did Marcus Aurelius Antoninus attain the rational soul of a Stoic? That is for historians to debate. But the undeniable earnestness that pervades the *Memoranda* strongly suggests that he mightily strove to.

APPENDIX: MARCUS, MAXIMUS, AND STOICISM IN *GLADIATOR* (2000)

Marcus Aurelius has appeared in two Hollywood films. In *The Fall of the Roman Empire* (Paramount, 1964) directed by Anthony Mann, he is portrayed by Alec Guinness. In *Gladiator* (DreamWorks SKG and Universal, 2000) directed by Ridley Scott, Marcus is portrayed by Richard Harris. The latter film stars Russell Crowe as Maximus, Joaquin Phoenix as Marcus' son Commodus, Connie Nielsen as Marcus' daughter Lucilla, Oliver Reed as Proximo, and Derek Jacobi as Senator Gracchus. Its twin opening weekends—May 7 in the USA and May 14 in the UK—*Gladiator* grossed $34.8 million and £3.5 million, respectively. It also received five Academy Awards including Best Picture. The impact of *Gladiator* (2000) on popular culture invites a short essay that explores the themes and characters of the film from a Stoic perspective.

The story begins in the winter of 180 CE, when Emperor Marcus Aurelius' twelve-year campaign against the barbarian tribes in Germania is drawing to an end. One last stronghold stands in the way of Roman victory and the promise of peace throughout the empire. The opening scene is a close-up of a man's left forearm, clad in a heavy leather bracer, with a rough, weathered hand wearing a wedding ring, lightly brushing the crowns of stalks of ripening wheat as the man slowly walks through a field. The man dreaming of his home, a farm in distant Hispania (Spain), is General Maximus. Dressed in battle armor and a fur cloak, he wears a short beard on his solemn face and stands in the mud amidst a burned forest. As he returns from his reverie, a tiny bird sitting atop a twig catches his eye. In an instant the bird flies off. Maximus smiles. The opening scene of *Gladiator* thus sets the stage for Maximus' anguished, violent, and trying journey to Stoicism.[1] Consider this passage from Marcus' *Memoranda*:

> Some things are rushing into existence, others out of it. Some of what now exists is already gone. Fluxes and changes constantly renew the world, just as the incessant march of time makes ever new infinite eternity. In this river, which of the things swirling around us should we value when none of them can offer a firm foothold? *Like a fond attachment to a sparrow: we glimpse it and it's gone.* (*Mem.* vi. 15; emphasis added)

"Some of what now exists"—the stand of trees before the Roman troops burned it away to create a battlefield—"is already gone." "In this river"—Maximus pleasantly imagines himself at home in a gentle river of wheat—"which of the things swirling around us should we value when none of them can offer a firm foothold?" Should Maximus value his battle-hardened legionaries in such a way as to count on them to win the imminent battle? Will the frosty forest floor offer a firm foothold to the cavalry Maximus will lead into combat? Maximus glimpses a small bird and it's gone. Fond attachment to a tiny bird is foolish, but no more foolish than a naive attachment to any of the fleeting things swirling around us, all of which are slipping away into eternity. Marcus' *Memoranda* often repeat this lesson about the perpetual flux, change, and transience of all parts of the world.[2]

Maximus and his lieutenants discuss the positioning of the catapults and await word from the emissary they sent to negotiate the peaceful surrender of the Germans. The Germans say "no" by returning the horse carrying the headless corpse of the Roman emissary. Maximus wishes his comrades "strength and honor," mounts his horse, and orders them to unleash hell on his signal. Beyond his love of family, at the beginning of the film Maximus' ethical guidance is limited to the creed of martial valor: *strength and honor.* But fortitude in facing dangers and preserving one's honor by doing one's duty constitute only one of the lessons Stoicism imparts. Maximus must learn more than "strength and honor" to progress on his journey to Stoicism.

Maximus rides off to join the cavalry. He exhorts the mounted soldiers: "If you find yourself alone riding in green fields with the sun on your face, do not be troubled, for you're in Elysium, and you're already dead. Brothers, what we do in life echoes in eternity." Both of the ideas expressed by Maximus in this scene are rejected by Marcus' Stoicism. Stoics do not believe in an afterlife. Marcus believes that eternity will erase us, all signs of our deeds, and eventually all memories of our lives. Fame is an illusion, he believes, and the echoes of even our greatest deeds in life fall silent. Throughout *Gladiator*, however, Maximus not only retains belief in Elysium, but is even shown at the end of the film reunited with his wife and son in an afterlife. In this respect, Maximus never attains a Stoic understanding of death. Yet he embodies strength and honor in leading his troops into the fray. During the battle Maximus is unhorsed, fights bravely, kills several enemy warriors, and is very nearly killed himself. Yet as the Roman legionaries dispatch the last few surviving barbarians, the battle is won. Maximus raises his sword and cries out "Roma victa!" to the cheering legionaries.

After the battle, Marcus approaches the bloodied, weary Maximus and praises him for again proving his valor. The Emperor asks how he can reward Rome's greatest general. "Let me go home?" Maximus plaintively replies. The victorious troops cheer as their general and emperor pass. Marcus observes that the soldiers honor not him, their emperor, but Maximus, their general. Maximus salutes his comrades in arms and they salute him. Commodus rushes to join them and promises to sacrifice a hundred bulls to honor his father's triumph. Marcus tells Commodus to save the bulls and honor Maximus for winning the battle. Commodus offers his arm to his aged father, but instead of taking it Marcus announces that he will leave. As the weak, fragile Marcus painfully mounts his horse, Maximus is quick to assist him. The Emperor wistfully remarks to Maximus, "So much for the glory of Rome." This line is true to Marcus' philosophy in the *Memoranda*, if we interpret it to suggest that glory, like fame, is fleeting and empty, whereas virtue is all that really matters.[3]

Later Marcus summons Maximus to his tent for a private conversation. Marcus is writing on a tablet, composing an entry in the *Memoranda*, perhaps? He says, "Tell me again, Maximus. Why are we here?" Maximus replies, "For the glory of the empire, Sire," to which Marcus responds, "Ah yes. Ah yes, I remember." This reflects Marcus Aurelius' need to write the *Memoranda* as an exercise in remembering. The Emperor asks Maximus to perform one last duty before he returns home—to become the protector of Rome after

Marcus dies, empowered to one end, to give power back to (the senate and) the people of Rome and to end the corruption that has crippled it. With all his heart Maximus declines this great honor offered by his beloved Emperor. What of Commodus? Marcus tells Maximus: "Commodus is not a moral man. You have known that since you were young. Commodus cannot rule. He must not rule. You are the son that I should have had. Commodus will accept my decision. He knows that you command the loyalty of the army." Maximus wants no such "honor" of absolute power and the responsibility of restoring the republic. He wants only to return to his home and family, which he hasn't seen in nearly three years while serving his military commission. He wants no more honors from Rome. Maximus craves to resume the humble roles of husband, father, and farmer once more. These desires are legitimate from a Stoic perspective, but only if circumstances allow him to resume those roles without being disloyal to his father-like Emperor, disregarding his civic duty to Rome, or committing any other injustice. Moreover, he can legitimately pursue those desires only if fate allows him that opportunity. Maximus asks for time (to deliberate about all his duties), and Marcus grants him until sunset.

Marcus summons Commodus and asks him if he is ready to do his duty for Rome. The Emperor announces that his son will not rule. Upon his death, the Emperor's powers will pass to Maximus to hold in trust until the senate is ready to rule Rome once more as a republic. Heartbroken, Commodus weeps that Marcus once wrote to him listing the four chief virtues: wisdom, justice, fortitude, and temperance. Commodus laments that as he read this list of virtues, he knew he had none of them. In their place, he explains, he has ambition, which can be a virtue when it drives us to excel, resourcefulness, courage (though not courage in battle), and devotion to his family. Commodus tearfully complains that Marcus didn't want him for his son. Saddened, Marcus replies that Commodus goes too far. Commodus, in anguish, wails that all he ever wanted was to live up to Caesar, his father. Marcus kneels before his son and confesses, "Your faults as a son is my failure as a father," and stretches out his arms, hoping for an embrace of forgiveness. Commodus accepts his father's embrace, but not his decision. Instead, the heir apparent repays Emperor Marcus with a lethal, suffocating embrace.

Commodus thus seizes the throne and lies that his father's breath gave out as he slept. He asks for Maximus' allegiance, with the warning that he will only do so once. Suspecting the patricide (and regicide), Maximus rebuffs Commodus. Commodus has Maximus arrested and orders him to be executed. Maximus must now learn that "strength and honor" is not sufficient to overcome every kind of setback. He has suddenly lost his high status as Rome's greatest general. The Emperor who loved him as if he were his own son has been murdered by a wicked usurper intent on killing him and his family. Maximus is now a criminal sentenced to death by the new Emperor, the despicable, craven Commodus. Maximus has been thrown into a new, chilling, violent river. He is forced to undertake a long, arduous, anguishing, and perilous march to Stoicism as a Stoic *prokoptōn* (progressor).[4]

Maximus' mettle is harshly tested throughout the rest of the film. He defeats the Praetorian Guard executioners but sustains a grievous wound in the fight. He travels hundreds of miles to get back home, but arrives shortly after Commodus' death squad has burned and crucified his wife and son while they were still alive. Devastated and weeping in anguish, Maximus buries the bodies of his beloved wife and son and collapses onto their fresh graves. Traumatized, badly wounded, and utterly exhausted, Maximus is easy pickings for roaming slavers drawn by the smoke rising from the scorched farm. General Maximus has become a captured, nameless slave called simply "Spaniard." The slavers and his fellow-slave Juba the Numidian clean Maximus' festering wound and he taciturnly recovers. Maximus rejects his former identity as a Roman soldier by defacing his SPQR[5] tattoo, lacerating his skin with a sharp rock. Proximo buys and trains Maximus, Juba, and the cadre of newly acquired chattel to be gladiators. Proximo is a former gladiator, and thus a former slave, who was liberated by Emperor Marcus Aurelius years before and awarded a *rudius* (wooden sword). Proximo teaches Maximus what an ex-slave is in a perfect position to teach a strong and honorable Roman ex-general. Proximo teaches Maximus *shadows and dust*, a vital lesson of Marcus' *Memoranda*: we are all mortals, living in a world of flux, as insubstantial shadows which arose from the dust, live out our brief lives, and descend into dust again as all animals and plants eventually do.

Earlier in the film, having escaped from the Praetorian executioners and rushing on the long journey back to the hills above Trujillo, Spain, Maximus rests beside a fire, nursing his wound. He recalls the prayer he made for the protection of this family the moment before the Praetorians' failed attempt to execute him: "Blessed father, watch over them with a ready sword, whisper to them that I live only to hold them again." To this Maximus then adds a new line containing a glimmer of the idea of "shadows and dust": "For all else is dust and air, whisper that I live only to hold them again, for all else is dust and air." Maximus has not yet learned that love of his wife and son is not the only thing that matters. His innocent wife and son have been butchered at Commodus' command and their bodies are returning to dust. But making good use of the days he has left after their deaths remains Maximus' responsibility. Taking the opportunity to act virtuously and promote justice is *not* dust and air. It is his duty. However, prior to becoming a slave and going to Rome with Proximo, Maximus has not progressed to gain this understanding of Stoicism. Juba nudges him out of his apathy by urging him that it is "not yet" time for him to die, which suggests that what he does with his life after his family is dead is not merely "dust and air." Juba also reinforces Maximus' un-Stoic belief in an afterlife.

Proximo contributes more to Maximus' progress as a Stoic than Juba. The slogan "shadows and dust" reflects the Stoics' emphasis on mortality succinctly expressed by Proximo's statement: "Ultimately, we're all dead men." But Stoics insist that our actions are not at all meaningless, because how we choose to face our deaths and how we choose to live matter immensely. Proximo explains to his gladiators that we can choose to face our deaths as men (that is, with fortitude), so that we will be remembered as men. That is, we can choose to be remembered not as slaves or gladiators or soldiers or generals, but as men who inevitably share the same fate, death, but face that fate in a manly,[6] not a cowardly, way. Fortitude matters, as do wisdom, justice, and temperance, the virtues Marcus Aurelius tried to teach Commodus in a letter.

Proximo's message is a bit off target for the Stoic archer, however, because Marcus denies that how we are remembered matters. What matters is that we act as virtuously as we can, not how or whether others remember us. After all, we will all eventually be forgotten anyway. This is why part of the speech Marcus delivers in his tent early in the film is so discordant with the philosophy in the *Memoranda*. Marcus says:

I am dying, Maximus. When a man sees his end he wants to know that there has been some purpose to his life. How will the world speak my name in years to come? Will I be known as the philosopher, the warrior, the tyrant? Or will I be remembered as the Emperor who gave Rome back her true self?

Marcus often reminds himself in the *Memoranda* that the world will stop speaking his name in the years to come and, in the fullness of time, he will be forgotten. Concern about his reputation is therefore utterly groundless and, in fact, base. What matters is doing the right thing when alive, becoming a good man (*bonus vir*), not what people say about you before or after your death. The purpose of his life is to use his powers of reason and intelligence to be a good citizen of the cosmos, to cooperate with others, be truthful, upright, modest, loving, compassionate, just, reverent, and wise. No Stoics, least of all Marcus Aurelius, worry about how they will be remembered or spoken of after they die. This speech in *Gladiator*, consequently, has no place whatsoever in the mouth of the Stoic philosopher and author Marcus Aurelius.

What would Marcus Aurelius think of Proximo? In the film we learn that Antonius Proximo operated his training lyceum for gladiators in Rome until Emperor Marcus Aurelius shut down all such schools. Why? Presumably because he judged gladiatorial "games" to be disgusting, violence-glorifying blood sport. Someone[7] may think that Proximo's choice of profession, buying able-bodied slaves to make them into profit-making gladiators,[8] is morally benign. But the film makes clear that Marcus rejected gladiatorial displays and expelled them far from Rome. Proximo is forced to relocate in the distant province of Zucchabar in order to set up shop. So, clearly, the Marcus Aurelius portrayed in *Gladiator* did not share the judgment that Proximo's chosen profession is unobjectionable. When Maximus promises to Proximo that he will kill Commodus, Proximo explains that he would not want that since Commodus makes Proximo rich. Proximo addresses Maximus respectfully as "General," and says he knows that Maximus is a man of his word, would die for honor, would die for Rome, and would die for the memory of his ancestors. In contrast, Proximo admits that he is an entertainer. Maximus needs Lucilla and Senator Gracchus to persuade Proximo, surely by means of a bribe, to set Maximus free. Thus Proximo's love of money is a powerful motivation for most of what he does.

Maximus, in contrast, never refuses to accept Marcus' decision to pass his imperial powers to Maximus after Marcus' death so that he can give power back to the senate and the people of Rome, restoring the republic. Maximus is merely reluctant to accept this position as protector of Rome offered to him by the Emperor. Commodus slays the Emperor before Maximus has had so much as a couple of hours to consider the Emperor's request.

Proximo teaches Maximus that "we mortals are but shadows and dust" and that to earn a chance to stand before the Emperor, Maximus must win the crowd. Maximus, however, needs time and help to relearn the Stoic lesson of "strength and honor" before he can teach it to Proximo. Initially, Maximus' motivation is hardly honorable, since his motive is not to promote justice by liberating Rome from a vicious tyrant. Rather, it's personal. Maximus wants to exact vengeance on the man who ordered the heinous murders of his wife and son. When Maximus' wish to stand before the Emperor is finally granted in the Colosseum, Commodus commands him to remove his masked helmet and reveal his identity. The music swells to a dramatic crescendo as Maximus declares: "My name is Maximus Decimus Meridius. Commander of the armies of the North, general of the Felix Legions, loyal servant to the true emperor Marcus Aurelius. Father to a murdered son, husband to a murdered wife, and I will have my vengeance in this life or the next." For all its dramatic effect, this speech is doubly un-Stoic. Vengeance is a fool's errand and fools lack not only wisdom but all other virtues, according to Stoicism. Moreover, Stoics deny there is any next life, as noted before.

Maximus needs help from Lucilla in order to think straight about what he ought to do. When Lucilla first visits him in his cell, Maximus wrongly interprets the idea of "shadows and dust" learned from Proximo to mean that since Maximus is a slave and could die in his cell that night or in the arena the next day, he can't possibly make a difference. Lucilla points out that the gods spared him and he had become a slave who is more powerful than Emperor Commodus. She thus tries to impart another lesson in his Stoic education: where fate leads, the Stoic follows willingly, like a sensible dog tied to a moving wagon. Though a slave, Maximus still has the power to consent to Lucilla's arrangement to meet with Senator Gracchus and plot to depose the unjust tyrant, Commodus. Maximus, however, only wants Commodus dead. He doesn't yet trust Lucilla or Gracchus, nor is he moved by justice to do what he can to realize Marcus Aurelius' dream that was Rome by restoring the republic. Lucilla reminds him of his lifelong commitment to "strength and honor." She says: "I knew a man once. A noble man, a man of principles, who loved my father and my father loved him. This man served Rome well." Resonating with the author's purpose of writing the *Memoranda*, Lucilla tries to stir Maximus' memory of himself, of his ideals, of his loyalties, of his loving bond with Marcus, and of his dutiful service to Rome. Maximus fails to realize that his identity and moral worth derive not from his status as a general recognized by the ruling emperor and the state, but from his power of assent, from his choices, decisions, judgments, intentions, and value-commitments. He need only accept Lucilla's help so he can *try* to achieve justice for Rome, leaving outcomes to the gods, to fate. Instead, Maximus rejects the ennobling potential of *recalling* "strength and honor" and tells Lucilla to *forget* she ever knew him. He needs more time to remember who he is. He is not commander of the armies of the North, not general of the Felix Legions, and not the Spaniard—an anonymous gladiator.[9] He is Maximus Decimus Meridius, and, if he so chooses, loyal servant to *the dying wish of* the true emperor Marcus Aurelius. He can choose to be a good man.

The turning point occurs the next day in the arena of the Colosseum when Maximus must fight Tigris of Gaul. He defeats the previously undefeated gladiator and the crowd shouts for the coup de grace. Commodus, disappointed that Tigris and two aimed tigers have failed to kill his nemesis, signals for Maximus to give the crowd the death they demand. Instead, Maximus defies the tyrant, disappoints the bloodthirsty crowd, and shows mercy to the fallen gladiator. Maximus takes a giant step on his journey as a Stoic progressor by combining the Stoic lessons of "shadows and dust," "strength and honor," remembering who he is, and remembering the kind of man he wants to be. Winning the crowd doesn't matter. Vengeance is not justice. Self-pity is disgraceful. Trust is noble. Doing the right thing, acting justly, being merciful, being trustworthy and trusting, is to be a good man. Being a good man, regardless of what others do or say, regardless of the circumstances or the consequences, is all that matters, according to Stoicism. Maximus' hard-won Stoic deportment even seems to inspire Proximo, who is in danger of becoming a good man when he enables Maximus to free his fellow gladiators. They fight off the Praetorian assassins long enough for Maximus to escape. Proximo and some of the gladiators are killed. The gladiators have learned "strength and honor" from Maximus.

The tyrant Commodus, for whom life is a frightful dream, has discovered the plot, holds Lucilla and her son Lucius hostage, and has the Praetorian guards ambush and capture Maximus. Commodus confronts Maximus, who is chained in a cell in the Colosseum. Commodus decides that only a famous death will do for Maximus, namely, dueling the Emperor himself in the arena. Maximus is surprised that Commodus would fight him. Commodus asks, "Why not? Do you think I am afraid?" Maximus replies, "I think you have been afraid all your life." Commodus retorts, "Unlike Maximus the invincible, who knows no fear?" Maximus chuckles, "I knew a man who once said, 'Death smiles at us all. All a man can do is smile back'." This man, Maximus tells Commodus, was his father, Marcus Aurelius. While this is not a quotation from the *Memoranda*, it fairly resembles the spirit of Marcus' view that death is not scary to the person who understands Stoicism.[10] Commodus taunts Maximus to smile as he stabs him in the ribs. Maximus' wound is concealed and his armor is strapped on. They duel in the arena. Maximus kills Commodus. Bleeding to death and unsteady, Maximus orders his men to be freed and Senator Gracchus to be reinstated. He says: "There was once a dream that was Rome. It shall be realized. These are the wishes of Marcus Aurelius." He falls hard to the sand. Lucilla runs to him, calls his name, and to her he speaks his last words: "Lucius is safe." Having given his life to honor the just wishes of Emperor Marcus, to do all he could to restore the republic, and to save an innocent boy, and the people of Rome, from an evil, murderous tyrant, Maximus has traveled far along the long, steep road to Stoicism. He has done so not by becoming an infallible paragon of virtue and godlike hero. Maximus is farther from being a Stoic sage than the actual Marcus Aurelius was. Rather, Maximus made enough moral progress to count as a *bonus vir*—a good man—and to be the imperfect inheritor of Marcus Aurelius' Stoic philosophy in *Gladiator*.[11]

NOTES

CHAPTER 1

1 *The Communings with Himself* of Marcus Aurelius Antoninus. Loeb Classical Library, Cambridge, MA: Harvard University Press, repr. 1987, p. xi. In his preface and introduction, Haines uses the title *Thoughts*, rather than the Loeb title page's clumsy *The Communings with Himself*, to refer to Marcus' work.

2 Marcus Aurelius, *Meditations*. New York: The Modern Library, 2002, p. lvi. Translations of the *Memoranda* are my own, though informed by Hays and Haines. I follow Hays' numbering of the entries of the *Memoranda*.

3 My account of Marcus' biography draws liberally from Anthony Birley, *Marcus Aurelius: A Biography*. New York: Barnes & Noble Books, 1999.

4 See the southwestern corner of the map Marcus' Roman Empire.

5 See the Genealogical Diagram.

6 See Chapter 2.

7 See the Genealogical Diagram.

8 See Chapter 3.

9 Ido Israelowich, "The Rain Miracle of Marcus Aurelius: (Re-) Construction of Consensus," *Greece & Rome* 55, no. 1 (2008): 83–102.

10 A Stoa is a covered walkway or porch. The *Stoa Poikilē* (Painted Porch), built in the fifth century BCE and located on the north side of the Agora (the chief marketplace) of Athens, is where Zeno of Citium expounded his teachings and founded the school of Stoicism.

11 See the Appendix, note 11 for more on Commodus.

12 "Soliloquy, or Advice to an Author," in *Characteristics of Men, Manners, Opinions, Times*, 113.

13 "Miscellany IV, Chapter I," in *Characteristics*, 423.

14 See the introduction by James Moore and Michael Silverthorne to *The Meditations of the Emperor Marcus Aurelius Antoninus*, translated by Francis Hutcheson and James Moor. Indianapolis: Liberty Fund, 2008.

15 "Natural History of Religion," *The Philosophical Works*, vol. IV, p. 350.

CHAPTER 2

1 See the map Marcus' Roman Empire.
2 See William O. Stephens, *Stoic Ethics: Epictetus and Happiness as Freedom*. London: Continuum, 2007.
3 See the map Marcus' Roman Empire.
4 I won't speculate about which of Marcus' philosophy teachers may have introduced him to Heraclitus' philosophy.
5 Charles H. Kahn, *The Art and Thought of Heraclitus*. Cambridge: Cambridge University Press, 1979, p. 21. Translations of Heraclitus' fragments are Kahn's, with some few, slight modifications. I follow his numbering of the fragments. My debt to his reading of Heraclitus is undisguised.
6 *The Art and Thought of Heraclitus*, p. 214.
7 See Chapter 4.
8 *The Art and Thought of Heraclitus*, p. 214.
9 See Chapter 5.
10 The Stoics commonly hold that God, Zeus, Providence, and Fate are different names for the same divine, active principle of right reason that pervades and orders the cosmos and is manifested as creative fire. See P. A. Meijer, *Stoic Theology: Proofs for the Existence of the Cosmic God and of the Traditional Gods*. Delft: Eburon, 2007.
11 See A. A. Long, *Epictetus: A Stoic and Socratic Guide to Life*. Oxford: Clarendon Press, 2002.
12 See Plato, *Crito* 46c and *Phaedo* 77e.
13 Compare with Marcus, *Memoranda* x. 34.
14 Epictetus appears to hold the orthodox Stoic view that the soul (mind) is physical in nature, being composed of *pneuma* (breath).

CHAPTER 3

1 An ancient Greek athletic contest that combined boxing and wrestling.
2 Other Stoics, in contrast, argue that the beauty and complexity of the human body is evidence of divine existence and Providence.
3 Marcus' disdain toward the body reflects a growing hostility toward the body in later Stoicism, whether this be due to the influence of Platonism or the medical tradition.
4 The Stoics are compatibilists who believe both that causal determinism is true and that rationality allows normal adult human beings to exercise freedom in their power of assent.
5 Since the human body is a microcosm within this macrocosm, one could fault Marcus for failing to similarly celebrate the body.
6 Strictly speaking, chance events are simply those that surprise us because we didn't predict them. From the cosmic perspective, there are no chance events.
7 Scott Rubarth has suggested to me a possible way to save Marcus from the fallacy of division here. At one level, the good of a plant is its own survival. Thus, its death will not be a good for that plant. But we could

consider the good of a plant to be the continuation of its species. On this view, the death of an individual plant may be good and necessary for that plant's species, even though the death is not a good for that particular plant. According to the Stoic doctrine of cosmic conflagration (*ekpurōsis*), periodically the entire cosmos is consumed in fire, out of this conflagration a new cosmos forms, and this renewal occurs perpetually. The conflagration would seem to be good neither for the individual plant nor for its plant species unless the cyclical nature of the cosmos is necessary for the continuation of the species *sub species aeternitatis*, "from the perspective of eternity."

8   Marcus follows Epictetus in using "God" and "gods" interchangeably.

9   Marcus does not explicitly address the situation of competing allegiances or adjudicating among them by appealing to a hierarchy of moral obligations.

10   The Stoics hold that since nature equips human beings with the power of reason, and though dying slowly and painfully from, say, bone cancer also counts as natural in a sense, reason can call for ending one's own life in order to end prolonged, irremediable, pointless suffering. Thus the Stoics believe that sometimes suicide is appropriate for the virtuous because in these circumstances it is contrary to neither nature nor reason, and thus is justified.

11   See Chapter 5: What is Owed to Others.

CHAPTER 4

1   See Chapter 2.

2   Marcus' philosophy of time is Presentism, the view that necessarily, it is always true that only temporally present objects exist.

3   See Chapter 5.

4   See Chapter 1.

5   See Chapter 5.

6   Presumably here Marcus means what *seems* locally to be bad. As we saw in Chapter 3, Marcus rejects the view that events in nature are *actually* bad from a global, cosmic perspective.

CHAPTER 5

1   See Chapter 4.

2   See Chapter 3: Death Harmlessly Transforms.

3   Does Marcus mean here our teaching and education of others or the teaching and education we received from others? He may mean both, but I suspect he means primarily the latter.

4   See Chapter 3: Limbs of the Social Body and The Bees and the Hive.

5   See Chapter 2: Heraclitus, River and Chapter 4: The Rushing River of Existence.

6   Plato's *Crito*, 49b.

7   See the Genealogical Diagram.

8 The Epicureans may be right that everything is composed of atoms moving mechanistically and purposelessly in the vacuous void of space.

9 For my account of Stoic love, see "Epictetus on How the Stoic Sage Loves," *Oxford Studies in Ancient Philosophy* XIV (1996): 193–210.

APPENDIX

1 Did director Ridley Scott, or the screenwriters David Franzoni, John Logan, and William Nicholson, or the producers Douglas Wick and Branko Lustig, explicitly intend Maximus' story to depict a journey to Stoicism? I am aware of no evidence that any of them intended *Gladiator* to have overt Stoic themes. I argue instead that the film can be fairly interpreted as Maximus' education in Stoicism and his journey of progress toward living in accordance with Stoic principles, whether he identifies those principles as constitutive of Stoic philosophy or not.

2 See Chapter 4.

3 See Chapter 5.

4 The early Stoics believed that there was nothing in between virtue and vice. Consequently, all who are virtuous possess all the virtues (the wise), while those who lack one virtue lack all the virtues. There are thus two classes of people, according to Stoicism: wise people (the sane), and fools (the insane). But later Stoics divided the class of fools into those who make progress toward virtue (the progressors) and fools who make no such progress.

5 *Senatus Populusque Romanus*: the Senate and the People of Rome.

6 In Latin *vir* means "man," *virtus* means "manliness" or "virtue." In Greek *andreia* means "courage" or "manliness," since *andros* means "man."

7 See John Sellars, "Stoics on the Big Screen: Marcus and Maximus" (unpublished). I am grateful to Professor Sellars for helping me detect some Stoic ideas in Proximo's remarks. However, I disagree with his judgment that Proximo adapts to circumstances in a Stoic manner, whereas Maximus fails to. Proximo appears to have chosen his role as "entertainer" and trainer of gladiators. In contrast, Maximus' roles as slave then gladiator were thrust upon him, not chosen, and yet Maximus adapts to his changing circumstances and roles. I also reject Sellars' judgment that Proximo is a Stoic character and Maximus is not because Proximo is not squeamish about death. Clearly, throughout the entire film, Maximus is no more squeamish about death than Proximo is. Sellars describes Proximo's death as a "noble suicide." Yet he evidently needed both a bribe from Maximus' "persuasive friends" and he needed *Maximus* to activate "Proximo's higher sense of debt and respect for the man who set him free" in order to abet Maximus' escape from the Praetorian assassins sent by Commodus. Consequently, Proximo's death, which is not a clear-cut suicide, is no nobler than Maximus' death.

8 Proximo tells his newly purchased slaves, "I did not pay good money for you for your company. I paid it so that I could profit from your death."

9 When Commodus asks the masked Maximus for his name, Maximus responds that his name is "Gladiator" before he reveals his true identity.

10 See, for example, *Mem.* xii. 35.

11 How historically accurate is the film *Gladiator*? Maximus is an entirely invented character and the plot departs significantly from history, but some of the film's elements are reasonably accurate. Commodus did become sole emperor after Marcus died, but there is no evidence that Commodus slew his father and Marcus had made his son co-emperor well before his death. The plot of the film is squeezed into three years, but Commodus ruled for twelve. Commodus was a cruel despot and his sister Lucilla did conspire against him. But Commodus exiled her to Capri and later executed her after he discovered her conspiracy to assassinate him, so Lucilla did not survive him. Commodus did participate in gladiatorial games in the Colosseum, but never risked his life in doing so. His able-bodied opponents would always submit to him and were spared. He killed wounded soldiers and amputees with a sword. Vain about his physical prowess, as Commodus descended into megalomania he assumed the persona of Hercules. In this role, he had Roman citizens who had lost their feet to accident or illness tethered together in the arena and he clubbed them to death, pretending they were giants. Commodus was also reported to have once killed a hundred lions in a single day, and on other occasions an ostrich, three elephants, and a giraffe. In November 192 he shot hundreds of animals every morning and fought as a gladiator every afternoon. December 31, 192, after Commodus vomited up food that conspirators had poisoned, his wrestling partner Narcissus strangled him in his bath. Commodus was also said to have had a harem of three hundred women and three hundred boys. Marcus did not ban gladiatorial displays in Rome during his reign, but he required the use of blunted weapons to reduce bloodshed among gladiators. He required wealthy Romans to sponsor gladiatorial displays in Rome while he was waging costly wars on the northern frontiers and contending with plague home and abroad. See Chapter 1: The Early Reign and A Stoic at War.

GLOSSARY

ancilium	a figure-eight-shaped shield.
apatheia	passionlessness; according to Stoic theory, the mental state of being free of pathological emotions.
Armeniacus	conqueror of the Armenians.
Armilustrium	Roman festival to Mars celebrated on October 19 which purified the army.
Arsacids	the Iranian (Persian) royal dynasty originally centered in Parthia, ruling from c. 250 BCE to CE 224, named after the tribal chieftain Arsaces. Members of the Arsacid clan were, with some interruptions, kings of Armenia until CE 428.
Astingi (Hasdingi)	an eastern Germanic tribe who lived in areas of present-day southern Poland, Slovakia, and Hungary.
auctoritas	clout, authority, prestige, command, conferred power.
aulicum fastigium	pomp of the court.
Aurelian Column	also known as the Column of Marcus Aurelius, a victory column with spiral relief depicting chronologically ordered scenes commemorating Marcus' military achievements. Nearly 40 m. tall, this monument still stands in Rome's Piazza Colonna.
bulla	a golden amulet worn around the neck of a child as a charm against the evil eye.
Chatti	a northwestern Germanic tribe who lived in the areas of the upper Weser, Eder, and Fulda river valleys and the Taunus mountains.

Circus Maximus	the most important Roman arena for chariot-racing, located in the Murcia valley between the Palatine and Aventine hills. Measuring about 650 × 125 m. and capable of holding as many as 250,000 people, it had parallel sides and one semi-circular end fitted with tiered seating, and twelve starting gates at the open end. The racing area was divided into two tracks by a long central barrier, marked at the ends with conical turning-posts and decorated with monuments. Four, six, eight, or twelve teams of horses competed under different colors, red, white, blue, and green.
Colosseum	medieval name of the oval-shaped Flavian Amphitheater dedicated in June CE 80 located in the center of Rome. Measuring 188 × 156 m. and 52 m. tall, it could hold about 50,000 spectators. It hosted gladiatorial contests and public spectacles such as mock sea battles, reenactments of famous land battles, animal hunts, executions, and dramas based on Classical mythology.
comes (comitēs) Augusti (Augustorum)	companion(s) of the Emperor(s).
consul	title of the chief civil and military magistrates of Rome during the republic (c. 508 to 27 BCE). Two were elected annually. During the imperial period (27 BCE to late third century) consuls continued but with attenuated powers and the Emperor either recommended the candidates or held the office himself.
Costoboci	an eastern European tribe who lived between the Carpathian mountains and the river Dniester around the river Don.
Cotini	a northern European tribe who lived in the area of present-day Slovakia and southern Poland.

crepundia	a rattle made of a string with tinkling objects attached to it.
de alimentis publicis	under state care.
decuriones	councillors who ran Roman local government in both colonies and municipalities. Recruited mainly from ex-magistrates, they controlled the public life of the community, its administration, finances, and the sending of embassies and petitions to the Emperor or provincial governor.
donative	an irregular monetary payment to soldiers, perhaps originally associated with distributions of booty. Donatives celebrated important events linked to the Emperor, including birthdays, dynastic policy, the defeat of conspiracies, military victories, and especially accession to power. They were not directly related to regular pay rates.
educator	he tutor of a Roman boy who supervised his moral welfare and general development.
enthymeme	an argument with one or more unexpressed premises or an unexpressed conclusion.
equites	the knights or equestrians; the second aristocratic order, ranked only below the senatorial order in status. They provided the officer corps of the Roman army and held a variety of posts in the civil administration.
equites singulares Augusti	mounted imperial bodyguards who acted as the Praetorian Guard's cavalry.
the Forum	the *Forum Romanum*, the chief public square and heart of Rome. Surrounded by monumental buildings, it was the center of public life, the venue for triumphal processions, elections, public speeches, and commercial affairs.

gens	family.
grammaticus (*grammatici*)	teacher(s) of both language and poetry, but rarely prose, who emphasized correctness of speech and avoidance of solecisms.
Iazyges	a tribe of the Sarmatians who migrated to present-day southwestern Ukraine c. 200 BCE.
imperator	originally a generic title for Roman commanders, it became a special title of honor. After a victory the general (or emperor) was saluted *imperator* by his soldiers. He assumed the title after his name until the end of his magistracy or until his triumph.
imperium	a quasi-religious type of power (superior to *potestas*) involving command in war and the interpretation and execution of law (including the death penalty), which belonged to the higher Roman magistrates. It represented the authority of the community in its dealings with the individual and the power to issue commands and exact obedience to them. Magistrates with *imperium* were consuls, praetors, proconsuls, propraetors and, in supreme form, the emperors of the imperial period.
Lacringi	a tribe who lived along the Danube east of the Marcomanni and Quadi.
Langobardi (Lombards)	a Germanic tribe from northern Europe who settled in the valley of the Danube.
manumission	the formal act of liberating a slave, done at the will of the owner.
Marcomanni	literally "men of the borderlands"; a Germanic tribe who lived in central Europe and formed a confederation with the Quadi, Astingi, and Sarmatians against the Roman Empire.
Medicus	conqueror of the Medians.

parataxis	the arraying of troops in a battle-line.
pater patriae	father of the fatherland.
patria potestas	paternal authority; the power of a Roman male ascendant, normally father or grandfather, over descendants through males and over adopted children.
patricians	a privileged class of Roman citizens. During the republican period, patrician status was conferred by birth or adoption. Patricians had once monopolized all the important priesthoods and high public offices, but by our period, the status was mostly honorific.
philostorgia	loving affection.
pontifex, pontifices	one of the four chief colleges of the Roman priests. It had general oversight of the state cult (sacrifices, games, festivals, and other rituals), advised magistrates and private individuals on the sacred law and recorded their rules and decisions.
pontifex maximus	the supreme leader of the college of the *pontifices*. He acted as a spokesman for the college, particularly in the senate. After Augustus added this office to the powers held by the *princeps*, it was always held by the reigning emperor.
praenomen	a Roman's first or "given" name. The most formal designation of a freeborn male Roman citizen consisted of five components, the *praenomen*, the *nomen* or family-name, the indication of the father's name, the indication of the Roman voting tribe to which the citizen belonged, and the *cognomen*. But the *tria nomina* or "three names" used in ordinary circumstances were the *praenomen*, *nomen*, and *cognomen*, for example Marcus Aurelius Antoninus. In our period aristocrats commonly held multiple *cognomina*.

praetor	the most junior office in which a man received *imperium* as a magistrate. A praetor performed civil jurisdiction, presided over criminal courts, supervised the games, financed major games, and occasionally presided over the senate.
Praetorian Guard	the elite corps of troops responsible for protecting the Emperor and the imperial family, suppressing disturbances, and discouraging plots. A detachment of the guard accompanied the Emperor on campaign.
prefect	a type of appointed military or civil official who had no *imperium*. A prefect could be in charge of a prefecture. There were prefects at the head of the Praetorian Guard, in charge of Rome's police-like *vigiles*, and in charge of the Roman fleet.
princeps	chief; with Augustus it became an unofficial title assumed by Roman emperors at their accession not conferred upon them by the senate. From *princeps* we get the English word "prince."
princeps iuventutis	the head of the equestrian order; originally loosely akin in meaning to "crown prince."
proconsul	a magistrate in place of a consul operating outside Rome and outside the regular annual magistracy.
Quadi	a Germanic tribe smaller than the Marcomanni who migrated, perhaps from north of the River Main, into the area of present-day Moravia, Slovakia, and lower Austria.
quaestor	lowest of the regular magistrates, charged with financial, judicial, and military duties. The *quaestores Caesaris* were chosen by the Emperor himself, were often patricians, and were always young men of distinction. Election to the office carried de facto admission to the Senate.

Quinquatrus	Roman festival on March 19 which opened the army's campaign season.
rescript	written answer from a Roman emperor to a query or petition in writing.
sacramentum	oath of allegiance, sworn on attestation by a Roman recruit, to the Emperor, and renewed annually on New Year's Day or the anniversary of the Emperor's accession.
Salii	priests associated with the worship of Mars, the Roman god of war. They had to be of patrician birth and have both parents living. They wore the uniform of an archaic Italian foot-soldier and played a prominent part in the Quinquatrus.
Sarmatians	an Iranian people, proficient in horsemanship and warfare, who migrated from central Asia to the Ural mountains between the 6th and 4th centuries BCE and settled in present-day southern European Russia and the eastern Balkans.
senate	the most important political and social body of the Roman Empire, its first estate. It acted as a source of binding rules, including rules of status and inheritance, and rules for maintaining public order. It formally conferred powers on new emperors and members of their families, and had the right to declare them public enemies.
sesterces	the *sestercius* was a unit of Roman currency; during the imperial period it was a large, bronze coin.
theriac	antidote; a medicine containing opium prescribed by the physician Galen.
toga virilis	plain white garment a freeborn Roman male wears upon entering manhood at the age of fourteen.

tribunicia potestas	tribunician power; during the republic tribunes were officials elected by the plebeian assembly empowered to convene the *plebs*, elicit resolutions, enforce decrees, and veto any act performed by a magistrate against elections, laws, or advice given by the senate to the magistrates. Under the empire the tribunician power to legislate, exercise judicial powers, and veto was divorced from the office but retained by the emperors to strengthen their personal power.
triumph	procession of a Roman general (or, under the empire, the Emperor) who had won a major victory to the temple of Jupiter on the Capitoline hill.
triumphator	conqueror.
tunica picta	painted or colored tunic.
Ubii	a Germanic tribe who lived on the Rhine and from 55 BCE on were mostly Roman allies.
vates	prophet of the Salii.
Victuali (Victohali)	a central European tribe that crossed the Danube into Roman territory with the Marcomanni and Quadi.

FURTHER READING

Birley, Anthony R. *Marcus Aurelius: A Biography*. New York: Routledge, 1966, 2nd edn. 1987, new edn. 2000.

Champlin, Edward. *Fronto and Antonine Rome*. Cambridge, Mass.: Harvard University Press, 1980.

Farquharson, A. S. L. *The Meditations of the Emperor Marcus Antoninus*, edited with translation and commentary. 2 vols. Oxford: Clarendon Press, 1944.

Hadot, Pierre. *The Inner Citadel: The Meditations of Marcus Aurelius*, trans. M. Chase. Cambridge, Mass.: Harvard University Press, 1998.

Haines, C. R. *The Correspondence of Marcus Cornelius Fronto with Marcus Aurelius Antoninus, Lucius Verus, Antoninus Pius, and Various Friends*. 2 vols. Cambridge, Mass.: Harvard University Press (Loeb Classical Library), 1919, repr. 1955.

Long, A. A. *Epictetus: A Stoic and Socratic Guide to Life*. Oxford: Clarendon Press, 2002.

McLynn, Frank. *Marcus Aurelius: Warrior, Philosopher, Emperor*. London: Bodley Head, 2009.

Morford, Mark. *The Roman Philosophers: From the Time of Cato the Censor to the Death of Marcus Aurelius*. London: Routledge, 2002.

Reydams-Schils, Gretchen. *The Roman Stoics: Self, Responsibility, and Affection*. Chicago: The University of Chicago Press, 2005.

Rutherford, R. B. *The Meditations of Marcus Aurelius: A Study*. Oxford: Clarendon Press, 1989.

Stephens, William O. *Stoic Ethics: Epictetus and Happiness as Freedom*. London: Continuum, 2007.

SUBJECT INDEX

action 25, 33, 47–8, 55, 59, 66, 77,
   81, 88, 93–5, 100, 101, 109,
   126, 130, 132–3, 138, 140–1,
   144, 151–2, 155–6, 166
  bad 25, 155
  good 152
  mind's 113
  right 40
  unnatural 47
  unselfish 115, 155
animals 50–1, 54, 56, 58, 63, 66–7,
   85, 106, 127, 136, 152, 159,
   165, 175n. 11
  herds of 54, 82–3, 89, 133–4
  rational 96
apatheia (passionlessness) 12, 16
atomism 105
  atoms 81–3, 104–6, 155, 174n. 8
  Epicurean 82
  of Leucippus and Democritus of
   Abdera 45
auctoritas (clout) 19
Aurelian Column 33, 37

birth 43, 46, 55, 58, 67, 77, 88, 91,
   106, 159
  childbirth 54, 86
  and death 84, 88, 100, 104, 111
  elemental 58
  of new bodies 54
  rebirth 85, 159
body 28, 57, 62–6, 75, 115, 117,
   119, 123, 131, 140–5, 148, 151,
   172n. 2, 172n. 3, 172n. 5

body parts 81, 92, 128
  and death 88, 113, 130, 132, 134
  Epictetus' view of 62–4
  social body 89–95
  and soul 66, 106, 113, 142
  world as a 79–80

change 55–8, 77–8, 83–7, 101–6, 111,
   114, 125, 127, 129, 149, 151, 162
  cycles of 43, 52–3, 55, 104
  death as 58, 66, 84, 87
  necessity of 78, 82–3
  seasonal 55, 74
  see also flux
Christians 28, 37–8, 39, 41
  Christianity 28, 40
comes (comitēs) Augusti
  (Augustorum) 22, 24
cosmic flux 43
  see also change; flux
cosmic holism 43, 46, 76–81, 115,
   117
  see also holism
cosmopolitanism 25, 96, 98–100, 136
  cosmopolis (cosmic city) 96–7,
   99–100
  and mereology 99–100

death 43–4, 48, 51–2, 54–6, 58,
   60, 63, 66–71, 97, 100, 108,
   110–12, 119–23, 129–30, 132,
   134, 136, 143, 145, 149–50,
   163–7, 169–70, 172n. 7,
   174n. 7, 175n. 8, 175n. 11

NAME INDEX